CADRES AND KIN

CADRES AND KIN

Making a Socialist Village in West China,

1921–1991

GREGORY A. RUF

STANFORD UNIVERSITY PRESS
Stanford, California

Stanford University Press
Stanford, California
© 1998 by the Board of Trustees of the
Leland Stanford Junior University
Printed in the United States of America

CIP data appear at the end of the book

For Nikos and Kalliopi

CONTENTS

ILLUSTRATIONS AND TABLES

Photos follow p. 150

PREFACE

For years, I kept a cartoon that seemed to epitomize my existence. In it, a man sits at a wide table, typewriter before him, piles of paper stacked high to each side. In the background, a woman, presumably his spouse, stands at a door atop a short flight of stairs. "Finish it?" the man is asking, with his head tilted quizzically. "Why would I ever want to finish it?"

After a while, I put the cartoon in a shoebox. I didn't find it funny anymore. My children, Nikos and Kalliopi, have spent their whole lives learning to cope with dissertations, books, papers, and articles. But they have been my principal source of inspiration, both in writing and in life. Now there will be more time to enjoy wildflowers. They, and their mother Tasoula, appreciate more than anyone else the difficult road I followed on this journey to Sichuan and the many detours made along the way, sometimes on paths less taken.

An opportunity to work in rural China presented itself in the late 1980s, when I was a graduate student in anthropology. Myron Cohen, my principal advisor, set up a multiyear collaborative research project on Chinese family organization with a grant from the Luce Foundation. The first year of that project, 1988–89, brought several Chinese colleagues from the Sichuan and Shanghai Academies of Social Science to Columbia University's East Asian Institute, where project participants planned a joint household survey. That fall, Cohen, Eugene Murphy (another graduate student), and I were to go to separate villages in China for a year of field research, but other events intervened.

The summer of 1989 found me in Greece, where Tasoula, pregnant with Nikos, was conducting her own fieldwork. With no word from colleagues in China and none of the letters of invitation necessary to procure a research visa, I found a job in Thessaloniki. We settled in for a winter in Macedonia, with the warmth of little Nikos now beside us. My favorite hours were the silent ones just before dawn. We would watch the indigo of night fade softly from the sky, and then Nikos would sleep in my arms as the sun rose and the city began to stir. I did not leave for China until August 1990, after we had moved back to New York.

In China, I was fortunate to have the sponsorship of the Sichuan Academy of Social Sciences (SASS). Mr. Zhao Xishun, director of the Sociology Institute, and Ms. Zhou Kaili, a veteran staff fieldworker, deserve special mention for their efforts and troubles in accommodating my many requests, and for accompanying me while I lived in Qiaolou. The staff at the SASS library warmly invited me to use their collections during my short periodic visits to Chengdu. The Meishan county government, and particularly Mr. Wang Zhichao of its Foreign Affairs Office, provided gracious assistance. Wang and his family offered their own hospitality in the winter of 1994–95, inviting me to stay with them during a return visit to Meishan. Of course, none of this work would have been possible without the cooperation and support of the Qiaolou party branch secretary. Yet I remain most grateful to the people of Qiaolou village and Baimapu township, who shared with me their lives and memories. In my heart I thank them individually, even though, in these pages, they must appear pseudonymously.

Events in China the previous summer shaped conditions of fieldwork. Although I had requested placement in a nonsuburban, middle-income village with "cooperative enterprises," Qiaolou's status as a model of rural socialist development was an important factor in its selection. In contrast to the "chaos" and unrest broadcast around the world in images of the 1989 demonstrations, Qiaolou was regarded by many county and provincial authorities as a paragon of stability, a place where "the collective" was alive and strong. It was also a site where those responsible for me were confident that adequate provisions could be made for my safety and well-being. Some authorities intimated that they would prefer I reside in the county seat and make daily visits, under escort, to the village. We did abandon the idea of working in three separate villages of the same township, but my SASS colleagues, much to their credit, insisted that we live in the countryside, according to the approved research plan. For eight months in 1990–91, we stayed in rooms rented in the village office building, secure in a guarded, walled compound with an iron gate that was padlocked at nightfall. I was generally not permitted to eat with village families in their homes. Instead, our research team formed a small, collective "mess regiment" and took meals together in a small kitchen attached to the building.

At the same time, the "stipulated parameters" (*guiding fanwei*) of our research restricted my activities to the confines of the village. On more than one occasion, for example, I was permitted to accompany wedding parties only as far as the village borders. Visits to the nearby Guanyin temple required prior approval from county authorities, one of whom usually accompanied me on such walks. Yet because Qiaolou bordered on the Baimapu township settlement, I was relatively free to wander the town's single street and to visit with people in their homes there. I often spent market days in Baimapu teashops, interviewing people from outside Qiaolou. Outside the village administrative compound, however, an escort was almost always with me.

It had been understood that I would be assigned a local assistant-consultant-guide. I had requested an elderly woman as an assistant, but local authorities selected a retired security chief, a party member and former production team leader who had a wealth of information about each village family. He had spent several years in other parts of China while serving in the army during the 1950s, and his standard Mandarin was invaluable to me during the first few weeks of work, when I struggled with the local dialect. I treasure the friendship that developed between us, and I am grateful for the affection and concern he showed to Nikos and Tasoula, who joined me for the last two months of my stay.

Security concerns shaped other aspects of my research as well. Workers in village collective enterprises such as the brick factories and the distillery were cautioned against revealing "state secrets" (*guojia mimi*). Qiaolou officials kindly permitted me to examine and copy the village household registry but only after provincial authorities assured them that no state secrets would be compromised. To my disappointment but understanding, I was unable to access any other official archives or documents, whether administrative records or economic accounts, at the village, township, or county level. The publication of a new Meishan county gazetteer (MSG 1992), a copy of which I obtained in 1995, was helpful in confirming (or refuting) information solicited during interviews and in reconstructing a broader context for the changes and continuities in local life over the course of the twentieth century. I have drawn on that text heavily, for better or worse, as a documentary reference.

The overwhelming majority of empirical material in this book, however, was derived from formally structured interviews and informal conversations, individual life histories and family genealogical reconstructions, and household surveys and village mapping. The opportunity to live in Qiaolou for an extended period of time was invaluable, facilitating observations and a rapport that probably would not have been possible through short-term visits. Most local residents soon grew familiar with my note taking, but there were always conversations that clearly would have died had I taken out my notebook. After such occasions, I did a lot of scribbling in latrines. Because I appreciate the reservations some scholars may have about the reliability of oral accounts, I have tried to cross-check information as widely as possible. As Voltaire put it, "Doubt is not a pleasant condition, but certainty is an absurd one."

I had hoped to do a broader study of cooperative family enterprise in the local "standard marketing community," an analytical unit proposed by G. William Skinner based on his own fieldwork in Sichuan nearly fifty years earlier. But constraints on my research activities obliged me to focus instead on the village alone. Qiaolou, like many Sichuan villages, consisted of individual family homes dispersed throughout the countryside, rather than clustered together in a single, nucleated settlement. The more I learned about local families, the more it became apparent that the village was actually a relatively recent creation. At the very least, its residents had come to share a sense of common identity only since the Communist revolution. This led me to question some of the assumptions embedded in notions of village community and in so-called community studies in general.

"Community" is one of those keywords, so prevalent in studies of culture and society, that carries with it a wide range of meanings. Raymond Williams (1983) traced its appearance in English to the fourteenth century, when it referred to shared relations or feelings, although its Latin roots convey notions of "together" and "under obligation." Its early uses also implied an organized social group or polity. We busily deconstruct imagined communities of nation, yet we rarely direct such critical attention to local or face-to-face communities, which are based on constructed imaginings no less than nations are. In a sense, the present volume is a study of community formation at the village level. This process entailed the mobilization of some—and the suppression of other—local alliances of interest, emotion, and exchange. It was also profoundly shaped by the institutions of state power, particularly those established in the Chinese countryside since the 1920s.

I begin with the setting of this study: the environs of the rural market town of Baimapu, which became a seat of subcounty township government after the fall of the Qing dynasty in 1911. Chapter 1 enters the social field of Baimapu by following a farmer who moved there looking for a new start. I attempt to reconstruct a history of settlement (or resettlement) in the area, or at least to describe conditions in the late nineteenth century, when the ancestors of the oldest and largest local descent groups apparently arrived. I then offer a view of the local landscape and the ways families marked their presence, physically and symbolically, both individually and in association with others.

Chapter 2 examines how families and individual residents cultivated various forms of alliance and cooperation during the early decades of the twentieth century, managing interfamily relationships to seek security in a time of heavy taxation, soaring inflation, and violent unrest. There I discuss aspects of family organization and management, marriage and affinal ties, descent group and lineage activities, popular associations and local administration, and offer some comparisons with other parts of China. I also explore issues of land tenure and social stratification, concluding with a look at local elites in the township arena on the eve of the Communist revolution.

Chapter 3 opens with the Battle of Baimapu, in which the People's Liberation Army (PLA) routed remnant Nationalist forces and secured the Liberation of Meishan some two months after Mao and other Communist leaders celebrated the establishment of the People's Republic of China (PRC) in Beijing. I recount the progress of the Land Reform campaign of the early 1950s, its creation of the administrative village of Qiaolou, and its iconoclastic assault on the vestiges of "the Old Society." The violent struggle of this period left a deep impression on the local population, whose relations were reshaped through the ascription of new political-status labels.

The organizational initiatives of cooperativization and collectivization are examined in Chapter 4. State authorities pursued ambitious urban industrialization plans by attempting to raise levels of agricultural production and by increasing state appropriation of rural surplus. They mobilized enormous numbers of laborers for construction projects and imposed a highly regimented system of communal life. This "Great Leap Forward" led to one of the worst famines in history, which profoundly affected how many farmers perceived their position in the Communist party-state order. After a brief respite of economic liberalization in the early 1960s, renewed efforts were made by radical political activists to promote village collectivism. They achieved mixed results in agriculture, where collectivist efforts were eventually abandoned, but had better success at nonagricultural enterprises, laying the foundations for a new village collective corporation that emerged under the post-Mao reforms.

Chapter 5 examines the strategies and tactics of Qiaolou's cadres in developing village industry. I explore how they mobilized economic, social, political, and symbolic resources to create a regime of managerial corporatism, and consider the relationship of local rule to state government. Shareholding, so fundamental to many forms of Chinese social organization, became an important aspect of property relations in collectively owned and operated village enterprises. Cadres drew on idioms of family and kinship to cultivate solidarity and labor discipline within the village corporation they managed. Loosened state controls during the reform era enabled them to increase their local power and create new roles for themselves as economic patrons.

Chapter 6 briefly returns to some of the major issues raised throughout the volume. I review the diverse ties through which goods, people, and services flowed between rural and urban areas. Maoist collectivism disrupted many of these relationships, attempting to monopolize control of rural-urban exchange and fostering a bifurcation of town and countryside. There were, however, important continuities with previous trends of the early twentieth century, including the institutionalization of state bureaucratic power in the countryside, the local dominance of young male activists practicing selective violence, and the use of corporate principles in organizing communities of interest and solidarity. I consider how alternative approaches to notions of corporatism help illuminate the social organization of power in present-day Qiaolou, and conclude with reflections on changing political consciousness among village cadres and kin.

For those familiar with his work, the influence of Myron Cohen will be apparent in the pages that follow. Over the years, his advice, challenges, and friendship have shaped my personal and professional development. While we do not always see eye to eye, his concern with empirical detail and his tireless efforts to purge my writing of jargon and vagaries have guided this book in many ways. The shortcomings that remain are certainly no fault of his, but only evidence of my own continuing stubbornness. Several others have also offered valuable critiques and suggestions on earlier drafts of this manuscript, including Anastasia Karakasidou, Jonathan Unger, Andrew Nathan, Madeline Zelin, Theodore Bestor, and George Bond. Muriel Bell at Stanford University Press has been a model of encouragement, patience, and support, and I appreciate her understanding throughout the unrelated difficulties that delayed my completion of this book. Nathan MacBrien deftly guided the manuscript through the production process, Victoria Scott devoted her careful attention to a detailed copy-editing of the entire manuscript, and Gerry Krieg prepared the maps.

Funding for this research was made possible by generous grants from the Committee for Scholarly Communication with the People's Republic of China (now cscc) and the Wenner-Gren Foundation for Anthropological Research. I was very fortunate to spend 1994–95 as the An Wang postdoctoral fellow at Harvard's Fairbank Center for East Asian Research. James Watson and Rubie Watson, two of the most generous people I know, shared with me so much more than friendship that it would be silly to try to express my gratitude. I have also enjoyed the support and encouragement of a great many other people over the years, including Gene Murphy, Jim Fenton, Steve Rubenstein, and Joyce Monges; Jean Oi, Andy Walder, David Zweig, Merle Goldman, and Michael Herzfeld; and Gene Cooper, Jing Jun, and Yan Yunxiang. Maris Gillette offered particularly warm assistance that was instrumental in helping to complete this project, closely reading a later draft of the manuscript.

Finally, a word of gratitude to my colleagues, especially Eli Seifman and Shiming Hu, and my students at the State University of New York at Stony

Brook, whose welcome and enthusiasm have provided a supportive environment in which to think, teach, and write near the quiet tidal marshes of Long Island Sound. Here Methodi can chase butterflies, Kalliopi can chase Methodi, and Nikos can chase Kalliopi. Ted Bestor once suggested that I decide on an audience for whom to write. The piles of paper on and around my desk contain a stratigraphy of samples from such efforts. In the end, I chose to write for my students here. Other material will appear elsewhere. In 1982, I had my first opportunity to spend a year in China as a SUNY undergraduate exchange student. When I returned to Cortland College for my senior year, I was introduced to anthropology by Sidney Waldron, who encouraged me to explore the alternative perspectives it offers on life. He warned me of the painful but invisible scars a career in academia could inflict, but he was also a source of inspiration and confidence. Without you, Sid, none of this would have been possible.

G.A.R.

Citations to Meishan gazetteers appear in parentheses as MSG (Meishan Gazetteer). In addition, the following abbreviations appear in square brackets in the text and notes to identify genealogical relationships between individual residents of the Baimapu area:

B	Brother	M	Mother
C	Child	S	Son
D	Daughter	W	Wife
F	Father	Z	Sister
H	Husband		

For example, "MeB" = mother's elder brother; "FyZ" = father's younger sister; and "S1S4" = fourth son of ego's first son.

The following units of measurement are used for weights, distance, and area:

1 catty (*jin*)	=	0.5 kg		
1 picul (*dan*)	=	300 catties	=	150 kg (pre-1949)
	=	100 catties	=	50 kg (post-1949)
1 *li*	=	0.5 km (0.3 mile)		
1 *mu*	=	0.164 acre		
6 *mu*	=	1 acre		
100 *mu*	=	6.6 hectares		

CADRES AND KIN

CHAPTER 1

A Topography of the Past

Shaping a Township Landscape in the Early Twentieth Century

Only those who make a living from the soil can understand the value of soil. . . . [To] country people, the soil is the root of their lives. In rural areas, the god represented in most shrines is Tudi, the god of the earth. . . . Tudi and his wife are an old white-haired couple who take care of all the business of the countryside and who have come to symbolize the earth itself.

—FEI XIAOTONG, *Xiangtu Zhongguo*

Violence was a stream that ran through China's rural landscape in certain well-defined beds: diked and controlled in the best of times, but at other times breaking forth to inundate local society.

—PHILIP KUHN, *Rebellion and Its Enemies in Late Imperial China*

In the early 1920s, Liang Jinyuan's father came to settle in Baimapu, a rural market township in western Meishan county, Sichuan. The area's low, wooded hillocks, terraced rice paddies, and small, meandering streams were not unfamiliar to him. The topography was much the same in his native Dongguachang, an adjacent market township a few hours' walk south. Liang's father had sometimes visited the Baima market. It met on odd-numbered days, while that in Donggua convened on even-numbered days. In this part of China, where farmers' homes were dispersed throughout the countryside, most families living in the vicinity of such settlements concentrated their social and economic activities there. Many visited other nearby markets as well, both in neighboring rural townships and in bustling Meishan town, a walled administrative center on the banks of the Min River less than 10 kilometers east of Baimapu. Yet when Liang's father moved to the area, he had only a small circle of social acquaintances there. Even his speech marked him as an outsider, for idiomatic inflections common in Baima were absent from the vernacular dialect spoken at the Donggua market, only a few kilometers away.

Liang's parents were poor farmers but had seven children, of whom Jin-yuan (b. 1929) was the fifth, and the second son. The first child, born six years earlier, was also a boy, as was the last, who died young. Liang's father died soon thereafter, leaving his widow and children on their own, along with a young daughter-in-law. Life in the 1930s was not easy for a widowed farmer with few relatives, particularly if she had seven other mouths to feed. Landowners faced heavy taxes, and tenants labored under high rents. Many market transactions were subject to various fees and surcharges, while spiraling inflation haunted an economy rocked by decades of banditry, civil unrest, and sporadic violence among competing local elites.

Shortly before or after the death of Liang's father, his mother had arranged for her eldest son to marry a young woman from a local family that lived nearby. The boy was ten years old at the time; his bride was twelve. Such "little daughter-in-law" marriages were common. They rarely entailed betrothal payments or other costs, aside from those of a small commemorative meal. But they were regarded as marriages, nonetheless, and created ties of kinship, or affinity, between families. Liang's new sister-in-law, Hao Suhua, came from a large and wealthy extended family, and this gave the Liangs, who were without other kin, a sense of acceptance and some hopes of security.

The ancestors of Liang's new affines had settled in the area five generations earlier. They had come from Meishan town, now the county seat, on the lowland Minjiang floodplain. Since their arrival in the mid-nineteenth century, the Haos had become one of the largest descent groups in the Baimapu area. The wife of an eldest son was a position of status, and Liang's new *saozi* [eBW] was a granddaughter of Hao Caiming (b. 1881), the only one of four brothers in the senior branch (*zhangfang*) of their descent group to have male descendants. Hao Caiming was a prosperous farmer married to two wives and the head of a family of more than a dozen members, which had included young Hao Suhua. His family estate included over 80 *mu* (more than a dozen acres) of paddy and supported a live-in domestic servant girl (*yatou*) as well as Hao Caiming's expensive opium-smoking habit.

A marriage tie to such a family did not promise riches and wealth, but it did offer potential advantages. Several Hao men were influential leaders in township administration, and by the time Liang's elder brother was in his late teens, he found himself appointed head of their *bao*, or ward, a subtownship administrative unit for purposes of policing, taxation, and conscription activities. Such a post, however, drew one into the realm of competitive politics, where, in the 1940s, lives as well as fortunes could be gained or lost. In 1937, the national government had relocated its capital to Chongqing (Chungking), in southeast Sichuan. With much of Eastern China occupied by Japanese invasion forces, taxes in Sichuan were raised even higher than before to support the war effort. Security measures were also tightened to counter a growing Communist insurgency. Large numbers of men were conscripted, some forcibly, as soldiers and laborers for army and militia units.

Although many of these administrative measures were mandated by the state government, they were enforced by local strongmen who dominated official positions in rural townships. Many used their formal authority and informal power to further their own family interests. Some profited from tax collecting; others offered private loans at usurious rates. Ruffians, associated with many of these same officials through "secret societies," enforced collection and imposed protection fees on market activities. Persistent inflation pushed many families into debt or tenancy. Less scrupulous local officials sometimes pressed people into their service under threat of death, while the wealthy hired bodyguards to protect themselves. Armed force became an icon of power as well as of fear.

Liang's elder brother served as local *bao* leader for only a short time before he had an angry falling-out with township officials. Unfortunately for the Liangs, the patronage and protection they had enjoyed through Hao Suhua's grandfather also diminished, following his death and the partitioning of his family into separate units. Hao Suhua's own father had also died, leaving her widowed mother struggling economically and socially with her teenaged brother. Two of Hao Suhua's younger sisters starved in a famine in the late 1930s; another scandalized relatives by refusing to marry, renouncing her kinship ties, and joining a celibate vegetarian association. Thus the Liangs and Hao Suhua were vulnerable to the machinations of powerful local bosses whom the family had recently antagonized. Then Liang's mother fell seriously ill:

> I was thirteen years old when my mother died [in 1942]. While she lay in the house awaiting a funeral, a conscription patrol came to take me. They always took the younger son because the elder was considered family successor (*jichengren*). My elder brother hid me when they approached, and I trembled as I listened to their voices in the room. My elder brother had served as a *bao* leader for a few years, but he had resigned the post rather than carry out some of the orders township leaders gave him. This had angered them, and they held a grudge against our family. But my elder brother would not yield. He refused to let them take me. He said that I had run away when I heard they were coming and that he did not know where I was. They demanded he pay the conscription substitution fee, but we had no money. They started to argue, and then they seized him as a conscript instead. He pleaded with

them to allow him to bury our mother before they took him away, but
they refused.

He returned home, quite unexpectedly, three months later. He had
deserted from the army. He said he had never seen any enemy and had
never fired his gun. He was emaciated from hunger. He told us that the
soldiers had to beg on the streets for food, or even took it at gunpoint
from the people if the officers so ordered. They were given three minutes to eat. If you did not finish your food, the officers would knock
your bowl to the ground. My elder brother was sick. The conscripts
had been made to sleep on the ground without so much as a reed mat
for bedding, no blankets, no change of clothes. He was covered with
sores and fleas. Not long afterward, he died.

Liang's elder brother died at the age of twenty-five. His adversaries, however,
continued to pursue young Liang even after they had seized his brother. His
saozi [eBW], Hao Suhua, with three sons of her own now, managed the family and sought assistance from her other patrilineal kin. She turned to a large
extended family headed by a junior cousin of her grandfather, another prosperous farmer also at odds with township leaders. This family looked after
Hao Suhua, her children, and their orphaned affine, helping Liang Jinyuan
evade the conscription patrols that continued to pursue him. But they all remained haunted by the specter of insecurity and faced an uncertain future.

Disorder Under Heaven

Sichuan's fertile Red Basin, and its position on the upper reaches of the
Yangzi River, have long made it a region of strategic importance to state
elites (Sage 1992; P. Smith 1988, 1991). Yet the tall mountain ranges that en-
circle the province have posed formidable natural barriers to communications and trade. "When all under Heaven is in order," as one popular expression put it, "Sichuan is the first area to fall into chaos. When tranquility
is restored across the land, it is the last region to achieve stability." Events
during the transition between the Ming and Qing dynasties in the seventeenth century, and again in the decades following the fall of the Qing and
the collapse of the imperial system in 1911, have reinforced such historical
hyperbole.

During the Ming-Qing transition, Sichuan had been a zone of war and
devastation on the inner frontiers of the empire.[1] In 1644, the same year that
the first Manchu emperor of the new Qing dynasty was enthroned in Beijing, forces commanded by Zhang Xianzhong, a famed bandit-turned-rebel,

entered Sichuan from neighboring Shaanxi province.[2] Fighting quickly spread to Meizhou (Meishan), which under the Ming had been a seat of prefectural government for three neighboring counties. For almost two decades, fighting continued between rebel forces, Ming loyalists, and Qing armies, each of which occupied Meishan for a time (MSG 1992: 3–4). Qing rule was not established in Meishan until 1662, a year before the last remnants of Zhang Xianzhong's once sizable army were finally defeated (Entenmann 1980; Li Shiping 1987: 146–48). But pacification came at a high price. Hundreds of thousands of people in Sichuan had been displaced, driven from their homes and farms, or killed, and much of the province's land was abandoned or fell out of cultivation.[3] The population of the entire Meizhou prefecture—which included Meishan, Pengshan, and Qingshen counties—stood at only 5,940 persons (MSG 1992: 116).

In the late seventeenth and early eighteenth centuries, the emperors Kangxi and Yongzheng promoted large-scale resettlement of Sichuan.[4] Millions of migrants were brought from elsewhere in China, especially from the south-central "Hu-Guang" provinces of Hubei, Hunan, Guangdong, and Guangxi. Not all settlers, however, came voluntarily. Oral traditions about ancestors brought forcibly, under guard, as new settlers or homesteaders were common in many parts of Sichuan (Sun, Jiang, and Chen 1989). In Baimapu, local legends of ancestral origins appealed to popular imagination through prominent events and figures from national history. "Our family ancestors came to Sichuan at the beginning of the Qing dynasty," asserted one elderly Hao grandfather, a local favorite among storytellers. "They were from Hunan province, Macheng county, Xiaogan township, and were brought here by Zhang Xianzhong. They were all tied up and roped together in a line." He stood, stooped, and crossed his hands behind his back to illustrate his point. "When they had to urinate, the guards would untie their hands. That's why we say we are going 'to free a hand' (*jie ge shou*) when we want to pee."[5]

Family genealogical reconstructions, however, suggest that the ancestors of Baimapu's larger and better established local descent groups, such as the Haos, more likely arrived in the area around the mid-nineteenth century. At that time, rebellions in many parts of China had again weakened the authority and power of imperial state government. By the 1850s, the Qing throne had acquiesced to the establishment of new civilian militia units, which were to help police bandits and pacify rebels in the countryside (Kuhn 1980).[6] In 1861, for example, such forces were used to quell a large uprising in the hills west of Meishan, not far from Baimapu.[7] Nevertheless, by the early twentieth century, many such militia groups were operating beyond their original purview. As the power of the imperial government waned, beset by domestic unrest and foreign incursions, influential elite families in urban as well as rural areas sought to control such militia or other irregular troops, sometimes deploying them for partisan purposes.[8]

After the fall of the Qing dynasty in 1911, violence and unrest continued to pervade many parts of Sichuan as armed and wealthy elite families competed for territorial dominance on regional as well as local levels. A militarization of the countryside, begun in the mid-nineteenth century, continued well into the twentieth.[9] A new class of large estate owners emerged: wealthy families that pursued their interests, amassed property, and projected their influence through both civilian government authority and armed force (Grunde 1976). From 1911 to 1915, Sichuan became a battleground for armies opposing then-president of the republic (and imperial aspirant) Yuan Shikai, until troops from neighboring Yunnan province occupied Sichuan and ousted Yuan's governor. What followed has been characterized as a "dismal period" in which the population of the province "suffered from nearly uninterrupted war, burgeoning opium addiction, economic disruption, and ineffectual or nonexistent provincial government" (Kapp 1973: 8). It was during this period that Liang Jinyuan's father moved from Dongguachang to Baimapu in search of a new start.

The establishment in 1927 of a new national government in Nanjing under the Nationalist Party (Kuomintang, or KMT) had limited impact on conditions in Sichuan.[10] Since the late 1910s, the province had been divided administratively into a series of garrison districts (*fang qu*), most of which were aligned with the forces of competing militarists, or "warlords" (*junfa*). Under this system, regional and local strongmen, as well as their allies and client-followers, found new opportunities for wealth and profit. They extracted from the population large sums of cash and grain to finance the administration of their districts and to defend them against rivals (Ch'en 1985). Not only did KMT authorities have difficulties extracting tax revenues from Sichuan, but by the 1930s each major warlord in the province was minting his own currency, often in vast quantities, thus contributing to spiraling inflation (Kapp 1973: 35, Bramall 1989: 27).[11]

Beginning in 1933, when Liang's elder brother married Hao Suhua, two years of drought exacerbated the heavy tax regime, leading to famine in the province. The following year, new grain levies were imposed in Meishan to collect famine-relief supplies (MSG 1992: 730). Hao Suhua's two younger sisters starved during this time. Meanwhile, a growing Communist insurgency—coupled with KMT efforts to interdict the Red Army as it passed through Sichuan on its Long March, and with the subsequent relocation of the national capital to Chongqing—prompted new initiatives to strengthen central government control over the province (Kapp 1973: 63, 98).[12] Among the most important of these measures for the present study were new offices of civilian state administration that were formally established for the first time in subcounty rural townships (*xiang*).

The men appointed to fill these new bureaucratic posts were often from wealthier, more influential families. Less affluent but well-connected newcomers, such as Liang's brother, were sometimes selected as leaders of *bao* administrative units below the township level, but they lacked the status of the newly empowered township officials, who were backed by the authority of the state. By the 1940s, local government and militia power in Baimapu were controlled by merchant-rentiers. These families owned commercial properties in the market town as well as large holdings, of 100 *mu* or more, in the surrounding countryside, and enjoyed social influence beyond the local marketing community.

Transplanting Roots

Many of these affluent, influential families were associated with descent groups such as the Haos, Wens, Xis, or Yans, whose ancestors had lived in the Baimapu area for as long as a century. Haos, for example, commonly asserted that their ancestors had settled in the area of Leshan (formerly Jiading) some twenty generations before, and that a junior branch or branches of their descent group had subsequently moved north to Meishan.[13] An important administrative and commercial center, Meishan was situated on the southern reaches of the Chengdu plain, a vast alluvial basin that had supported intensive, irrigated rice cultivation for more than a thousand years (see Map 1).[14] It was best known to many as the native place of the Song dynasty scholar and statesman Su Shi (Su Dongpo), who, with his father and younger brother, comprised the Three Sus (San Su) of Chinese literary history. Built on the west bank of the Minjiang, one of the four great rivers after which Sichuan is named, Meishan lay midway between the provincial capital of Chengdu and the city of Leshan, which were 80 to 90 kilometers— or a three-day walk—to the north and south, respectively.

Described by one late-nineteenth-century foreign visitor as a "large and busy place" (Bird 1899: 457), Meishan was a transfer point for bulk trade along and across the Min River.[15] No fewer than sixteen ferries operated near the town (MSG 1923: 52). A walled seat of prefectural government, Meishan had an imperial magistrate's office (*yamen*) and army garrison, as well as numerous temples and ancestral halls. At least three separate daily markets convened within its walls, offering the services of doctors, fortune-

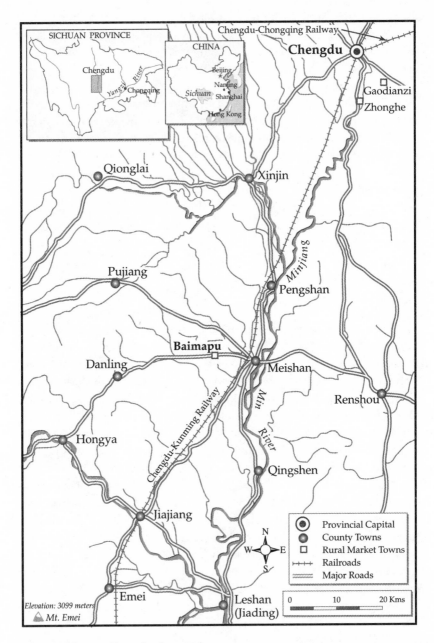

MAP 1. Western Chengdu plain, Sichuan

tellers, guest hostels, pawnshops, restaurants, teahouses, and a variety of other enterprises. Laborers and merchants in Meishan channeled the flow of goods between market towns on the lowland floodplain, as well as to and from rural markets in the hills to the east and west. Large blocks of brine salt, for example, were brought up the Minjiang via Leshan and off-loaded at Meishan, along with kerosene, foreign textiles, and other imports. Local products, such as grain, cotton, tobacco, sugarcane, and minerals such as mirabilite (Glaubers salt), which had been carried in from the rural hinterland, were shipped out on shallow-draft sailing barges or small pole-driven boats.

One of the most important of these rural transport routes ran due west from Meishan into the hills toward Danling and Hongya counties.[16] Leading out from the town's west gate, this footpath, constructed of meter-long rectangular slabs of dark red stone placed two abreast, crossed a narrow floodplain and skirted paddies, ponds, and cane fields. After about 8 *li*, or roughly an hour's walk, the path began to climb into the first set of hills as one approached the rural market town of Xianger (see Map 2). There it forked, with a branch leading northward to the rural market township of Shangyi (formerly Hanjiachang).

West of Xianger, the footpath continued around low, wooded hillocks and terraced paddies. Dispersed throughout this countryside were small groves of bamboo, often shading family homes.[17] Wet rice was the principal crop, and nearly all low-lying areas adjacent to ponds and streams were cultivated as paddies, most of which yielded a single harvest each year in the fall. The lower slopes of hills, where the soil was less suited for rice, were sometimes terraced into small fields of rapeseed, from which oil was pressed. Upper slopes were often left uncultivated, or bore small plots of sweet potatoes, soybeans, peanuts, cotton, or vegetables. Hilltops were covered with a variety of deciduous trees. Some were valued for their firm white wood, preferred for furniture, tool handles, and roofing beams; others, with thick dark trunks, were considered excellent for coffins. Many of the local poor foraged in the forests of these low hills, collecting dry brush and kindling wood that could be sold or bartered in Meishan.

Some 8 kilometers west of Meishan, the flagstone path traversed a broad expanse of flat paddy and crossed a narrow bridge spanning a small stream. The bridge, made of three tree trunks set tightly side by side, was flanked at each end by two large banyan trees, the branches of which intertwined to form a low, rooflike cover over the span. The passage beneath was so difficult to negotiate that here, it was said, "Civilian (*wen*) officials must descend from their sedan chairs; military (*wu*) officials must dismount from their horses" (Zhou 1993: 277). Beside the bridge stood a small two-story building, referred to by local inhabitants simply as the Bridge Building (Qiao-

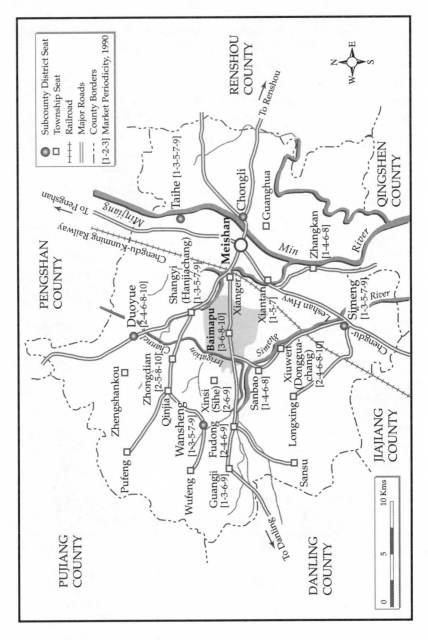

MAP 2. Meishan county

louzi), which at different times housed guards, toll collectors, or a maintenance crew. Beyond the bridge, the path ascended one last hill before approaching the rural market settlement of Baimapu.

It was along this route that a man named Hao Daixiu was said to have come from Meishan with his two sons to settle near Baimapu. Although the younger son eventually returned on his own to Meishan, his father and elder brother, Hao Tianyan, remained on their new family farm. Almost all Haos in present-day Baimapu traced their ancestry to these two men, who apparently arrived in the mid-nineteenth century (see Figure 1).[18] Like other residents of Baimapu, the descendants of Hao Daixiu and Hao Tianyan claimed that when their ancestors had settled in the area six or more generations before, they had found a sparsely populated countryside of wooded hills, wild fields, and marshy swamps. With great effort, it was said, they harnessed the resources of the land, draining the wetlands and terracing the lower hillslopes for cultivation. Through perseverance they transformed uncultivated "barren hills" (*huangshan*) into property for their progeny, and after death came to be commemorated as ancestral founders. The transplanting of their roots was celebrated in local legend, and the claims they established to the land were enshrined in the vernacularly named topography of the local landscape.

Marking the Land

The ancestors of the Wens, Xis, and Yans, who, together with the Haos, comprised four of the largest descent groups in Baimapu township, were said to have come to the area around the same time as Hao Daixiu. Over generations, as sons and brothers divided and established their own families, their houses gradually spread across the hillsides, either alone or in small clusters inhabited by patrilineal kin. A few descendants of these early settlers became wealthy and influential elites in the local market town. Others fell into economic decline or even lost their land. Yet the topography of the area continued to be marked with the patronyms of those whose ancestors had converted the land to productive use, transforming it into property. Through their labors, they created place out of space.

The high ground on which Hao Daixiu and his son chose to settle, for example, came to be known as Big Hao Hill (Hao Dashan). It was in the vicinity of this rise, about a kilometer south of the Baimapu settlement, that Hao Daixiu's descendants first built their homes, opened their fields, buried their dead, and established a commemorative hall in honor of their ancestors (see

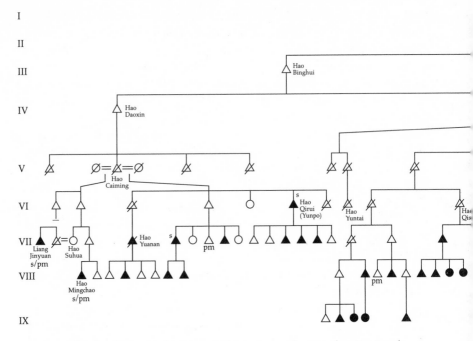

FIGURE 1.   Qiaolou Haos: A selective genealogy. △ = male, ○ = female, ◬ = deceased, ▲ = employed in village enterprise, s = enterprise staff, and pm = party member (CCP).

Map 3). Just north of Big Hao Hill lay the twin rises of Xi Lower Slope (Xi Xiapo) and Xi Upper Slope (Xi Gaopo), which bore the surname of another large local descent group. A small stream, also marked by the Xi name, flowed through a narrow vale between the two hills and meandered northeastward. As it crossed a small plain and headed toward the Bridge Building on the Meishan footpath, it skirted the bulk of Big Xi Hill (Xi Dashan) where the earliest Xi families had established homes and, later, an ancestral hall and cemetery.

Big Xi Hill was the highest point in the area. Even though it rose only 500 meters above sea level, it nevertheless towered more than a hundred feet above surrounding paddies. It was said that from its commanding heights one might—early in the morning, on a rare clear day, free of clouds or haze—glimpse the peak of sacred Mt. Emei rising above the southern horizon. North of Big Xi Hill and the Meishan footpath lay Yan Grave Hill (Yan Fen Shan), where many family homes and ancestral remains of another large descent group were located, and to the west was Yan Pond (Yan Haizi). Directly north of the Baimapu settlement was Upper Wen Slope (Wen Shangpo) and Big Wen Pond (Wen Datang), where the homes, ancestral hall, and cemetery of yet another major local descent group were located. Thus the vernacularly named topography of the local landscape symbol-

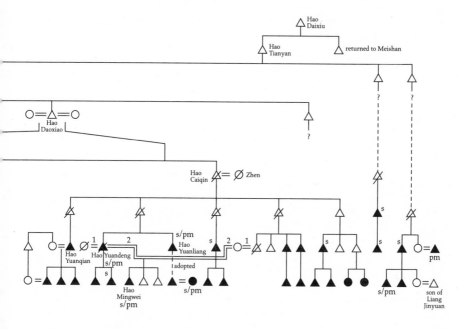

ized the proprietary claims that these ancestors had once made to the land. The forms their descendants built on that landscape, such as houses, ancestral halls, and graves, marked the continuing presence of these patrilines across time.

Virtually all built forms were fashioned out of the earth itself. The walls of houses and temples, for example, were constructed of mudbricks, large rectangular blocks about a foot and a half in length, cut or pressed from the local soil, dried hard in the sun, and sealed together with clay paste. These heavy blocks insulated homes, keeping them relatively cool during the hot, humid summers and trapping warmth in the near-freezing winters. The roofs of most homes were made of dried rice stalks, by-products of the harvest that were also used to feed water buffalo, the principal draft animals in the area. Families that had attained greater affluence, however, often converted to tiled shingles purchased from kilns near Xianger. Tile-roofed homes were a symbol of status, even for families that subsequently suffered an economic downturn, because they conveyed permanence. They also better withstood rains and offered no hiding places for many of the insects that nested in thatched roofs. Tiled roofs were common on the homes of merchants in the Baimapu market settlement, but relatively rare in the surrounding countryside.

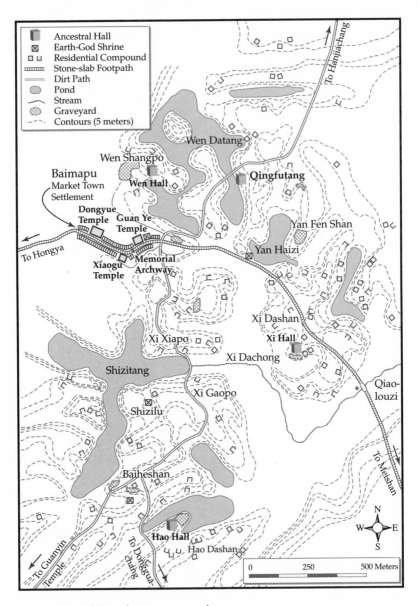

MAP 3.   Second Bao of Baimapu township, ca. 1940

The homes of poor families were often little more than small huts, some-times even a single rented room, but most houses were based on a U-shaped model. The core structure was a rectangular hall, often divided into three rooms: a central main room (*zhengfang*) flanked by a kitchen and a bedroom. Families that grew and prospered added wing rooms perpendicular to this central hall, creating an open courtyard where crops were dried and threshed, children played, chickens ranged, and family feasts were held. Such wing rooms might be built for a newly married son and daughter-in-law, for storing produce, grain, and farm implements, or even for domesticated animals such as hogs or water buffalo. Another set of rooms might be added directly opposite the main hall, fully enclosing the courtyard.

Such four-cornered compounds (*siheyuan*) could contain upward of a dozen rooms. They symbolized the unity of large, extended patrilineal families and the ideal of five generations living under the same roof (*wudai tongtang*).[19] Although few families approximated such ideals, some did manage to create *siheyuan*, which stood as prestigious monuments to their prosperity and enduring presence across generations. A four-cornered compound with a "dragon's gate" (*longmen*) entry-portal conveyed significant status.[20] As a popular local expression put it, "A dragon's gate is worth 1,000 catties, a regular house door but two ounces" (*Qian jin longmen, er liang hu*).

Family Times

Inside the house, the kitchen was of central importance, and its field of social activity was dominated by women. Meals were prepared and often eaten there, and children heard many stories from mothers and grandmothers during time spent in the kitchen. During the winter, the kitchen was also the warmest room of the house. Its stove was an important symbol of family commensality, and it defined social boundaries.[21] Although the term "family" (*jia*) conveyed notions of a patriline of ancestors and descendants continuing across genealogical time, in a more immediate sense family was regarded as an economic unit, a corporate group with its own property and collective finances. When a family divided into separate economic groups, a new stove was constructed, even if a new house were not.[22] In fact, the phrase "to divide the stove" (*fenzao*) was synonymous with "family division" (*fenjia*). The sight of smoke rising simultaneously from different parts of a house was a telltale sign that a family was in an advanced stage of partition.

The main room of a house was larger than the others. Its central location, along the meridian of the household compound, symbolized its formal status. It was here that the family's ancestral spirit altar (*shenkang*) was located and that guests and visitors were received. Nevertheless, in many homes the main room was used on a daily basis for informal activities or even for storage. Spirit altars consisted of a square Eight Immortals table (*baxianzhuo*), sometimes with intricately carved trim, pushed against the center of the rear wall. Candles, food, and incense were set there as offerings to family ances-

tors and sometimes to religious deities. This evoked a spiritual tie of commensality between living descendants and patrilineal ancestors, reaffirming
bonds of reciprocity beyond death. Above the altar, a large red paper bearing
the family's surname hung on the wall. Whereas the stove symbolized the
unity of family as a corporate economic group, the ancestral scroll expressed
the ritual identity of family as patriline.[23] Denoting the spiritual seat (*shen-
wei*) of collective ancestral spirits of a particular surname, scrolls in Baimapu
monumentalized genealogical time as a generic, almost atemporal, continuity between the past, present, and future.

Ancestral halls (*citang*) were architecturally patterned on *siheyuan* homes,
each with a dragon's gate entry-portal leading to an open-air inner courtyard.
Much as they did for individual families, such four-cornered compounds
symbolized the identity and prestige of local descent groups as extended
families writ large.[24] Ancestral halls were the site of major ritual activities
and important group deliberations. Three times a year, special rites and communal banquets were staged there to commemorate patrilineal ancestors
(see Chapter 2). Such halls were also repositories for handwritten genealogical lineage histories, as well as storehouses for grain harvested from land
held corporately in ancestral trust.

These halls were smaller and less grand than some found in other parts of
China, such as the Southeast Coast and the lower Yangzi valley, where lineage development had long historical roots and attained more elaborate organization (cf. J. Watson 1975b; R. Watson 1982; Ebrey and Watson 1986;
Siu 1989). But they were, nonetheless, impressive monuments to the status
of the larger and wealthier local descent groups. More than thirty surnames
were represented among the families living in the subtownship *bao* that
Liang Jinyuan's brother briefly headed. Of them, only three had ancestral
halls in the area: the Haos, the Wens, and the Xis.

The Wen hall and adjacent ancestral cemetery were situated on Upper
Wen Slope, just north of the Baimapu market settlement. The largest and
most impressive ancestral hall in the township, it reportedly had eighteen
rooms. It was covered with a tiled roof and had been built with more than
ten thick wooden pillars, two feet in diameter, said to have been hewn from
primordial forests (*yuanshi senlin*) and transported at great cost and effort
to Baimapu.[25] In the main room of the hall was a ceremonial altar, on which
a single large ancestral tablet (*shenzupai*) was set in a plaster base.[26] The Hao
ancestral hall sat at the base of Big Hao Hill, also overlooking a pond and
adjacent to an ancestral cemetery. It, too, was a tile-roofed *siheyuan*, but
consisted of only seven rooms. The Xi hall, built on Big Xi Hill, was similar
in size, and likewise flanked by a (smaller) cemetery. Although the Xi surname featured prominently in the vernacularly named local topography,

Xi ancestral trust properties were relatively modest, and by the 1940s few Xi families were still large landowners.

Spiritual Ties

The presence of particular families and patrilineal descent groups was also marked by the raised mounds of ancestral graves, which had powerful spiritual importance. Death was seen not as an end, but as a transition. To attain ancestral status, one needed not only male descendants but also a proper funeral, a ritual process heavily focused on the containment, absorption, and eventual cleansing of the polluting influences of death (J. Watson 1988). Ideally, a rite of passage with such monumental significance called for the services of hired specialists, as well as specially constructed coffins, commemorative feasts, and tombstones.[27] Failure to perform minimal ritual obligations was regarded as an unfilial act of potentially serious consequence, for an unsettled spirit might return as a ghost (A. Wolf 1974). It was at just such a critical moment that the adversaries of Liang's elder brother raided the family home, forcibly removing the eldest son and ritual family head before he could perform their mother's funerary rites.

After death, part of the spirit or soul of an individual ancestor was believed to reside in the grave with the deceased's mortal remains. If situated in an optimal location, a grave might bring health, longevity, prosperity, and good fortune to descendants. As with all the forms built on the local landscape, graves were sited in accordance with beliefs about local *fengshui*, or geomancy.[28] Because bones were believed to be particularly powerful, or efficacious (*ling*), conductors of the energy forces, or vital airs (*qi*), flowing through the earth, ancestral burial sites were chosen with special care. Just as a well-placed grave might channel natural energy forces to the benefit of descendants, a poorly sited one might be interpreted as the cause of unfortunate or ill-fated events. In some cases, ancestral graves associated with families in particular branches (*fang*) of local descent groups came to be clustered together on a site where the conflux of *fengshui* forces was deemed to be particularly auspicious.[29] The Wen ancestral cemetery, for example, was nestled at what was said to be the mouth of the Baimapu "*fengshui* dragon,"—a curved hill that was considered a prominent site of great symbolic power. Graves represented a key link in the conceptual continuity and unity of a patriline, and were periodically the focus of important ritual activities.

Deaths, like other major transitions of the life cycle, such as births and marriages, were also reported to local earth gods (*tudi gong*) through ritual offerings at their shrines. These small monuments, standing less than a meter high and containing a small statuette, dotted the countryside at irregular intervals.[30] In the popular religious pantheon, earth gods were local tutelary deities with jurisdiction over specific territory. As intermediaries between the living and the powerful, official gods who ruled the Underworld, they were approached with petitions for favorable weather, plentiful harvests, and general good fortune, and were also offered sacrifices at important family rituals and major festivals, such as the Lunar New Year and the Grave Sweeping festival (Qingming). Uniting families and individual residents of different surnames in symbolic exchange relations with the spiritual forces governing the fate of the land, earth gods marked ritually defined territorial units of social interaction (Sangren 1987: 61).[31] Elsewhere in 1940s Sichuan, earth god shrines were a principal focus of identity for "natural groupings" of families dispersed across the countryside (Skinner 1964–65: 6). In the subtownship administrative *bao* to which the Liangs belonged, there were three such shrines: one located near Yan Pond, another not far from Big Hao Hill, and a third on the west side of Upper Xi Slope (see Map 3). Another reportedly stood in the Baimapu market settlement.

Earth gods were believed to report directly to city gods (*chenghuang*), who ruled from urban administrative centers such as Meishan. In the bureaucratic hierarchy of the Underworld, city gods wielded powers analogous to those of county or district magistrates in secular imperial administration. As subordinate authorities, earth gods were responsible for delivering the souls of the deceased to the appropriate city god in preparation for passage to the courts of judgment and punishment in Hell. But they were also believed to hold their own punitive powers, and if offended could bring drought, flood, hunger, or other misfortune to the residents within their domain.

Close symbolic parallels between the organization of power in the supernatural Underworld and that in secular state administration were an important ideological foundation of the imperial system. When state power waned, local "cults" sometimes developed around other deities with popular followings, although officials often attempted to co-opt such religious movements (J. Watson 1985; von Glahn 1991; Katz 1995; Szonyi 1997). A number of popular deities enjoyed large followings in turn-of-the-century Sichuan, and there were several temples in the small Baimapu market settlement itself.

Marketing Communities

The rural market settlement of Baimapu was built on a small hillock, 18 *li* (9 km) west of Meishan. There, a strip of several dozen single-story mud-brick houses, built wall to wall, crowded along each side of the flagstone path that constituted the town's only street. The streetfront rooms of these homes were used as small shops, some only a few meters wide, their interiors blackened by the smoke of oil lamps. To the rear lay the open courtyards and dimly lit rooms of family living quarters. The tiled eaves of these houses extended outward across the street, almost to the point of touching. Through this narrow passage, partially sheltered from sun and rain alike, foot traffic along the Meishan path moved daily. But every two or three days this space became a marketplace, a bustling center of exchange and interaction that drew such large crowds as to render the street almost impassable for much of the morning.

Market was both time and place; it embodied movement, as a center of periodic economic exchange and social interaction. Working in a small, rural market town on the Chengdu plain during the 1940s, Skinner (1964–65) noted how "local marketing communities" formed around such settlements. Others, such as Highbaugh (1948), Treudley (1971) and Crook (n.d.), have described daily life in such market towns and the significance of rural periodic markets in the lives of local families.[32] Markets such as Baimapu were a major arena of social intercourse, a theater for political maneuvering, and a stage for symbolic display. These diverse activities formed the basis of exchange communities that included not only town residents but also farm families living in homes dispersed throughout the surrounding countryside.

Baimapu was a fairly important market in rural Meishan, convening four times during each ten-day cycle, on a 3–5–7–10 schedule. Each day of the lunar month ending with the number 3, 5, 7 or 0 signaled market day at Baimapu, and brought not only market-goers from the surrounding countryside but also itinerant merchants from Meishan and other towns. In similar rural settlements, markets convened on alternate days. This made it possible for traders to buy goods or produce at a particular market one morning and sell them elsewhere on another.[33] Most families living within a 10-*li* (5-km) radius of Baimapu regularly conducted their marketing activities there.[34] Some came simply to sell fresh vegetables, others to buy a hog, secure a loan, have a smith repair a farm tool—and, of course, to visit with friends at a favorite teashop, exchange news, or gossip. But even on so-called cold days (*hantian*), when market was not held in Baimapu, one could walk to an alternative market settlement—and another set of social contacts—only a few hours away.

Although rural markets offered a range of basic goods and services, many were known as particularly good forums of exchange for specific commodities. Baimapu, for instance, was a well-known grain market (MSG 1992: 705), and its frequent periodicity, convening every two or three days, suggested its relative importance in the regional marketing system. Even along

Baimapu Street, certain areas were dominated by the barter and sale of particular items. Fresh produce, for example, was peddled along one section, eggs
and live fowl along another, and likewise for cotton, fruit, grains, hogs, seed,
tobacco, and wood and bamboo products. Butchered meats, mainly pork,
were sold from several different stalls.

In the 1940s, Street Village (Jiecun), as Baimapu also came to be called,
was home to several dozen families, including most large landowners in the
area. But unlike farmers living in the surrounding countryside, most market town residents engaged in retail or artisan activities. Here there were numerous general-goods stores retailing a variety of items, such as bowls, jars,
cooking utensils, tools, baskets, kerosene, and cooking oil. Other family businesses offered dried foods, cakes, sweets, sugar, and salt. A few shops specialized in particular commodities, such as cloth bolts and clothing; writing materials, almanacs and calendars; or statuettes, candles, incense, and "spirit
money" (*zhiqian*; literally, "paper money") used in ritual ceremonies. There
were half a dozen teahouses, twice that number of restaurants or small eateries (*xiao chidian*), several barbers, and at least two hostels offering secure
lodging for travelers and long-distance itinerant traders with their goods or
animals. The market town also contained the workshops of potters, weavers,
cloth dyers, and blacksmiths.

Honors, Riches, and Wealth

Near the center of the Baimapu settlement stood a large Dongyue temple
dedicated to the God of the Eastern Peak. Dongyue temples were found in
many Sichuan market towns (e.g., Skinner 1964–65; Treudley 1971).[35] Popularly viewed as the god of the dead, with power over the determination of
life, death, and rebirth as well as the award of riches and honors, the God
of the Eastern Peak was believed to preside over the courts of Hell beneath
Taishan (Mt. Tai) in eastern China's Shandong province (Goodrich 1991:
170–71).[36] The Dongyue temple, it was said, had been commissioned jointly
by the Wen and Xi lineages to commemorate an important marriage alliance
between them. Its main hall was dominated by two large clay statues of the
god (Dongyue Gong) and his wife (Dongyue Niang), symbolizing the Wen
and Xi lineages, respectively, whose members were described as "cousins"
(*laobiao*) related through marriage.[37]

Each year, on the sixth day of the third lunar month, the union of the god
and goddess (and the alliance between the Wens and Xis) was celebrated
in an elaborate ritual procession of these effigies throughout the township

countryside. The route followed a circuit that stopped at several smaller local temples, as well as at a much larger Guanyin temple, before returning to the Baimapu market settlement.[38] The procession of the God of the Eastern Peak symbolized the projection over residents of the marketing community of cosmological authority from an officially sanctioned deity who was associated with honor and riches, life and death. It also provided visual pageantry that enhanced the prestige of the Wen and Xi lineages, whose leading members were prominent local notables in the area.

A tall memorial archway (*pailou*) made of stone straddled the flagstone path near the eastern end of Baimapu (see Map 3). Similar commemorative monuments were found along roads and at the entrances of settlements in many parts of Sichuan, and throughout China in general. They were sometimes erected to honor the memory of a local hero, a successful candidate in the imperial civil service examinations, or perhaps a "virtuous widow" who refrained from remarrying.[39] Although memorial archways were often commissioned by a particular wealthy family, lineage, or temple association, many other local residents also took pride in them, viewing them as a mark of distinction for the marketing community as a whole.

Near the archway stood a temple in honor of Guan Ye (Guan Di), the god of war, wealth, and the military (*wu*) wing of the bureaucracy.[40] This temple was described as a beautiful structure, the eavetips of its tiled roof angling gracefully upward. Two large banyan trees flanked its open courtyard, where the earth god shrine of the Baimapu market settlement was said to have been located. Based on the historical figure of Guan Yu, warrior-hero of the Three Kingdoms period in the third century, "Grandpa Guan" (as Baimapu inhabitants referred to him) had been posthumously elevated to the status of a deity and officially given the symbolic title of emperor (*di*). Becoming the focus of a popular temple cult during the intense commercialization and large-scale population movements of the early Qing dynasty, the symbolism of Guan Di promoted "an ethic of trust and camaraderie to hold together 'a society of strangers'" (Duara 1988b: 782).

In the early nineteenth century, Guan Di was a popular patron deity in many market towns throughout China, especially in the north (Gamble 1968; A. Smith 1970). A symbol of power and authority, loyalty and filial piety, and protective patronage, Guan Di transcended local territorial communities, such as those marked by earth god shrines, and linked the locale to broader society through the idiom of the marketplace (Duara 1988b: 786).[41] When, in the early twentieth century, formal offices of state administration were extended from the county level to that of rural townships, the new Baimapu township government was headquartered in the Guan Ye temple.

State Strengthening and Local Empowerment

During the Qing dynasty, Meizhou had been an administrative prefecture (*zhou*) with an imperial magistrate who controlled an army garrison and held jurisdiction over Meishan and three other neighboring counties (*xian*). After the Republican revolution in 1911, however, the prefecture was abolished and its former counties were administered separately (MSG 1992: 37). In 1920, as part of an effort promoted by national and provincial authorities to curb the growing power of local and regional civilian militia, each of Meishan's five officially recognized towns (*zhen*) and four rural townships (*xiang*) became a seat of subcounty district (*qu*) administration, with jurisdiction over three to five rural market settlements surrounding it (ibid., p. 37). Baimapu, which had officially become a township in 1913, when troops were stationed there (p. 51), was one of these new district centers. Local leaders of many civilian militia units, which were coordinated around market towns, had been assuming increasingly broad powers of tax collecting and policing, and it was hoped that subcounty district offices would improve state control.[42]

Although the KMT opened its first offices in Meishan in May 1927, national government influence over county affairs remained relatively weak for another ten years. Recall that, during the 1910s and 1920s, Sichuan had been divided into garrison districts dominated by competing military leaders.[43] Although regional militarists commanded large armies of troops, their control over local militia forces within their domains was often challenged. In 1925, for example, troops of the powerful general Yang Sen battled forces loyal to a local army chief for several days in the area of Meishan (MSG 1992: 8). Two years later, *The West China Missionary News* reported that the army of Liu Wenhui, who by then controlled most of Sichuan south of Chengdu, had fought a "pitched battle" against "local militia forces" in Meishan after the latter had set up independent tax stations along roads in the countryside (Kapp 1973: 53).[44] In rural areas such as Baimapu, new taxes, levies, and surcharges proliferated as county authorities, district leaders, and militia chiefs competed for revenue control.

For example, in addition to the land tax (and a new surcharge on that tax), there were levies imposed on salt (both its production and sale),[45] on commerce (alcohol, grain, hogs, kerosene, sugar, paper, and tobacco taxes, as well as transit fees and the like), and on professional services (e.g., deed notarization). Other surcharges included "bullet taxes" and collections for "winter defense funds," "Northern Expedition funds," and "national defense funds" (Kapp 1973: 40–41). Opium became a major source of revenue, through its retail sale as well as through production and sales taxes.[46] Taxes also began to be collected several years in advance. Conditions varied from one area to another, but by 1934 there was no region in Sichuan where tax levies were running less than twenty-two years in advance (Ch'en 1969: 31–32; Sheridan 1975: 294). As early as 1919, annual land taxes in Meishan began to be collected three to four years at a time, and later as much as six years at a time; by 1933, they already had been collected through the year 1998 (MSG 1992: 729–30, but cf. p. 9; see also Liu Jun 1988: 89). Moreover, actual levies were alleged to be as much as three times officially reported revenues (Xiong 1988: 131). Many small landowners were pushed into debt or tenancy.

After 1937, when the national capital was relocated to Sichuan, formal offices of subcounty government were extended to the township level in an attempt to reduce further the territorial power of rural district officials and militia leaders. But these "state strengthening" efforts aggravated the economic burden on rural inhabitants because the operating costs of subcounty bureaucracies were paid largely through new local tax levies (Duara 1988a). Irregular fees and surcharges burgeoned while public works projects and grain reserves often declined. Many newly empowered local officials colluded with rural militia leaders to increase their family wealth or pursue their own partisan interests.[47] The result was "the domination of local state forms by entrepreneurial brokers who derive[d] their power and profit from the functions they perform[ed] for the state, but who [were] not easily accountable to the formal agencies (or democratic processes) of the polity" (ibid., p. 75). Acting in the name of government authority, new township officials extracted even more revenue from rural inhabitants while extending their power further and further beyond their official duties. But even though efforts to develop new formal institutions of state administration in the countryside were hampered by such informal patterns of local dominance, this did not lead to "anarchy" in local society (cf. Duara 1988a: 73); rather, it fostered new forms of local empowerment as local elites employed directed violence in pursuit of additional wealth.

With much of the country under Japanese occupation, the KMT government stepped up taxes and conscription in Sichuan to support its operations and war effort (Bramall 1989: 14).[48] From 1936 through 1947, at least twenty new types of tax levies were introduced in Meishan (MSG 1992: 726), some of which were collected several times a year.[49] Inflation, exacerbated by the overminting of currency, spiraled upward. In 1941, county tax authorities began to accept payments only in grain (ibid., p. 12). In fact, from 1937 through 1945, the commodity price index for Sichuan in general rose at an annual rate of 130 percent (Bramall 1989). By 1948, prices for some goods in

Meishan were 12,000 to 40,000 times their levels seven years earlier: a catty of tea leaves cost Y160,000; a catty of tobacco leaves, Y80,000; a catty of salt or of plain liquor (*baijiu*), Y60,000; a catty of pork, Y44,000, and a catty of husked white rice, Y12,500 (MSG 1992: 417–418; 763).

While KMT rule did bring new social services, particularly schools, to rural areas, large numbers of men were forcibly conscripted for military service. Some were assigned work as construction laborers or transporters, others as foot soldiers fighting first against the Japanese and later against the Communists.[50] Threat of conscription hung heavily over many families. Conscription regulations enforced in Baimapu under the authority of the wartime Nationalist regime stipulated that families with three sons provide at least one son for military-related service; those with five or more sons were obliged to send two. But as Liang Jinyuan's account illustrates, even families below the threshold for mandatory conscription quotas sometimes had their young men or boys seized. The wealthy, however, could buy their way out of conscription by paying a substitution fee (*paikuan*) of five to ten *dan* (roughly half a ton) of unhusked rice to township leaders. Some among the poor, in contrast, sold themselves as substitute conscripts (Endicott 1980: 190–91).

At the turn of the century, there had been a regular, daily flow of men, women, and youngsters heading east for the markets of Meishan, shouldering or hauling by cart or wheelbarrow loads of grain, cotton, peanuts, bamboo products, timber, or, most commonly of all, kindling wood. But by the 1940s, fear of conscription was so prevalent that many men avoided open travel. Few dared go to Meishan, and some even stayed away from market in Baimapu. Most marketing was performed by women. The flagstone path to Meishan was traveled largely by women and children carrying large bundles of brush and firewood down to the county town to barter for a few handfuls of rice. Along the way, they commonly encountered local militia patrols or KMT army roadblocks, with armed soldiers seeking to replenish troop strength.

Not surprisingly, it was often the poor, driven to market by hunger, who were victims of such arrests and seizures. As one elderly Yan man recalled:

> My father died when I was still a child, and my mother remarried and moved away. That was common among many rural women at the time. I was raised by my paternal grandparents in Meishan. As a boy, I worked as a small peddler during the War of Resistance against Japan. My *yao-bar* [patrilineal junior cousin] learned a trade as a tailor. In 1937 or 1938, my grandfather died and my grandmother went back alone to her natal place [Baimapu], where she rented a room in the house of a farm family. I remained in Meishan with my *yaobar* and earned a liv-

ing making shoes. In 1947 or 1948, my grandmother called me to come and help her cut wild grasses and collect firewood to sell in Meishan. Of course I went right away. But one day I was careless and gambled away all the money I had earned for her. I was scared. I did not know what to do. I found a job pulling carts all over the area, even as far as Chengdu, a journey of three days. I was given some food and clothing for this work, but no wages. One day while I was hauling a cart along the road, I was stopped by a KMT army patrol. They took me away to serve in the army. Just like that. We left the cart in the middle of the road.

Such incidents were common enough to earn the Kuomintang the pun name of Zhuamindang (literally, "People Grabbing Party").[51] In Baimapu, conscription and taxation became two of the most feared powers of the new local township officials.

Administering the Rural Township

Among the most important newly empowered official positions in Baimapu were those of militia group leader (*tuanzhang*), township head (*xiangzhang*), deputy township head (*fu xiangzhang*), and granary supervisor (*liangzhang*).[52] The men who filled these posts were from wealthy local families that enjoyed considerable influence within the Baimapu marketing community. Many used their affluence to finance political maneuvering. Some enjoyed close ties to county elites in Meishan and were able to position themselves for appointment to the new posts created in rural township administration.[53] Most of the township officials empowered through the state strengthening reforms were from the larger and better-established local descent groups, such as the Haos, Wens, Xis, and Yans.

In the countryside surrounding the township settlement, administration of tax collection, conscription, and policing was conducted through the *baojia* system of collective security.[54] Rural market towns were the organizational focus of this system. Baimapu township, for example, was divided administratively into twenty separate *bao* units, the leaders, or heads (*baozhang*), and deputies (*fu baozhang*) of which were appointed by township officials. Liang Jinyuan's family lived in what was known as Second Bao (Er Bao). Each *bao* was itself comprised of ten *jia* units, ideally composed of ten administrative households (*hu*) each.[55] Second Bao included *jia* units located to the north and south of the Meishan footpath. Each *jia* leader (*jiazhang*) was selected by the headman of the *bao* and confirmed by township officials.[56] Such men were responsible for transmitting government regulations to each household in the *jia*, notifying each of its obligatory taxes and other fees, and assuring each one met its tax and conscription obligations.

During the Republican era, a new position was added to the *baojia* structure. This *bao* representative (*baomin daibiao*) served in the township government, participating in administrative affairs as well as in tax and security matters. By local accounts, this was a powerful and influential position.[57] Originally selected by the *bao* leader and the headmen of each *jia*, *bao* representatives were later elected by local families. Hao Youyu, a wealthy landowner, was elected as a *bao* representative after he hosted an enormous banquet in the Baimapu settlement, with tables of diners reportedly stretching half the length of the town. In fact, all the men who served as leaders of Second Bao and its constituent *jia* units came from families with some landholdings, suggesting that landownership was a criterion for office.[58] *Bao* leaders, in particular, tended to come from relatively wealthy families. The man who apparently replaced Liang's brother as *bao* head, and the man appointed as deputy head of the *bao*, were both wealthy (Yan) landowners married to two wives each.

Many officials and scholars have noted that the *baojia* system tended to divided local society, subverting "natural" loyalties by enforcing mutual surveillance and collective group responsibility (e.g., Hsiao 1967; Kuhn 1980: 59–63, but cf. p. 94). Although Second Bao was a territorial unit of administration, it did not correspond to local notions of territorial community, which were oriented around several different foci, including family farms, ancestral property, earth god shrines, and the local market. The administrative subunits of Second Bao also crosscut local descent groups, although several administrative *jia* were demographically dominated by families of particular descent groups, such as the Haos, Wens, Xis, or Yans.

Patrilineal kinship with *baojia* leaders, however, was no guarantee against harassment. One elderly Yan man, who had been appointed as his local *jia* leader in the 1940s, described how he had been forced from his position by a patrilineal kinsmen who wanted it for himself. "He told me, 'From now on, I am *jia* head, and you are not.' Then he went around and told everyone that I was dead. He warned me to stay at home and never to show my face, not even at market, or else he would have me conscripted. What could I do? He had good relations with township leaders, and they turned a blind eye to this."

"Local Notables" in the Township Arena

Even though the establishment of formal administrative offices in rural townships was intended, in part, to check the power of local elites over militia organization and deployment, in Baimapu civil authority and armed force were both controlled by the same group of wealthy families, most of whom owned large landholdings and commercial shops in the market settlement. In the early twentieth century, such prominent families were often referred to by the honorific, "local notables" (*dizhu*).[59] They often managed the trust properties owned by temple organizations and ancestral associations, oversaw rural schools, and served as guarantors, creditors, and moneylenders for other local residents. Their family tombstones were usually large and elaborate, their homes tile-roofed *siheyuan* compounds, their sons generally educated, and most of their children married with grand banquets and large betrothal payments. Many such senior men maintained expensive opium habits and grew their fingernails long as a symbol of their ability to avoid the drudgery of manual labor.

Consider the case of Wen Shisan, a wealthy merchant-landowner and geomancer (*yinyang xiansheng*) who served for many years as Baimapu township head as well as a period as *bao* leader. Wen was the head of a prosperous joint family of over a dozen members who lived in a large tile-roofed *siheyuan* north of Baimapu settlement. They possessed one of the few private wells in the area, whereas most families drew their drinking water from nearby ponds and streams. They also owned 20 *mu* of land, most of which was rented out to tenants, as well as several shops in the market town run by Wen's three married sons. The eldest son, who ran a profitable beancurd (*doufu*) business, also served as a *jia* headman and tax collector. The second son served for many years as a *bao* head and *bao* representative. Like many such local notable families, the Wens played an influential role in the management of their descent group's ancestral association, as well as in the prosperous Dongyue temple alliance.

Some local notables were viewed as charitable patrons who looked after the interests of friends and relatives. For example, Xi Bailian, whose family owned a mid-sized farm of some 10 *mu*, served as both deputy township head and the local KMT representative in Baimapu. He was remembered by some as having arranged shelter for a number of poor and propertyless families on the grounds of the Dongyue temple, which he also helped manage. Yet not all local notables and township officials were enlightened or restrained in their economic and political activities, and some were notorious for the strong-handed way they exercised power. As Liang Jinyuan's experiences show, the less scrupulous were known to pursue adversaries with conscription patrols. They also manipulated the adjudication of disputes, seized property when debtors failed to repay loans, arrested people on trumped-up charges in order then to demand ransom for their freedom, and even used their authority as township officials to press men into their service under threat of death (*xin si bi pei*).

One wealthy landowning merchant, who had made a fortune as a government tax collector in another county and then served a term as Baimapu township head, employed armed ruffians to ensure his election to the county assembly in 1947. On election day, his sons and associates took guns and surrounded the polling station in Baimapu, permitting only those who supported his candidacy to go inside (see also MSG 1992: 212). The continuing importance of militia power throughout the 1940s was underscored in many local accounts of the most powerful man in the township, a wealthy landowner named Hao Yuntai, who was said to have declined the post of township head when it was offered to him by county authorities, opting instead for the office of militia group leader. Hao Yuntai also served as granary supervisor and head of the new township public school, positions that gave him access to sizable cash and grain resources. He allegedly loaned grain privately from public reserves, making a large profit from high interest rates.[60] Apparently such practices were common in Meishan. In 1949, a provincial investigator reported that there was more grain missing from official granaries in Meishan than any other county in Sichuan (ibid., p. 730).

Hao Yuntai's power was based in part on the alliance he formed with two patrilineal cousins, the brothers Hao Youyu and Hao Yuru, both wealthy landowning merchants who held important posts in the township administration: the former was a *bao* representative, while the latter was head of local conscription patrols. Together these three Hao cousins, who in local kinship terminology addressed one another as "brothers," formed one of the most powerful cliques in the township government. It was widely alleged that they used their power and authority for personal and family gain, manipulating tax and conscription procedures to favor their allies and clients or to harass potential rivals.

The most infamous expression of local notable power in Baimapu was an incident involving these men and one of their uncles, Hao Caiqin—head of the same family that came to the aid of the young orphan Liang Jinyuan as he desperately tried to evade the conscription patrols. I turn to this event in Chapter 2. The conflict between these two patrilineal kinsmen was to have profound implications for future social and political developments in Baimapu, for reasons that were probably unforeseen by the participants and observers themselves.

Shaping a Township Landscape

Herzfeld (1991) drew a distinction between social time, comprising the "grist" of everyday experience, and monumentalized time, a generic construction that attempts to reduce social experience to "collective predictability." He argued that the monumentalization of time through calibration into discrete, well-defined periods is an important aspect in the processes of community building. Although Herzfeld was principally concerned with the imagined communities of nations, similar monumentalizations of time can take place among less grandiose collectivities. Marking the land with their surnames and family farms, with their houses, graves, and ancestral halls, with temples and earth god shrines, residents of the Baimapu countryside created symbolic monuments of their own social communities.

In the 1940s, roughly 130 families lived with the Liangs in the area of Baimapu's Second Bao. More than 30 different surnames were represented among this population. Residents of this administrative unit, however, did not share a collective sense of identity as a single local community. The *bao* represented a view of the landscape that was projected from the state, as did the administrative *xiang*, or rural township. But unlike the *bao*, the township was based on an actual focal point of social and ritual interaction: the rural periodic market. The new township offices were even situated at the temple of Guan Ye, the patron deity of many marketing communities.

The *bao* had no such foundation. In fact, by local accounts there had been little regular direct interaction between families in Second Bao living to the north and those living to the south of the Meishan path. They conducted no rituals as a collective social group, rarely intermarried, and in some cases did not even know the names of those living in more distant areas of the *bao*. To the extent that people associated themselves, and their fates, with a particular place or territory, those sentiments generally focused on ancestral halls, family property, earth god shrines, and the local market, each of which was evocative of a spiritual bond that families shared through the land.

There were no "village communities" in the early-twentieth-century Baimapu countryside. Individual family farms and homesteads dotted the land at irregular intervals, dispersed among the wooded hilltops. From the perspective of officialdom, only clustered market settlements such as Baimapu were recognized places in the countryside. But for local inhabitants, the vernacularly named topography of the local landscape marked their ancestral roots, and the houses, ancestral halls, and graves that they and their ancestors had built on the land stood as monuments to forms of social community that had developed and endured despite the pervasive insecurity that haunted many families over time.

CHAPTER 2

Alliance and Antagonism

Family Associations in an Era of Insecurity

In the courtyard were two basins for storing water. The recluse
pointed to them and said, "This one has an ant-sized drip; from the
other we get rid of a pint a day. Which will empty first?"

—SU SHI, *Literary Collection of Su Donpo (1079)*

Time flows downstream, Life moves upstream.

—CHINESE FOLK SAYING

In the early years of the twentieth century, a young farmer from the southern part of Second Bao married a woman, née Zhen, whose family lived
several *li* to the west in an adjacent *bao*. The groom, Hao Caiqin, was the
fourth and youngest son of Hao Daoxiao, whose grandfather [FF] and great-
grandfather [FFF] had come up the road from Meishan to settle in Baimapu.
Big Hao Hill, near which he lived, had been named in honor of those ancestors, to whom the nearby Hao ancestral hall was also dedicated. Yet unlike
his brothers and many of his patrilineal cousins, who spent most of their
lives in the homes of their fathers, young Hao Caiqin and his wife Zhen
moved to a house in her *bao* after they married.

Hao's father had headed a family that owned more than 20 *mu* of paddy.
After their father's death, he and his brothers divided the family, and each
received 5.2 *mu* with which to start his own independent family. It was
not a poor legacy, but with the subsequent births of five sons and at least
two daughters, Hao and Zhen sometimes struggled to make ends meet. Yet
they eventually prospered, owing largely to the weaving skills of Zhen. As
a youth, she had been apprenticed by her parents at the Guanyin temple in
her native *bao*, where resident Buddhist disciples—all women—ran a cloth-
weaving enterprise with some thirty unmarried apprentice girls. Hao and

Zhen purchased several looms and established a profitable home industry under Zhen's direction. Although they did not buy additional land, they later rented another 40 *mu* from a family in Xianger that owned property in the Baimapu area.[1] They not only farmed grain and cotton but also raised a large number of hogs, which provided valuable night soil to fertilize their fields.

By the late 1930s, Hao and Zhen had created a large joint family (*da jia-ting*) of more than thirty people, including five married sons and daughters-in-law, as well as at least twenty grandchildren, all living on a common budget. Adult children and even young grandchildren, male and female alike, were put to work in the fields, at tending animals, and on the family's looms. In 1939, Hao bought three houses (and later a fourth) in a southern corner of Second Bao, a short distance from the Hao ancestral hall and the home of his late father. His extended family ate, slept, and worked in four separate households but prepared meals in a single kitchen and distributed cooked food among the residences. This eventually proved too unwieldy, and separate stoves were set up in each house. Yet family members remained united as a single economic unit. Their production and consumption activities, as well as their purchase and allocation of foodstuffs, remained centrally controlled and funded from a common budget.

Hao Caiqin's fortune brought him influence and may also have led to growing aspirations in local politics. Or perhaps the aid and sanctuary he and his family gave to their young orphaned affine, Liang Jinyuan, antagonized township officials. Whatever the cause, tensions mounted in the late 1940s between Hao and his nephew [eBS], Hao Yuntai, a wealthy rentier and leading township official. Hao Yuntai, whose father was a half brother of Hao Caiqin (born to a different mother), had five sons of his own and headed a family that owned 40 *mu* of paddy. Hao Yuntai was also a leading member of the local lodge of Gowned Brothers (Pao Ge), a not-so-secret society that dominated affairs in the Baimapu market town. Owing in part to his close ties with county elites in Meishan town, he had received appointments as chief of the township militia, supervisor of the township granary, and headmaster of the local public school.

The growing antagonism between these two families of close patrilineal kin assumed a new and public dimension when Hao Yuntai ordered his uncle to comply with conscription regulations and submit some of his sons or grandsons for military service. Old Hao Caiqin not only refused but also declined to pay the customary conscription-substitution fee, which in his case would have been substantial.[2] Outraged, Hao Yuntai dispatched the armed conscription patrol of Second Bao, headed by his cousin Hao Yuru, to their uncle's home with orders to seize the proper quota of conscripts. But Old Hao Caiqin, it was said, had anticipated the move and had sent his sons and grandsons to hide among the wooded hilltops. They posted lookouts to warn of a patrol's approach and fled in other directions. This apparently continued for some time, so that Old Hao Caiqin's sons and grandsons had to maintain a constant state of vigil, day and night, for signs of a patrol.

They took with them young Liang Jinyuan, whom the patrols were also pursuing. Recall that Liang's elder brother had married a distant niece [FeBSSD] of Hao Caiqin. As an elderly grandfather, Liang recalled the terror that had gripped him one night when, while running in the darkness, he had become separated from the others:

> I used to run with the group of Hao Yunzhou [the youngest of Hao Caiqin's five sons]. I was only sixteen or seventeen at the time. Sometimes we used to run to a different *bao*, outside the jurisdiction (*fan-wei*) of the patrol. There they could do nothing about us (*guan bu liao*). Sometimes we also hid at the Guanyin temple. Conscription patrols never dared to go there. One night they came after us, and we had to go out running in the rain. We would watch for the light of their torches and then run the other way. In the darkness and confusion, I became separated from the group. I hid behind a grave mound and waited. I was terrified. After a while, I saw a light moving toward me. I trembled all over, but I could not move. I did not know whether it was a ghost or the KMT, and I did not know which I should fear more. It took all my effort to keep from shutting my eyes in panic. Suddenly, the light fell upon me. "There he is!" a voice shouted. My heart jumped. But it was the Hao brothers. They had come looking for me, fearful of what might have happened.

Liang never forgot how Hao Caiqin's family saved him that night. He remained their loyal ally for the rest of his life, providing support that would prove critical during the political crises of the Communist era.

Rumors of the standoff between Hao Caiqin and Hao Yuntai circulated widely throughout the township. The situation grew increasingly embarrassing to the powerful militia chief, who was said to have regarded his uncle's attitude and behavior as a personal affront to his official authority. The showdown came one spring in the late 1940s, during the Grave Sweeping festival of Qingming, an occasion when patrilineal ancestral associations gathered for rituals of collective identity and solidarity. Hao families from throughout the Baimapu area came to the ancestral hall at Big Hao Hill to participate in annual rites and a large communal banquet. When Hao Yuntai appeared, he surprised everyone by arriving with a contingent of armed militiamen. In front of a large crowd of astonished onlookers, he ordered the elderly Hao Caiqin seized, bound, and taken to the township lockup at the Guan Ye temple. One of Hao Caiqin's grandsons, who is now the village Communist Party secretary of Qiaolou, recalled the incident in a rare moment of candor:

> One year at the Qingming festival, we had all gathered at the Hao ancestral hall for rituals and a banquet. Suddenly, Hao Yuntai appeared with his soldiers. He was a big landlord from whom we all rented land.[3] He did not even stay and eat. Hmph! He just gave us all a strong warning and left. Then his henchmen seized my grandfather, tied him up, and took him away to the township gaol. They held him for seven days. We tried to exercise some influence to get him released, but to no avail. All the elders (*zhangbei*) of the township, from every family and surname, were aghast at what had happened. At our Qingming festival yet! Hmph! They told Hao Yuntai that he had been excessive (*tai guofen*), but he would not listen to reason. And still my grandfather would not give in to the conscription orders. Finally, we had no choice but to appeal through intermediaries to beg for grandfather's release. [Another grandson of Hao Caiqin asserted that this appeal had been handled through the intercession of the local Gowned Brothers.] The terms were harsh. He demanded fifteen *dan* of unhusked rice. That is twenty *dan* [roughly a ton] by today's standards. We had to sell all our hogs to raise that kind of grain. We got our grandfather back home, but there was nothing left to do but divide the family. We had nothing left.

The drama between Hao Caiqin and militia chief Hao Yuntai became a critical moment in local history, as Chapter 3 will show. In a broader sense, Hao Caiqin's rise to fortune, and the subsequent decline of his family following its confrontation with armed power, may illuminate how Baimapu residents managed their lives and social relationships. In quest of security, or even prosperity, men and women drew on various aspects of social organization, both within and beyond their families, along and across lines of patrilineal descent. Some of those associations created important alliances; others generated antagonisms. But all were generally perceived to lie within the context of family relations.

Managing Interests and Sentiments

Notions of family lie at the core of Chinese social organization. By situating each person within both a contemporary economic unit and within a continuous patriline across generations, relations within and between families framed social identity in material, spiritual, and emotional ways. As Medick and Sabean (1984) have shown, both emotions and material interests are socially constituted in relationships of property, labor, and domination, and notions of family often serve as a symbolic and organizational idiom for broader communities of interest and emotion. In Baimapu, patrilineal families (*jia*) were both the principal property-owning units and the primary domain in which production, consumption, and reproduction were organized and managed.[4] Patrilineal descent ideology structured each person's formal status within a family hierarchically, defining his or her relationships to ancestors and orienting his or her views of the afterlife (A. Wolf 1970; Baker 1979). Sentiments of emotion and obligation instilled during childhood socialization formed the basis of interpersonal relationships between family members and other kin (M. Wolf 1972; Stafford 1995). Memories of how such relationships developed and changed over the years were imbued with affect and antagonism.

The family head (*jiazhang*) was a formal position ascribed to the senior male of each patrilineal family. All major decisions, particularly those relating to property transfers, required his seal of approval.[5] Yet strictly speaking, a family head held more symbolic authority than real power; he represented the "face" of the family in official matters. Far more influential was the informal position of family manager (*dangjia*), for it was she or he who ran the practical affairs of a family, organizing production tasks, directing errands, handling finances, and making most everyday decisions about consumption, investments, and expenditures. Status as family manager was achieved rather than ascribed and could be attained by any adult, female or male. In some instances, a senior male was both family head and manager, but more often senior women exercised managerial authority in Baimapu families. In fact, it was not uncommon for a family head to be an aged or even infirm grandfather, while his spouse or even daughter-in-law acted as family manager.

Formally, women had an ambiguous position under patrilineal descent ideology, with its popular rituals, literary traditions of Confucianist moral philosophy, and male-dominated property regime.[6] Although women were crucial to the perpetuation, status, and even influence of a patriline, they were often the forgotten or "nameless" links between ancestors and descendants (R. Watson 1986).[7] Hao Caiqin's wife, Zhen, for example, was remembered only by her (father's) surname, despite the contributions she herself made to the family's success. A woman also faced greater social, physical, and even psychological displacement at marriage, finding herself in an unfamiliar environment of strangers, surrounded by her husband's kin, and burdened with discomforting scrutiny, demands, and expectations.

With motherhood, a woman's status formally rose, as did her prospects

for future security. As principal caregivers, mothers cultivated strong emotional bonds with their children, forming "uterine families" (*niangniangmu*)
around themselves (M. Wolf 1972).[8] The affective bonds of emotional sentiment and filial loyalty that a woman fostered in her sons as well as daughters were sometimes her best hope for support, as either a family manager
or an elderly widow. As wives and mothers, many women came to exercise
strong influence over the economic and social affairs of patrilineal families,
despite the fact that they held few formal rights to property.[9] One of the few
forms of property to which women did have popularly recognized ownership
rights was "private room money" (*sifangqian*), which consisted of cash, jew-
elry, and other valuables presented to a bride at her family wedding feast
by her parents (especially her mother), matrilateral relatives (especially her
mother's brother), and, often, her father's sister.[10]

Managing a family entailed not only the control of finances, supervision
of labor, and deployment of assets but also the crafting and maintenance of
relationships with other families, individuals, and associations, from marital
affines and patrilineal kin to friends, neighbors, and officials. Some of these
relationships were largely informal; others involved more stylized rituals.
Most were marked by commensal banqueting, which symbolized communities of exchange and reciprocity. Families facing a labor shortfall, for example, often practiced "labor exchange" (*tiaogong*) and "help" (*bangmang*)
to avoid the cost of hiring temporary laborers.[11] Others cultivated "dry kinship" (*ganqin*), ritualized relations similar to godparentage practices in other
societies, that could be expanded or contracted as desired (see Fried 1953).[12]
A person could have several "dry" parents, and a man or woman with several "dry" children often enjoyed status as a patron, broker, or social inter-
mediary. As a whole, these diverse forms of association, cooperation, and alliance constituted the fields of interaction through which families and individuals managed their lives.

Most of these communities of exchange and identity centered on activities at family farms or in the local market settlement. Status in the township
arena was linked primarily to popular perceptions of how successfully a family managed its economic and social security. As the case of Hao Caiqin
shows, even a thriving family economy was no guarantee of a secure future.
Family associations were also needed with marital affines, patrilineal kin,
and matrilateral relatives, or with teahouse friends, ritual kin, and local notables. Managing such associations of alliance, local residents wove the warp
and weft of what Fried (1953) called their "social fabric."

The pervasive insecurity of the early twentieth century fostered a high
degree of economic and social mobility, although in the Baimapu area the aggregate trend appeared to be downward. To build a large extended family

such as that headed by Hao Caiqin was no small accomplishment; maintaining it over time was an even greater challenge. The burdens of rents, taxes,
and high interest payments; the costs of weddings, funerals, and opium addiction; the threats of banditry, conscription, and violent retribution; and the
inevitable process of family division—all these presented formidable obstacles. Families pawned or sold property. Some family members were hired
out as boarding laborers or domestic servants. Moreover, as inflation and the
growing proliferation of counterfeit currency prompted first tax collectors
and, later, even landlords and merchants to demand payment in grain rather
than cash, the importance of land took on added significance. Access to land
meant access to grain, without which a family had little hope of security.

Landholdings and Social Status

Land tenure, including both ownership and usufruct rights, was an important marker of status, although by no means the only one. Scholarly studies
of agrarian China have often relied on statistical surveys and government
archives to reconstruct patterns of landholding and social stratification.[13]
Although synchronic data from a particular point in time may suggest the
broad contours of landownership, they do not in themselves explain how
stratification developed and changed over time. Fixed-time surveys may be
helpful in tracing strati*fied* (action completed) access to land, but do little to
illuminate how such processes emerge in the context of dynamic family relationships spanning years and generations.

   According to present-day local officials, in the 1940s, Baimapu's Second
Bao encompassed an area of more than 2,000 *mu* (over 130 hectares), roughly
a quarter of which was under cultivation. Reconstructing patterns of land
tenure and how they change over time is difficult, and not only because of a
lack of archival documentation. Not all land within the *bao* was owned by
families living in the *bao*; not all landowning families in the *bao* owned all
their land within the boundaries of the *bao*. Family histories suggest that in
the 1940s most land in Second Bao—perhaps more than 80 percent of it—
was owned by individual families.[14] Of the 130-odd families living in Second
Bao, about 80 percent owned at least some land. More than a third of these
families had holdings sufficient to meet their subsistence needs and to cover
the costs of basic expenditures. These families enjoyed a degree of recognized independence. However, most families had small holdings of only a
few *mu*. Families with many mouths to feed and those that pursued more
ambitious farm enterprises were obliged to lease additional parcels in Second

Bao or elsewhere. Roughly 20 percent of the families living in Second Bao were tenant farmers who owned no land of their own.[15] A few even worked entirely as hired hands on farms owned by others.

The most prominent landowning families in the township owned 100 *mu* or more of paddy and were often regarded as local notables. Generally living as rentiers, they leased their holdings to tenants at rents as high as 80 percent of the main harvest.[16] Many resided in the Baimapu market settlement, where they also ran commercial businesses. At harvest time, they dispatched collection agents to their farms to supervise the threshing, weighing, and bagging of rice.[17] A few prominent landowning families, however, lived in large tile-roofed *siheyuan* homes in the countryside and took an active role in managing their farms. Rather than renting out their holdings, these wealthy landowners hired agricultural laborers to work their land, usually on annual contracts that provided room, board, and either wages or a share of the harvest. Other large landowning families worked part of their holdings while renting out another portion to tenants.

Families that owned upward of 10 *mu* of paddy were often able to live as independent owner-cultivators. Generally secure in their subsistence needs—those with fewer mouths to feed might even prosper—such independent farm families lived without renting additional land. They usually supplemented their agricultural livelihoods through subsidiary activities, such as animal husbandry, cotton spinning, or foraging.[18] Nevertheless, the minimal size of a viable independent family farm varied, based on such factors as family size, ratio of productive laborers to dependent consumers, quality or fertility of the soil, tax assessments on the property, availability of fertilizer and irrigation, and the extent to which family members pursued nonagricultural ventures.[19]

By far the largest land tenure cohort consisted of those families that farmed a few *mu* of their own land while also leasing supplemental holdings. Some of these owner-renter cultivators, such as the family of Hao Caiqin, were more well-to-do and rented additional land to expand their agricultural enterprises. Most, however, leased additional plots to meet their subsistence needs. For example, Jin Shaoyun and his family of ten farmed 3 *mu* of their own land in southern Second Bao, while leasing another 4 *mu* from an absentee rentier who owned several hundred *mu* of land in the Baimapu area but resided in Meishan. The Jin family paid their landlord rent of 1 *dan* of unhusked rice (*guzi*) per *mu*. This was nearly 80 percent of the crop family members could reasonably expect to harvest from those plots. Because most rental contracts stipulated payment in grain, leased land was generally devoted to rice cultivation. The Jins also owned a water buffalo and a hand-driven winnowing machine (*fengmiche*), use of which they sometimes rented out for a little extra cash. They tried to make ends meet by trading rice (*zhengmi*)—carrying husked or polished rice (*mi*), ready for cooking, down to Meishan to barter or trade for a slightly larger quantity of unhusked or unpolished rice (*guzi*). Yet occasionally they were still obliged to borrow grain from other landowners with more secure surplus. Interest rates on such loans ranged from 50 to 80 percent and were higher on those issued during the spring and summer when grain supplies were lower. Loans were customarily due after harvest, when the price of grain was at a low.

Owning land, however, provided no guarantee that a family could keep it. There was an active land market in early-twentieth-century Baimapu. As politically influential local notables colluded to hide family property from official tax registers, the burdens of escalating land taxes fell increasingly to smallholders and the less well connected (Grunde 1976). One elderly farmer from northern Second Bao, for example, claimed that his father had owned 50 *mu* of paddy but had been obliged to sell more than half of it in 1933 because he had been unable to afford the tax assessments imposed by township authorities.[20] Not only were local levies high, but weddings and funerals, illness and opium addiction all posed potential economic burdens. Even once-independent owner-cultivators could find themselves slipping into debt and mortgaging their property. As another elderly farmer from southern Second Bao recalled:

> My father owned over 10 *mu* of land on which we grew rice, cotton, peanuts, and soybeans. We lived in a ten-room *siheyuan*. But my father smoked opium. We never had enough grain to cover his debts and still feed ourselves. Each year we borrowed grain from a landlord [nearby]. . . . He charged us 60 percent interest. We had to put up our land as collateral. If we failed to repay the loan any year, we would lose our land.

Faced with unanticipated major expenses, families might turn to affines or "dry kin" in search of a loan. There was also at least one pawnshop (*dangpu*) in Baimapu, and many more in Meishan and other nearby market towns.

Contracts for loans and leases were drafted by a third-party scribe (*daibiren*). They were signed by family heads or their designated representatives (the illiterate affixed a thumbprint), who also pressed an imprint of the family head's seal in the presence of two recorded witnesses (*jianzhengren*). Without property as collateral, a guarantor (*baozhengren*) from a property-owning family had to assume responsibility for the debt in the event of default.[21] Negotiations were often conducted in Baimapu teashops on market days, as were many contract signings, and concluded with a banquet. When a debt was paid in full or a rental agreement terminated, the contract was turned over to one of the signed witnesses, who destroyed the document in the presence of all parties.

Leasing Land and Hiring Labor

Tenancy contracts varied in length but were usually one-, two-, five-, or ten-year leases, all of which required a deposit (*yajin*).[22] In some cases, fixed-rate rental contracts set at 1 *dan* (300 catties, or 150 kg) per *mu* of paddy were used. More often, contracts were based on a percentage of the harvest, with the landowner claiming between 50 and 80 percent of the main rice crop (see also Buck 1980; Barnett 1963; Crook n.d.). Elderly farmers recalled that families who enjoyed closer, more personal relations with their landlord might have their rents discounted as much as 20 percent (Fried 1953).[23] In contrast, some rentiers obliged tenants to assume the burden of land tax payments, although legally this was the responsibility of the landowner (Crook n.d.).

The burdens of renting land left most tenant families, who leased just a few *mu*, with only a slim margin of subsistence or even mired in debt. Without supportive intercession by patron guarantors, tenants in default faced eviction, forced servitude, or imprisonment in the township lockup. Consider the account of Old Master Yue, an elderly widower:

> My father, Yue Shiwen, was a farmer in Shangyi. My mother, née Yan (Yue Yan Shi), was from Baimapu. She belonged to the Yan family. I don't know her name. Before Liberation, women took their husbands' surnames. By the time I was born [in 1921], my family already had five mouths to feed. There was also a lot of opium smoking. We rented 10 *mu* of paddy from a landlord living in Xianger and lived in a house he owned. . . . In Shangyi there is more flatland (*pingba*) [than in Baimapu]. We had double croppings of rice [there] each year. *Dachun* [the main harvest in the fall] was given to the landlord. We had to feed ourselves with whatever we could get from *xiaochun* [a second, smaller harvest in the spring]. But it was not enough, so each year we would borrow rice from him at 50 percent interest. The loans were due each fall at *dachun*. We tried to grow peanuts on barren hills (*huangshan*). The landlord did not care about that. He was only concerned with the grain.
>
> My father died in 1932, and my mother [soon] married off my younger sisters. They had no dowries, not even a banquet. They were

ten and eleven years old at the time. I ran off to my mother's natal family (*niangjia*) [in Baimapu's Second Bao]. My mother's father (*waigong*) arranged for me to work for an elderly friend of his, a petty landlord [in a nearby *bao*]. [The landowner] had a family of eight, and I and two other farm laborers worked their 8 *mu* of paddy. I was rehired each year. They gave me 2 *dan* of polished rice (*mi*). We [hired hands] lived and ate at the landlord's house. [Twelve] years later, I returned [to Second Bao] and got married. How old was I? Between twenty-five and twenty-nine; I don't remember these things. My mother's father arranged for me to rent 13 *mu* of paddy for 10 *dan* [of unhusked rice a year] from a local notable [a large landowner and township official]. My mother then returned [from Shangyi] to join us. Grain yields at that time were not like they are now. We gave nearly all our grain to the landlord. Again we did not have enough left over to feed ourselves! Each year, I borrowed 500 catties of grain from him without any real hope of ever paying it back. By the time of Liberation, I was indebted to him for 1,500 catties [about 750 kg]: 1,500 catties! Can you imagine how many lifetimes it would have taken me to pay that back?

Through the patronage of matrilateral kin, Yue had found employment as a boarding farmhand. Over the course of a decade, he saved enough to marry. Once again, through his mother's father, he leased a sizable farm of over a dozen *mu*. The close associations and friendships his maternal grandfather shared with wealthy local notables was evident in the discount terms of the lease, which gave Yue 13 *mu* at a price most paid for 10. Nevertheless, his account suggests that tenants could still totter on the brink of debt.[24] Some families found themselves obliged to hire out one or more of their members as laborers on the farms of others.

It was common for men and women from both small-landholding and tenant families to hire themselves out as short-term laborers (*duangong*) during periods of peak agricultural activity. They would gather at various teahouses in the Baimapu market settlement, waiting for landowners or their farm managers to select work crews. Most were paid with a percentage of the harvest and provided with their daily meals, usually of vegetables, rice, and alcohol. Meat was generally served to short-term hired hands only after completion of the harvest, or once every three days for longer jobs. Many families looking for extra income sought work elsewhere, especially in Dongguan and Wansheng townships, after the harvest was brought in from their own fields.

Others, however, were obliged to seek substantial commitments, contracting themselves out for a year or more. For the landless, long-term labor (*changgong*) contracts offered a marginal sense of security. They usually provided meals, a place to sleep, and sometimes a pair of straw sandals or even a pair of pants. Depending on the terms of the contract, laborers might also received a measure of grain from the harvest. It was not only the landless or destitute who turned to such arrangements. There were also owner-cultivators with small farms and large families who sought to defer costs by negotiating for their children year-round boarding labor jobs, such as tending the water buffalo and hogs of a more well-to-do family. Any wages or grain earned by such children were paid to their families, and some family managers found such arrangements economical. But many who had been so employed in their youth recalled the experience with bitterness.

Jin Yuzhen was the daughter of a landless laborer from a neighboring *bao* who had earned his living as a long-term hired farmhand. Her family had been desperately poor. When Jin was born in 1924, her mother left to become a wet nurse in the household of a wealthy family, but died within the year. Jin's father tried to care for her on his own, feeding her watery rice porridge to stretch their meager resources. Later, he was conscripted by the Nationalist army but managed to have alternative military service arranged for him in a local militia controlled by a large landowner. Soon after, apparently through the patronage of his benefactor, Jin's father remarried. Jin claimed that her new stepmother quickly asserted control over the family's management. They rented living quarters in a house belonging to another landowner, paying him one *dan* of unhusked rice per room. But to do so, they borrowed heavily and soon found themselves so deeply in debt that they were unable to secure a guarantor and thus rent land.

As a young child, Jin was sent by her stepmother to beg in the Baimapu market settlement. When she was older, she worked for wealthy families, washing clothes and tending water buffalo. She also collected firewood to sell in Meishan and dog feces to barter as fertilizer at Baimapu. At one point, in order to service a debt, her stepmother indentured Jin to a wealthy family as a domestic servant girl (*yatou*). She remained there until the age of ten. Eventually her stepmother secured a lease for another house, along with a few *mu* of paddy. Although the contract was signed by her father, as family head, its terms had been negotiated by her stepmother. In 1943, when Jin was nineteen, her stepmother arranged her uxorilocal marriage to the eldest son of a poor Xi family of owner-renter cultivators in Second Bao. Jin's new husband soon went to work as a long-term laborer in another market town. She saw him only rarely, usually on major holidays, when he would return for a brief visit. Jin bore him two sons and a daughter, but he died of hunger and malnutrition in 1948. As she recalled, "He came home just in time to die."

Prolonged misfortune could ultimately spell the demise of a family. Not only would it lead to formal partition, but in more extreme cases, as family members physically dispersed to seek shelter or employment, they lost track of one another. Sometimes children were adopted out, given an early and inexpensive betrothal, or even placed in servitude.[25] Others among the very poor sought sanctuary at temples or turned to begging, vagabondage, or even banditry. A few men, such as the grandson of a once-wealthy Xi rentier who had squandered almost his entire family estate on opium, volunteered for military service in the hope of finding food and shelter. For such people, simply to marry and produce descendants was challenge enough.

Both the continuity of a man's family patriline across time and the long-term security of a woman's uterine group were dependent on the marriages that parents arranged for their children. Descendants were needed to offer the necessary ritual sacrifices to the memory and spirits of parents after death, and the filial devotion of offspring was often the only promise of security for the elderly, especially women, once illness or infirmity crept up on them. Decisions about betrothal had important consequences for a family's future, and women played a prominent role in arranging marriages.

Contracting Affines, Creating Kin

Transfer of labor and other forms of property, creation of affinal alliances, and latent expectations for the continuing reproduction of descent lines all converged in a complex of ritualized practices surrounding betrothal and marriage. Marriage was a mechanism of social maneuverability, a vehicle for the creative structuring of relationships between families (Peters 1976). Through marriage one acquired affines (in-laws), who could be active allies or mere acquaintances. Moreover, the passing of genealogical time transformed affinal relations as the marital relatives of one generation became the bilateral kin of the next. In essence, marriage creates kinship (Lévi-Strauss 1969; Bourdieu 1977). Many families, in fact, had extensive contact with their affines and matrilateral relatives, often helping one another during peak labor seasons, using their introductions to broker new business deals, and even seeking loans from them.[26]

The rituals surrounding betrothal and marriage in Sichuan were similar to those widely described for other parts of China (cf. Freedman 1979c; Guo 1990). Most marriages in early-twentieth-century Baimapu had been arranged (*baoban*) unions in which responsibility for finding a suitable spouse was entrusted to a special broker or matchmaker (*meiren*), usually a woman.[27] The principal contracting parties were the two families rather than the bride and groom themselves. Often, initial inquiries and overtures were made, introductions brokered, gifts exchanged, betrothal payments negotiated, and contracts finalized without any direct involvement of the young people concerned. In some cases the betrothed did not even see each other until the rituals were complete and they were ushered into their conjugal "new room" (*xinfang*).[28]

Because the interests of families were paramount, some arrangements were less than appealing to the bride or groom. One woman complained with good humor about the marriage arranged for her to a Wen man in Second Bao. "My husband is not even as tall as a double pile of cow dung!" she was fond of exclaiming.[29] A man from a tenant family who had been orphaned as a youth and raised by his eldest brother recalled that his marriage had been arranged by his brother and sister-in-law in 1946. Poverty had obliged them to put off his marriage until he reached his mid-twenties, whereas most married by their mid- or late teens. Even then, the wedding was simple: no banquets, no bridewealth, no dowry; in his words, "not even a pair of pants." Yet he claimed that he was most astonished of all to lift his bride's veil and discover that she was blind.

As elsewhere in China, negotiations about the formal exchange of gifts and payments between the families of a bride and groom were the most crucial, complex, and time-consuming aspect of the betrothal process (see R. Watson 1981; Gates 1996; Yan 1996). Major betrothal gifts from a groom's family took two forms. Bridewealth—gifts of cash or grain referred to as the "arrangement for claiming the bride" (*la niang yue*)—was presented shortly after negotiations were finalized. If a bridewealth settlement were large, or if the groom's family faced economic difficulties, such payments might be made over several years. Once completed, a date was selected for the actual transfer of the bride, and a second set of items, known as "gifts of splendor" (*caili*), was presented to her family. These were typically bolts of cotton cloth that were then used to make her wedding clothes.

A bride's natal family was expected to present the new couple with a dowry (*peijia*) at the time of the wedding.[30] Although dowries varied in size and value, they consisted largely of everyday household items such as bedding, toiletries, and perhaps furniture, as well as a trousseau (*jiazhuang*) of cloth and clothing for the bride. Dowries were carried on public display to the home of the groom's family, usually by a party of the bride's *biao* kin [i.e., those related to her FZ, MB, and MZ], representatives of families whose own ties to the bride (and now also to the groom) were themselves based on marriage. Some families tried to enhance their social status through large betrothal payments, but such strategies were constrained by a number of factors, including common expectations that the value of a dowry should, ideally, be two or even three times that of the bridewealth.[31]

Marriages also involved the expenses of the feasts that each family hosted to mark its new ties through public recognition. In fact, the prestige of particular weddings was popularly linked less to the value of the bridewealth and dowry than to the affluence and influence a family projected through the number of guests invited to banquet. (The groom's family traditionally hosted several banquets over three or four days.) This was calculated in terms of the number of tables (*zhuozi*) hosted, each of which seated eight diners.[32] The potentially high costs of weddings—which included not only bridewealth, dowry, and banquets but, ideally, rented sedan chairs, hired musicians, firecrackers, and other gifts as well—led to many early betrothals. Negotiations often concluded while the future bride and groom were still children, giving their families several years in which to save or borrow for upcoming expenses.

Sometimes, decisions were made to marry one child (typically a daughter) first, in a less costly and less prominent union, thus conserving family resources for the marriage of another child (often a son) in a more important affinal alliance. Jin Shaoyun's family of small landowners, for example, married their first two children (both daughters) with modest dowries and small banquets in order to finance a more elaborate and costly marriage for their third child, the eldest son. With twelve mouths to feed (nine of them children) on only 3 *mu* of paddy, they had been obliged to lease an additional 4 *mu* and to borrow grain each year from different landowners simply to meet their subsistence needs. It took family members five years to raise the grain necessary to finance their eldest son's wedding, at age eighteen; even so, the expenses incurred left them in such debt that his younger siblings were not married until they were well into their twenties.

Adopting Future Brides, Calling in Sons-in-Law

In early-twentieth-century Baimapu, many young people were married by the time they were in their early teens. Liang Jinyuan's brother, as mentioned in Chapter 1, married at the age of ten, and his wife, Hao Suhua, was only two years older. More than one-third of all marriages involved "little daughters-in-law" (*xiao xifu*), or "daughters-in-law raised together [with a son]" (*tongyangxi*)—pre-menarche women who were adopted into a family and raised to become a daughter-in-law within it.[33] Such arrangements customarily entailed no betrothal gifts, bridewealth, or dowry, thus saving both families considerable expense.[34]

Although adopting a future bride meant another mouth to feed, in Baimapu most such daughters-in-law were already old enough to do various chores, from babysitting and cleaning to farm work and carrying firewood down to Meishan. Moreover, such young women grew up "eating the mother-in-law's rice" (*chi popo fan*), as it was said, and supposedly formed stronger filial sentiments toward their foster affines.[35] One elderly woman who had married into a Baimapu family at the age of fifteen considered herself an adopted daughter-in-law. She recalled that her natal family had been so poor that she was offered her first taste of steamed rice by her mother-in-law.

The marriage between Hao Caiqin and Zhen (described earlier) was unusual in that the couple moved away from Hao's patrilineal family home and took up residence in the neighboring *bao* where Zhen's family lived. Most often, couples resided with the patrilineal family of the husband's father. Men usually grew up, married, and grew old within the familiar social and physical surroundings they had known since childhood. Perhaps, as some claimed, Hao Caiqin had been a "called-in son-in-law" (*zhao nuxu*)—a man who married uxorilocally, taking up residence with his wife's natal family. Most families who called in a son-in-law were without a son of their own. Uxorilocal marriages were rare, often spoken of pejoratively, and considered to be of lower status than virilocal marriages.[36] Nevertheless, in certain contexts, uxorilocal marriage might present an attractive option to a family with many sons. Such arrangements usually involved neither bridewealth, indirect dowry costs, nor the banqueting expenses commonly associated with idealized notions of wedding ritual.[37] Because uxorilocally married men sometimes forfeited inheritance rights to their patrilineal family property, larger shares might be left for their brothers.

As the youngest of four brothers, Hao Caiqin's birth order increased the likelihood that a uxorilocal marriage might be arranged for him. But some of his descendants denied vehemently that he had married uxorilocally, asserting, rather, that the couple had lived on their own, neolocally, in a separate residence.[38] Hao had also inherited his quarter share when his father's family divided. Moreover, uxorilocal marriages were usually arranged by families in difficult economic circumstances, and Hao's father had been a well-to-do farmer with more than 20 *mu* of paddy, a respectably sized family estate. His father also had been married concurrently to two wives, and polygyny was commonly regarded as a symbol of wealth and status.

At least twelve men in early-twentieth-century Second Bao had been

married to two or more wives concurrently; five of these were wealthy rentiers, while the other seven were well-to-do owner-cultivators.[39] Co-wives
in polygynous marriages often competed for status, despite the formal authority usually enjoyed by the first or senior wife (*da taitai*). For example,
two brothers with the surname of Jin were said to have resettled in the area
south of Baimapu from the hills to the west sometime in the 1890s. When
the elder died, leaving his widow childless, the younger brother permitted
his widowed sister-in-law to adopt one of his four sons, presumably the
youngest. Most adoptions involved families of patrilineal kin (J. Watson
1975a). The widow raised the boy to maturity and eventually arranged for
his marriage to two wives. The first was a daughter of Hao Caiqin. This was
a high-status marriage of considerable expense for both families, but it succeeded in forging strong links between descendants of the two families that
continue today. The weaving skills brought into the family by Hao Caiqin's
daughter, who also bore six children (three sons), supplemented the few *mu*
they owned. Some years later, in a move that apparently antagonized her
daughter-in-law, Jin's mother arranged for him to marry a second wife, who
bore him two sons as well as a daughter. Relations between the two wives,
and between Hao Caiqin's daughter and Jin's mother, were poor, however. Jin
was obliged to build a separate house for his secondary wife (*xiao taitai*), her
children, and his mother. Nevertheless, the two households continued to
maintain a single family economy, with Jin's first wife weaving cloth and her
co-wife peddling it at periodic markets in the area. It was only after the death
of Jin's mother that a rapproachment was possible between the two wives and
the family reunited as a single residential household.

Widowed Wives and Second Husbands

Although it was always hoped that a marriage would produce both descendants for the ancestors and filial heirs for aging parents, a widowed woman
faced an uncertain and sometimes precarious future, especially if she had no
sons. As assertive wives, or mothers of married sons, many women acted as
family managers, but if left without a husband or son their links to most
forms of property became more tenuous. Even widows with sons were often
obliged to remarry (many to widowers) in the hope of finding some security.

For example, in the 1920s a woman from Second Bao named Xi Yuhua,
born into one of the area's more prominent descent groups, married a local
tenant farmer named Tian. In the mid-1930s, the couple moved with their
infant son to Sihe (now Xinsi) township, west of Baimapu, where they rented
7 or 8 *mu* from a "petty landlord" (*xiao dizhu*). In 1936, however, shortly

after the birth of their second son, Xi's husband died. A year later she re-married. Her new husband lived back in Baimapu's Second Bao, enabling Xi Yuhua to return to the area and social ties she had known as a young woman. Xi's second husband was also a tenant farmer named Tian, a close patrilineal cousin of her first husband, although he was more prosperous than his late kinsman and ran a farm of 34 *mu*. He was also married already, and his pri-mary wife had borne him a daughter. By marrying Xi Yuhua, he gained sta-tus as a polygynous family head and became the stepfather of his two neph-ews, thus acquiring heirs.[40] He also gained affinal ties with a major local descent group, some of whose members were in the township government. He marked this auspicious event with a large banquet of over twenty tables (160 guests).

There were, in fact, several other cases in which widows or widowers re-married close patrilineal relatives of their former spouses. Recall the local *fengshui* master and powerful township head, Wen Shisan, who headed a wealthy joint family of merchant-landowners in Second Bao. When the wife of his second son (who himself served nearly twenty years as head of Sec-ond Bao) died childless, Wen arranged for her cousin to replace her. Appar-ently he asserted that the first daughter-in-law had failed to produce an heir and demanded that his affines replace her. In another instance, when one of Hao Caiqin's grandsons [S4S1] died childless, his widow was remarried to an-other of Hao's grandsons [S2S1], himself a recent widower (see Figure 1).[41]

Such examples are drawn from large extended families, organized and managed as corporate domestic groups. Controlling sizable assets of produc-tive resources, such families often enjoyed influence and respect within their local exchange communities. Attaining a patrilineal family of "joint" form was difficult and brought significant status. Because married sons, as heads of their own conjugal branches (*fang*), had the right to claim their share of the patrilineal family estate and to divide out independently, extended fami-lies were even harder to maintain across time. Such efforts required judicious management of material and social resources. The fines imposed on Hao Caiqin's family devastated its economic base, rendering it impossible to sus-tain such a large domestic group. But every family faced division sooner or later, dissolving to form newly constituted corporate economic groups.

Divided Fortunes

Like marriage, family division (*fenjia*) was a fundamental aspect of social or-ganization. Whereas marriage created a new conjugal branch (*fang*) within a patrilineal family (*jia*), division marked the termination of a patrilineal family as an economic unit and the fissioning of its branches into independent families. Division was a contractual agreement that formally partitioned corporately held family property. Negotiations, usually involving fathers and married sons but sometimes between brothers, were often mediated by the mother's brother or another matrilateral relative. Such a man had no claim to the property in question but did presumably have an interest in assuring that his sister (or cousin) was adequately provided for in her old age and that each of his nephews received an equitable share of his natal *jia* estate.[42] Agreements were ritually concluded with a small banquet and often marked by construction of a separate stove.

Family division formally terminated jural relationships between brothers, so that one brother would not be responsible for debts incurred by another. Although some brothers who set up their own independent families remained on friendly or cooperative terms—many even continuing to share a house but using different stoves—other partitions created a sharp and bitter break. One woman recalled with distress how her paternal uncle [FyB] had refused his own widowed mother's request for support. He had divided out with his own wife and children several years earlier, breaking with his mother, widowed elder brother, and three nieces. When the elder brother was forcibly conscripted by the Nationalist army in the 1940s, the aging mother was left alone to care for three young granddaughters. But her second son allegedly ignored her pleas for help, insisting that the terms of their division settlement had given his elder brother an extra share of property to cover her expenses and that he had no further obligations to her.[43]

Some division settlements entailed written contracts (*fenjia dan*) signed by the principal parties and a witness. For the poor, however, family division was a much simpler process in which an oral agreement sometimes sufficed. As one man from a family of landless laborers put it, "Write what division contract? [My brother and I] simply divided and forgot about it. We each went our separate ways." But the partitioning of wealthy families was often a complex process with detailed clauses about the redistribution of existing assets and liabilities. Recall, for example, the family of Hao Suhua's grandfather, the wealthy Hao Caiming, who was a senior cousin of Hao Caiqin. Born about 1881, Hao Caiming was a great-grandson of the ancestral founder of the Baimapu Haos. His father was the eldest of three brothers, as was his grandfather, but Hao Caiming was the only one of four brothers in the genealogically senior branch of their local descent group to have male descendants (see Figure 1). Married to two wives, father to six sons (one of whom died in infancy) and one daughter, and grandfather to at least seven grandchildren (two of whom died young), Hao Caiming headed a joint fam-

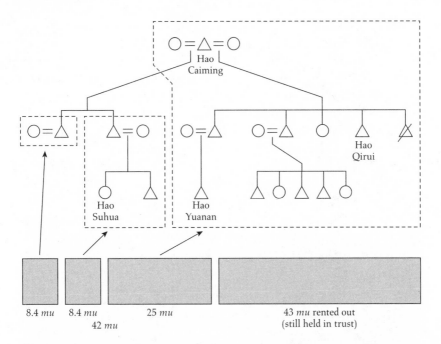

8.4 *mu*   8.4 *mu*   25 *mu*   43 *mu* rented out
            42 *mu*   (still held in trust)

FIGURE 2.   Hao Caiming family partition, stage one, 1941. The two eldest of Hao's
five surviving sons, both married, divided out. Their newly independent families
each received a one-fifth share (8.4 *mu*) of the 42 *mu* originally farmed by their
natal family. Another 43 *mu* of land rented out to tenants continued to be held in
corporate trust, with a one-fifth share of the annual rent going to each of the two
eldest sons.

ily estate that totaled 85 *mu* of paddy. (Altogether, Hao had at least eighteen
grandchildren, but not all had been born by the time of his death.)

The family's land, however, was dispersed in two different administrative
bao units. Family members cultivated 42 *mu* situated closer to their residence, in southern Second Bao, while leasing to tenants another 43 *mu* located a bit farther away, in another *bao*. In 1941, Hao Caiming's two eldest
sons (both born to his first, or primary, wife) divided out (see Figure 2). Under the settlement, the two older brothers established their own independent patrilineal families, each of which took ownership of a one-fifth share
(8.4 *mu*) of the 42 *mu* they had been farming together. The three younger
sons, however, continued to cultivate jointly the remaining three-fifths
(25 *mu*) of family land in Second Bao. At the same time, a new shareholding
arrangement was devised to divide the rent from the 43 *mu* leased to tenants.

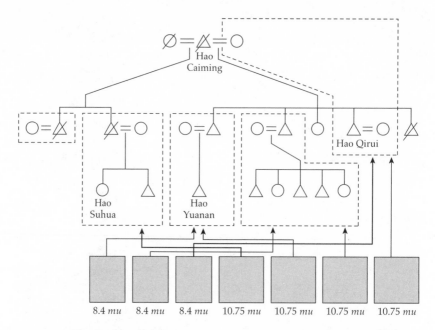

8.4 *mu*   8.4 *mu*   8.4 *mu*   10.75 *mu*   10.75 *mu*   10.75 *mu*   10.75 *mu*

FIGURE 3.   Hao Caiming family partition, stage two, ca. 1945. After Hao's death, the remaining 25 *mu* of land farmed by his family was divided equally among his three younger sons, who set up their own separate family units. At this point, the 43 *mu* of corporate trust land was also partitioned, into four equal shares—one for each of Hao's three younger sons, and one for the family of his eldest grandson. Hao's eldest son had died without an heir, and his widow was excluded from the division settlement of the trust estate.

That land became held in corporate trust, and each son—including the two eldest—received equal shares each year.[44]

Following the death of Hao Caiming a few years later, a second division settlement was negotiated (see Figure 3). From the 25 *mu* they had continued to cultivate jointly as a family, Hao's three younger sons each received a one-third share (8.4 *mu*), equal those allotted their elder stepbrothers a few years earlier. But the partitioning of the 43 *mu* of trust land was more complicated, since the two elder brothers had also died. The eldest left his widow without an heir, and she was excluded from any share in the property. Instead, the land was divided into four equal shares of 10.75 *mu*, one each for Hao's three surviving younger sons, and one share for the family of his deceased second son, who was survived by a widow and an infant son (Hao Suhua's brother).

Corporate shareholding principles were the foundation of many forms of social organization in early-twentieth-century Baimapu, including not only patrilineal families but also popular associations (Sangren 1984). If managed effectively, trust properties could provide steady revenue. Because they were usually dissolved only by consensus or bankruptcy, they often provided an institutional base for more enduring interfamily relationships. Families that sought to strengthen their alliances with others sometimes established shareholding trusts or purchased shares in existing corporate associations. Such strategies enabled a family to access or mobilize resources in economic alliances of larger scale.

Consider, for example, the voluntarily organized, rotating grain-credit societies (*qiguhui*)—contract-based shareholding associations set up among local market acquaintances.[45] Skinner (1964–65: 20) noted that in Sichuan such associations tended to be restricted to resident members of a particular "standard marketing community." To participate in such associations in Baimapu, a family needed to own at least some land as collateral against default. Most rotating grain societies were comprised of a core group of members, often a market town teashop cohort, who had better than average knowledge of one another's economic situations. They usually were formed by ten families and ran on a ten-year cycle. Participants invested initial contributions of either 300 catties (so-called one-*dan* associations) or 150 catties (half-*dan* associations). Drawing lots at a banquet each summer, a different family claimed the grain in the association's collective coffer, which it then had to repay at 10 percent interest for the remaining years of the cycle.[46] Participants might thus have an opportunity to meet unanticipated or major expenses, such as a wedding, funeral, house building, land purchase, or business deal, while avoiding the 60 to 80 percent interest rates commonly charged by local usurers. For many, the social connections offered through these and other, broader associations were a source of security in uncertain times. Some corporate shareholding associations became important foci of identity, symbolizing the communities of exchange that crosscut the local population.

Ancestral Associations

One of the most common idioms of community organization in early-twentieth-century Baimapu consisted of ancestral associations (*Qingminghui*) of patrilineal kin. Based on notions of common descent from a founding (male) ancestor, these associations offered an arena and framework for agnatic community building and social alliance. They were named after the

Grave Sweeping festival of Qingming (literally, "Clear-Bright") held each spring, a season symbolizing renewed life and vitality. Three times a year, but most importantly at Qingming, ancestral associations drew together patrilineally related families for collective ancestral rites and communal banquets that celebrated their common identity and promoted solidarity.[47] Rituals were conducted in honor of ancestors, grave mounds were cleaned and repaired, and a commensal feast was held, with the leftovers divided up into shares (*fen*) and distributed to member families.

Some *Qingminghui* had characteristics of lineage organizations described elsewhere in China, such as ancestral halls, corporate estates, genealogical record books, and collective ceremonial rituals. Other ancestral associations were more a community of mind than a patrilineal corporation.[48] Their members shared sentiments of common descent and converging interests but lacked the economic base, social prestige, and political influence of better-established *Qingminghui* in Baimapu or lineages in other parts of China. Among the larger local ancestral associations, for example, the thrice yearly gatherings of all patrilineally related families at their respective ancestral halls were an occasion for enforcing the lineage code, or family law (*jiafa*). After sacrifices were presented to the ancestors and the local earth god, junior members were expected to kneel and bow before elders. Children were required to recite the names of local ancestors and to identify by name particular elders present at the ceremonies. Those unfortunate enough to err were spanked, many recalled, usually with a bamboo stick or cane. Unfilial children and disrespectful daughters-in-law were also publicly humiliated and punished at such gatherings.[49] After being subjected to scoldings, ridicule, and beatings, they were forced to kneel in front of the entire assembly for the duration of the banquet.

There had been three ancestral halls (*citang*) in the area of Second Bao, owned by ancestral associations of Haos, Wens, and Xis. These halls or, more properly, these associations possessed modest estates of corporate trust property, ranging in size from 4 to 20 *mu*; each also maintained a genealogical history book (*jiapu*) as well as an adjacent ancestral cemetery on landforms named after ancestral settlers. The founders of even the oldest of these local lineages had apparently arrived no earlier than the mid-nineteenth century, and by the mid-twentieth century most of their descendants living in Second Bao were still within the five mourning grades (*wufu*) of primary kin. Hao Caiqin, for example, was a grandson of Hao Binghui, said to be the eldest of three brothers born in Baimapu after their father and grandfather resettled there from Meishan. Hao Caiqin's own grandchildren were *wufu* kin of all descendants of Hao Binghui, who together constituted the entire Hao population of Second Bao (though not of the entire Baimapu area).

The banquets and rites held by ancestral associations were also attended by patrilineally related families living in other areas of Baimapu township. The size and prestige of an ancestral association, like that of a marriage, were based largely on the number of tables served at the feast.[50] Local descent groups without ancestral halls or corporate property nevertheless maintained their own *Qingminghui*. The Yans and Lins, for example, each pooled contributions of rice, meat, and vegetables from individual families and gathered thrice annually at the home of the oldest man of the most senior generation. This senior elder was sometimes also called the "lineage master" (*zuzhang*), a position of ritual status that could rotate among different branches of a local descent group.[51] Wealthier *Qingminghui* also elected an "association chief" (*huishou*) or a committee of managers. Often these were prominent kinsmen of independent means and considerable business experience who oversaw administration of trust properties and settled association accounts each year at the Qingming feast (Hazelton 1986: 152; MSG 1992: 999). In ancestral associations without corporate property of their own, an association chief was often responsible for planning the next year's banquets, soliciting contributions, and coordinating ritual activities. Such men often had little more than ritual authority, particularly if their own families were poor. But occasionally a man of property and wealth such as Hao Caiming succeeded to the position of lineage master and commanded considerable influence.

Almost every family in the Baimapu area ascribed to membership in a *Qingminghui*, either one based nearby or one whose ritual activities were held in another township or county.[52] Membership, however, required active expression. At least one representative of each family was expected to attend the rites and feasts of the association, otherwise the affiliation might be considered suspended. Some families, generally those that were larger and more prosperous, simultaneously maintained membership in several *Qingminghui*, each based in a different locale, of different size, and focused on a different ancestor within a progressively broader and more distant genealogical framework (see Figure 4). Large (*da*) associations were distinguished from small (*xiao*) ones not on the basis of size (i.e., number of tables hosted) but of whether or not a particular ancestral association was regarded as an autonomous ("small") subunit of a higher-order ("large") association focused on a genealogically more distant common ancestor.[53] Within a particular local descent group there might exist several *Qingminghui*, and several corporate local lineages might also be included within the broader frameworks of higher-order ancestral associations.

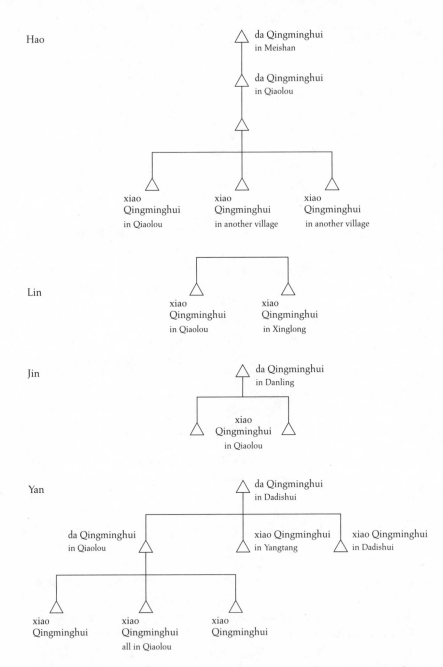

FIGURE 4. Early-twentieth-century *Qingminghui* (ancestral associations) in the Baimapu area (selective examples).

Lines of Identity

Each family's banqueting attendance reflected membership, position, or status within a larger series of kin-based social ties. In some cases, a family representative (what James Watson calls a "designated eater") would make a brief appearance at the (smaller) early morning meal of a higher-order association before attending the major banquet and rituals of the family's principal *Qingminghui* at midday. Families endeavoring to maintain stronger ties among a wider circle of patrilineal kin sent representatives to the (main) noon feasts of one or more higher-order *da Qingminghui*, while dispatching others to more restrictive or localized *xiao Qingminghui*.

For example, several Hao families—including Hao Caiqin's—made a brief appearance at the smaller, early morning meal (*zaofan*) of the higher-order *da Qingminghui* at the Hao great ancestral hall (*zong citang*) in Meishan before returning to Baimapu for the principal banquet and rituals at the local Hao branch ancestral hall (*fen citang*) on Big Hao Hill.[54] Yet for other Hao families living elsewhere in Baimapu township, the *Qingminghui* that met at the Hao hall in Second Bao was itself a higher-order ancestral association (see Figure 4). These families would come to the Hao ancestral hall for the smaller morning meal and the collective sacrifices to Hao Daixiu and his son Hao Tianyan, from whom all Haos in the area traced descent. Later, they would head back for a main banquet and rituals at the homes of the men who headed their small *xiao Qingminghui*, which focused on the two younger sons of Hao Tianyan (see Figure 1). The Haos in Second Bao, who were descended from Hao Binghui, the eldest of Hao Tianyan's three sons, remained at the local Hao ancestral hall for their large midday feast.[55]

The Xues, in contrast, were descendants of three brothers who had moved to the area of Second Bao in the 1910s from another part of Baimapu township where their ancestral hall was located. These families did not have their own autonomous *xiao Qingminghui*; instead, they walked a few *li* to banquet at the nearby Xue ancestral hall. Similarly, there were only a handful of Jins living in Baimapu, patrilineally related families with no common, corporate ancestral trust property or local ancestral hall (see Figure 4). They would sometimes send representatives to the Qingming celebrations at their ancestral hall in Danling county to the west, although they had their own *xiao Qingminghui* in Qiaolou, commemorating two brothers who had come down from Danling several generations earlier. Two Lin brothers had also settled in the Baimapu area during the late nineteenth century, but their descendants subsequently split into two separate branches (*fang*), each with its own *Qingminghui* (see Figure 4). The senior of the two was localized in northern Second Bao. In contrast to the Haos, who hosted more than a dozen tables of banqueters, small associations such as the Lins fed only four tables.

Not all families sharing a common surname traced descent from a common ancestor. There were, for example, at least two unrelated Yan descent groups (see Figure 4). One was a small branch of a larger lineage with an ancestral hall in the nearby township of Dadishui. Although they lacked a branch ancestral hall of their own, these Yan families did hold shares in a local trust estate of several *mu*, including an ancestral cemetery. Yet they themselves were segmented into three distinct (sub)branches, each with a *xiao Qingminghui* focused on one of three brothers. Members of these three small ancestral associations would travel to their common ancestral hall in the nearby township for morning ritual activities, then return to Second Bao for their separate midday feasts and rites at the homes of their respective (sub)branch elders.

The feasting, commemorative rituals, and festive atmosphere surrounding *Qingminghui* activities and events fostered sentiments of collective patrilineal identity and solidarity. Ancestral associations also provided an institutional field of interaction within which individual families could develop particular alliances. But as the conflict between Hao Caiqin and his nephew Hao Yuntai shows, agnatic solidarity had its limitations (R. Watson 1985). Although prominent members of Baimapu's largest descent groups—the Haos, Wens, Xis, and Yans—dominated township administration and military security, not all their patrilineal kin acted as a unified political force. In fact, alliances between families across local descent groups were often more important than those within local lineages.

Gods of Alliance

The Dongyue temple in the Baimapu settlement was a symbol of interlineage alliance between the Wens and Xis. It was said that a compact had been formed through an important marriage between two prominent Wen and Xi families at some past time, now forgotten. In commemoration of the alliance, each lineage had contributed funds for the construction or restoration of a temple dedicated to the God of the Eastern Peak, who was popularly believed to have power over life, death, and rebirth, as well as the award of riches and honors.[56] The temple was frequented by many inhabitants of Baimapu. The association that funded and operated it was managed by a committee of elders from the Wen and Xi lineages who also arbitrated disputes and mediated conflicts among local families, particularly (though not exclusively) Wens and Xis.[57] This offered an alternative to more formal proceedings at the township offices, where lawsuits were alleged to be costly, time-consuming, and influenced by bribery.

Inside the temple were two large clay statues of the God of the Eastern Peak (Dongyue Gong) and his wife (Dongyue Niang), symbolizing the Wen and Xi lineages, respectively. Each year, shortly before Qingming, the temple association sponsored an elaborate ritual procession of the god and goddess throughout the township, headed by several monks (*heshang*) and temple assistants who rang gongs and called for contributions to the gods. The procession was conducted in the form of a good-natured footrace between the two lineages, each of which sponsored a team of four men to carry the effigy of its deity.[58] Victory was a matter of honor and a source of pride for the entire lineage. Spectators lined the route and cheered the contestants, often wagering on the outcome. The procession concluded with an enormous banquet for several hundred guests back at the temple.

Of all the local temples visited in the course of the Dongyue procession, the Guanyin temple was the grandest, larger even than the Dongyue temple itself. Dedicated to the Buddhist goddess of mercy, it was the largest architectural structure in the township and the largest institutional landowner. It was located a few kilometers south of the Baimapu settlement, roughly a twenty-minute walk (or a few minutes run) from Hao Caiqin's houses in Second Bao. According to the 1923 Meishan gazetteer, the Guanyin temple dated to the reign of the Ming Tianshun emperor (1457–65), but it was popularly believed to be much older.[59] It was also a well-known stopover for pilgrims en route to Mt. Emei, a few days walk to the south. A ground-surface survey supported local claims that the temple had been a complex of three large halls (*dian*) and two courtyards, with numerous wing rooms and dormitories covering more than an acre of land. The Guanyin temple also owned an estate of more than 200 *mu* (30 acres) and was managed by women.[60] During the Republican era, it had hosted a primary school with "several tens" of students, run by a single teacher.[61]

The women who ran the Guanyin temple hired male laborers from the ranks of the local poor to cultivate rice, vegetables, and cotton. Many of these workers, it was said, were army deserters or young men trying to evade conscription who had been given sanctuary at the temple. Cotton was used in the looms of a sophisticated cloth-weaving enterprise run on temple grounds. In any given year, upward of thirty young unmarried women resided at the Guanyin temple as apprentice weavers. Most, like Hao Caiqin's wife and her daughters, had been sent by their families to learn this valuable skill, which could enhance their families' incomes and improve their own marriage prospects. These women lived and worked together on the temple grounds, taking their meals in a large communal kitchen and dining room. They shared this space with elderly women, many of them spinsters or widows, who had come to live at the temple as Buddhist disciples or lay nuns.

This women's community was formed around Guanyin, a female deity popularly believed to have been a princess who, against her parents' wishes, refused to marry and became a nun. Symbolically, Guanyin mediated the forces of *yin* and *yang*. In certain contexts, she could represent a subversion of orthodox legitimacy, refuting the hierarchical relations between men and women (Sangren 1987: 155, 179).[62] Given this powerful symbolism, and the apparent strength of the women's association centered on the temple, it is perhaps not surprising that the Dongyue procession stopped at the Guanyin temple. Draped in a scholar's gown, with eyeglasses perched on his nose and an open book on his lap, and carried aloft by representatives of local patrilineages, the Dongyue god, who held official rank, projected the authority of the orthodox, state Confucianist cult over the potentially unorthodox power of Guanyin.

Unorthodox Practices

There was one religious hall in the township, however, that the Dongyue procession deliberately avoided. The Qingfutang, or "vegetarian hall" (*zhaitang*), as it was also called, was a small religious association of strict vegetarians who had taken vows never to marry. Hao Suhua's elder sister had joined this hall as a young girl. Physically, the hall (*tang*) was a large *siheyuan* compound, similar to a large family home or ancestral hall, located just northeast of the Baimapu settlement in northern Second Bao. Socially, the hall consisted of roughly a dozen men and women of mixed ages who had broken with their patrilineal families, renounced the institution of marriage, and taken vows of celibacy. They moved into the compound, adopted vegetarian diets to purify their souls, and created new ritual kinship ties with each other.[63]

The Qingfutang was headed by a woman whom other members addressed as grandmother (*zumu*) or father's mother (*nainai*). She was assisted by a man who was addressed as elder brother (*gege*). The "grandmother" managed the association's 40 *mu* of land, an estate larger than that of any local lineage in the area.[64] Some of its paddy was rented out; the rest was farmed by two long-term hired laborers. The association also employed a domestic servant girl (*yatou*) for cooking, cleaning, and other chores. It further supported itself by loaning out grain at 40 percent interest, a rate significantly lower than the 80 percent often charged by usurers in the area. Members of the Qingfutang, who had no descendants, drew on notions and practices associated with the patrilineal ancestral cult to create a ritually celebrated "descent group" based on their institutional affiliation. Each year at the Qingming festival, these ties of association, ritual kinship, and collective solidarity were marked by a communal banquet with ritual sacrifices to "ancestors" (*zuxian*) within the Qingfutang.[65] Younger members cared for elderly ones, and after a death the association saw to it that proper ritual sacrifices were offered to the spirit of the deceased.[66] New members were admitted only on the recommendation of current members, and initiates swore oaths never to marry and to adopt a vegetarian diet.

These vows were central to the collective identity shared by members of the Qingfutang. Women combed their own hair in a particular style, a practice reminiscent of marriage resistance movements in Southeast China, while the group's vegetarianism was a metaphor of purity and cleanliness.[67] Members observed a ritualized abstinence from meat, fish, poultry, and eggs, subsisting instead on rice, beancurd, peanuts, and vegetables cooked with vegetable oil. Whereas pork was a central symbol in many patrilineal rituals, at the Qingfutang even the use of pork lard as cooking grease was forbidden. Scallions (*cong*) and garlic bolts (*suanmiao*) were also avoided because it was said that these might make one pregnant. This last taboo was particularly noteworthy because it emphasized the Qingfutang's utter rejection of women's role in biological reproduction, the very quality for which women were honored and valued in patrilineal descent ideology and agnatic culture.

The ritual complex surrounding the Qingfutang drew on elements of Confucianism as well as institutional Buddhism and Daoism, but its particular combination was clearly unorthodox. This suggests affinities with syncretic religious sects, particularly those associated with the White Lotus millenarian movement (Naquin 1985; Perry 1976).[68] Topley (1978: 254) has noted that although vegetarian halls in rural Guangdong province were often residential establishments for lay practioners of Buddhism, they sometimes provided cover for semisecret religious sects associated with a millenarian syncretic religion known as "the Great Way of Former Heaven" (Xiantian Dadao). Many such sects preached that a supreme female deity, the Eternal Venerable Mother, ruled the cosmos and offered salvation to devotees. Her blissful paradise represented a refutation of the supposedly endless cycle of birth, suffering, death, suffering after death, and rebirth that lay at the heart of state-sponsored religious orthodoxy (Cohen 1988). This inversion of the hierarchy of patriliny, and of the state-sanctioned, orthodox patriarchal cosmology, prompted authorities to label such sects heretical.[69]

Although the religious affiliations of the Baimapu Qingfutang remain unclear, the association offered its dozen or so members hope of security, remembrance, and perhaps even salvation. For those with "bad fates" who found themselves exposed and vulnerable on the margins of the patriarchal order, it provided a sense of community, albeit a rather insular one that was subject to the scorn of many local residents.

Gowned Brothers Under the God of War

Whereas the ritual kin of the Qingfutang were ostracized from mainstream local society, those of the Elder Brothers' Society (Gelaohui) largely dominated local affairs. Based on the idiom of "sworn brotherhood" (*jiebai xiongdi*), these men pledged oaths of loyalty and assistance to one another and were ritually initiated into a hierarchical fraternal association. The bonds between them cut across lines of patrilineal descent. In fact, their vows of brotherhood explicitly superseded all other kinship loyalties.

Like similar so-called secret societies throughout China, the Gowned Brothers (Pao Ge), as they were also called after the long robes many wore, had their origins in a covert movement against Manchu rule.[70] By the early 1900s, they formed a loose organization of substantial size with autonomous local chapters, or lodges, operating in many parts of the country. During the Republican era, the Elder Brothers' Society exercised formidable influence in many areas of Sichuan.[71] In the countryside, local lodges were organized around periodic market towns, which they often controlled. As Skinner (1964–65: 37) observed in the 1940s: "The positions of grain measurers, pig weighers, livestock middlemen, and certain other commission agents were reserved for society members, and a portion of each agent's fees was claimed for the coffers of the lodge."[72]

The influence of the Gowned Brothers in Meishan county had been profound.[73] By the 1930s and 1940s, there was little "secret" about their activities or membership. In Baimapu, Gowned Brothers controlled economic exchange in the marketplace, extracted protection fees from local merchants, and ran gambling dens. Many men from mercantile families of the market settlement were said to have been members, as were some from farm families in the countryside.[74] The leaders also dominated township government and militia forces, holding official positions as township officers, *bao* headmen, and militia-group leaders.[75] Even those who were not members were well aware of who among their neighbors were, because they were often obliged to interact with them. Some were compelled to pay protection fees; others sought loans, work, conscription waivers, or tax discounts. Recall that Hao Caiqin was ransomed only after his family appealed to the Gowned Brothers to intercede with Hao Yuntai, a prominent leader in the Baimapu lodge.

The rituals and banquets of the Gowned Brothers were held in the Guan Ye (Guan Di) temple. During his human incarnation, Guan Di was said to have been a mighty warrior of great courage and deep loyalty. In fact, the temple's main statute of this god of war and wealth was said to have been flanked by those of Liu Bei and Zhang Fei, his two "sworn brothers" of the famous Peach Garden oath whose exploits are immortalized in Luo Guanzhong's fourteenth-century classic, *The Romance of the Three Kingdoms.*[76] When township offices were established inside the temple, a tall screen was erected in front of these effigies, and a large rectangular table was set before the screen. There, in the shadow of the most famous sworn brothers in Chinese history, prominent Gowned Brothers met as township officials to discuss local affairs, hear lawsuits, and judge accused criminals.

The symbolism was not lost on local residents. Although Guan Di was revered in many rural communities as a patron of wealth and prosperity, in 1940s Baimapu he was associated with autocratic township authorities. Many elderly men and women recalled the Guan Ye temple as dark and imposing, widely feared and much to be avoided. Although rice was traded and taxes were collected in its open courtyard, the banyan trees that towered over this space were said to have been home to poisonous snakes that would drop down on and bite the *laobaixing,* or "commoners of a hundred surnames."

Drawing on various popular organizational idioms, early-twentieth-century residents of the Baimapu area sought ways to ensure their economic well-being in a period of great instability and uncertainty. The pervasive inflation, taxation, and violence of the Republican era encouraged the rise of new local elites who often pursued aggressive, even predatory entrepreneurial strategies. The quest for security and prosperity required rich and poor alike to cultivate a wide variety of interfamily alliances, many of which were institutionalized in ritual relations of exchange. Following their own interests and emotions, residents wove together a fabric of society that stretched between town and countryside. Although the Communist revolution tried to suppress many of these independent channels of resource mobilization, local social organization and the history of interfamily relationships in the Baimapu area had a profound influence both on how revolutionary power was projected and on how the socialist transformation of rural society was orchestrated.

CHAPTER 3

Creating a New Village Order

Revolutionizing Identity Through
Liberation and Land Reform

A revolution is not a dinner party, or writing an essay, or painting a picture. . . . It cannot be so refined, so leisurely and gentle, so temperate, kind, courteous, restrained, and magnanimous. A revolution is an insurrection, an act of violence by which one class overthrows another.

—MAO ZEDONG, *"Report on an Investigation of*
the Peasant Movement in Hunan"

To fifteen-year-old Xi Xueming, the early morning of December 17, 1949, seemed like any other cold winter market day. Often, when he had time on his hands, he would visit his uncle who worked at the Guan Ye temple as chief of township security. Although a visit to the Baimapu settlement promised excitement on almost any market day, young Xi Xueming also enjoyed spending time at the township office on off-market, or "cold days." There were people to see and things to hear even when the town was relatively quiet and most shopowners kept their storefronts boarded closed.

And things to hear there were. For several weeks, there had been rumors throughout the area of approaching Communist armies. Some local laborers, carting goods on the six-day roundtrip trek to Chengdu, had returned with reports that the Communists had declared a new government in Beijing. There was even talk that President Chiang Kai-shek and other KMT leaders had fled the country, or at least the Mainland. But rumors, it was said, were as reliable as the price of grain, which could rise and fall by 400 percent in the course of a single market day at Baimapu. In Meishan town, the KMT was still in power, although increasing troop movements and new concentrations of defensive forces prompted growing anxiety about the future. Recently, airplanes had begun to fly over Baimapu. A few years earlier, in 1944, a Japanese plane had dropped a bomb over nearby Qinjia township, destroying homes and fields and causing several casualties (MSG 1992: 12). Ever since, a plane overhead had been viewed as an ill omen in Baimapu. Now there were whispers at market about Communists, and the stories exchanged were often frightening.

More than two months earlier, Mao Zedong had proclaimed the establishment of the People's Republic of China from atop the Gate of Heavenly Peace in Beijing. Yet large parts of the country, including much of the Southwest, remained outside Communist control. By early December, the People's Liberation Army (PLA) had secured eastern Sichuan, including the former wartime capital of Chongqing, a few days' journey downriver from Meishan. Advancing on the Chengdu plain, Communist forces moved first westward, to Leshan in the south. In response, three divisions of KMT troops took up positions around Meishan, along the Min River and the major north-south road that ran from Leshan to Chengdu, the provincial capital. One division was posted along the Chengdu-Leshan road, while two companies were dispatched to Baimapu to defend the county's western flank and the road between Meishan and Hongya.[1]

By mid-month, the situation had become critical. Underground Communist organizers stepped up their activities, hoping to incite a popular rebellion.[2] In a brazen move, they put a sign on the door of the county opera house announcing the formation of a "Meishan People's Liberation Committee." The proclamation reportedly drew a large number of local intellectuals and young students who joined in the dissemination of propaganda and pasted up signs welcoming the PLA (Liu 1990). County authorities, for their part, had assembled a local security force of nearly four thousand, composed of local militia troops, police, Gowned Brothers, and armed private retainers of large landowners.

Late in the afternoon of December 16, county authorities dispatched a lorry of troops to protect government offices from an incipient rebellion. From atop the vehicle, soldiers opened fire on demonstrators. The crowd dispersed but found that the gates of the walled town had been shut to prevent escape as security forces rounded up protestors and suspected ringleaders. Word spread through the town that KMT authorities were threatening to burn Meishan to the ground in retaliation. Deeply alarmed, local civilian elites mobilized their own force of some thirty armed volunteers, called the "Meishan People's Self-Defense Committee," to aid authorities in maintaining security.[3] While the town was spared a conflagration, leaders of the aborted uprising were able to slip across the walls and retreat to the hills in the north.

Meanwhile, larger troops movements in the countryside focused attention on the county's western flank. Earlier that same day, the PLA had crossed the Min River and entered Meishan at Simeng township, near the county's southern border with Qingshen. KMT forces retreated and regrouped at Dongguachang (present-day Xiuwen), the market town just south of Baimapu from which Liang Jinyuan's father had come. Others established new defensive positions along a 7-kilometer front stretching from Qiaolouzi, the Bridge Building near Baimapu, to Sanbao township in the west. A field-radio communications post was set up at the Xi lineage hall, with its commanding view atop Big Xi Hill (MSG 1992: 390). Operations were headquartered in the Guan Ye temple. Young Xi Xueming, however, knew nothing of these developments when he set off early the next morning to visit his uncle at the township offices.

As he walked from his family's home in southern Second Bao, Xi wondered what news he might hear from his uncle or other local officials. But there would be no market at Baimapu that day. As young Xi reached the market settlement and approached the Guan Ye temple, he inadvertently surprised a group of armed guards who challenged him brusquely, weapons raised and ready. "*Ni ganma*?!" they demanded. "What do you think you're doing?!"

Their agitation was understandable. For these remnant KMT supporters, the future may have looked uncertain but the end must have seemed inevitable. In fact, PLA advance units had reached Baimapu township the previous evening, to scout local defenses in preparation for the main assault force due to arrive the next morning from Simeng and Dongguachang. They found that KMT troops and local militia had set up a series of defensive works near the large "Cross-Shaped Pond" (Shizitang) in southern Second Bao (see Map 3). There, the path dipped between two hills—Xi Upper Slope and Xi Lower Slope—and crossed a narrow plain of rice paddy before climbing to the Baimapu market settlement another kilometer to the north. The defenders had felled trees from surrounding hillsides and had piled the trunks, some more than a foot thick, in a series of barricades across the path. In the gully, winter water ponds (*dongshuitian*), which farmers relied on for irrigation at spring planting, had been drained to create a long field of deep mud that, it was hoped, would slow an assault. Fortified positions were set up on Xi Lower Slope, looking south over an intended field of fire.

When the opposing forces clashed on the morning of December 17, the engagement was brief. After losing several men in a frontal assault on the footpath barricades, the PLA launched a second attack from the flank. They successfully dislodged the defenders, who broke rank and scattered. Few local residents were eyewitnesses to the engagement. Most had sheltered themselves under beds and tables behind the closed doors of their homes.[4] Young Xi Xueming fled from the Guan Ye temple at the first sounds of gun-fire and lay hiding, terrified, in the fields north of the market settlement. "I wanted the ground to open and swallow me," he recalled. "But it would not let me in." Eventually, cold and hunger overcame his fear, and he ventured home. There he found chaos among anxious family members. The Battle of Baimapu, which lasted no more than an hour, was over. "Liberation" had come to Meishan.

The Moving Frontier of Liberation: Creating and Negating the "Old Society"

The Chinese Communist movement may have cultivated a homegrown ver-sion of Marxism, but it was outsiders who brought revolution to Baimapu. It was incumbent upon party work teams to elicit popular support for their agenda and to recruit, train, and anoint new local leaders who would admin-ister the revolution once party organizers departed. To arouse the poor and to incite those with grievances to speak out against their former antagonists, the political work teams introduced a new vocabulary of revolution. At pub-lic meetings and in teahouse conversations, these organizers and propagan-dists announced the end of what they labeled the "Old Society" (*jiu shehui*), a "semi-feudal" system led by a corrupt "landlord class" that "exploited" the "masses" through "tyrannical" rule and "superstitious" beliefs. In the "New China," they said, the people would "stand up" and "turn over" their lives to govern themselves, creating a "new democracy" of the people under the guidance of the Communist Party, their "revolutionary vanguard."

The invention of "Old Society" was part of an attempt to repudiate and to distance the former social and political order through the very way in which it was defined. The past became, in a sense, a "foreign country" (Low-enthal 1985). Recast as an alien time and place, it was redefined as a cultural and political Otherland, and hence became the object of selective remem-brance and collective amnesia (e.g., R. Watson 1994; Jing 1996). The term "peasant" (*nongmin*) was one of several modern neologisms popularized by the Communists to evoke the "backward" character of China's Old Society (Cohen 1993a; see also Hayford 1990).[5] The first major efforts to distance New China from its cultural past came with the Land Reform campaign of the early 1950s, a movement that entailed much more than the redistri-bution of property. Land Reform was also an ambitious attempt to reorga-nize the communities of interest and sentiment with which local residents identified, as well as the cosmologies of social and spiritual life within which they lived.

To accomplish such goals, the local population was "mobilized." Through their action and rhetoric, political work teams of the Chinese Communist Party (CCP) attempted to shape and direct class consciousness.[6] They convened mass meetings at which the poor were encouraged to denounce the former township elite, "speaking bitterness" (*shuoku*) against landowners, usurers, and local strongmen. The work teams also orchestrated the violent destruction of prominent architectural symbols of the old order, literally deconstructing the monuments of the past to clear ground for the creation of new local communities. Earth god shrines were demolished. Some temples and ancestral halls were torn down, others converted to new uses. The campaign culminated with public execution of condemned "tyrant landlords" (*eba dizhu*), whose family homes and properties were parceled out to the local poor.

As elsewhere in China, Land Reform was a major political watershed. Its property redistributions were instrumental in creating popular legitimacy for the new Communist government. Yet the long-term significance of the campaign lay not in its heralded land-to-the-tiller reforms, which were effectively annulled a few years later with the advent of collectivized agriculture (see Chapter 4), but in its creation of a new social and political order. Land Reform introduced new typologies of identity and created new forms of community organization. It attacked the cosmologies of power, authority, and social relations in popular religion and promoted a new interpretation of the social order based on notions of class exploitation. It also established new institutions of rural government that profoundly influenced family opportunities, social status, and economic security for decades to come.

These revolutionary upheavals were initiated from "above," under the direction of the new party-state authorities. In the process, however, certain families and individuals became empowered, both materially and symbolically, with new forms of authority and new patterns of dominance over their kin and neighbors (Friedman, Pickowicz, and Selden 1991). These new cadres and their fellow villagers became both the "agents and victims" of revolution (Siu 1989). Obliged to carry out the policy directives issued by party-state authorities, they often interpreted and implemented instructions and orders in terms of particular agendas. Although the revolutionary transformation of society was conditioned by larger political and economic forces over which the residents of Baimapu had little control, for them its meaning and significance were ultimately understood in the context of their personal and family relationships. Despite its national scale, the Communist revolution was profoundly local in character.

Pacifying the Countryside

The gunfire that raged between the heights of Xi Upper Slope and Xi Lower Slope in Second Bao that December morning echoed, figuratively and literally, throughout the township. Heralding the establishment of a new order, these first sparks of revolution represented powerful new forces that were to alter dramatically the lives of local residents. The PLA soldiers who marched into Baimapu on December 17, 1949 were followed by CCP political work teams. As the Communists gained control over more and more territory, the number of cities, towns, and townships requiring the immediate attention of their work teams grew inordinately (Shue 1980). Along this moving frontier of Liberation, understaffed political organizers moved as quickly as possible to pacify the countryside and to stabilize the economy (MSG 1992: 351). They set up "mass organizations," started training classes for local activists, recruited and armed new militia units, collected grain taxes, and suppressed so-called bandits and counterrevolutionary activities. Before moving on to other "newly liberated" areas, they mobilized the poor to take up the banner of revolution and to become dependable, if not effective, basic-level cadres (*jiceng ganbu*).

In the months following the arrival of the Communists, tensions in the Baimapu area remained high as the PLA sought to secure the region for the political work teams. Township officials and *bao* leaders were detained or kept under a watchful eye. Local militia that had operated under the KMT were disarmed. Attempts were made to disband the Gowned Brothers, or at least to suppress their activities. Physical movement was curtailed and tightly controlled, requiring authorized travel permits. Concerns over possible counterrevolutionary activity mounted after Hao Yuru, former conscription patrol chief, was caught attempting to flee the area disguised as a PLA soldier.

That winter, at least eight separate "bandit" (*tufei*) groups—totaling more than three thousand KMT operatives, secret-society members, hooligans, former rural officials, and "backward masses" (*luohou qunzhong*)—continued to roam and pillage rural Meishan (MSG 1992: 14, 241). In February 1950, an attack on Duoyue, a rural town north of Baimapu, left at least a dozen PLA soldiers and cadres from a grain-collection work team dead, as raiders made off with weapons and more than ten tons of grain. Those responsible reportedly then linked up with larger groups operating in neighboring Pengshan county to stage a "counterrevolutionary" uprising that was not suppressed until September (Liu Chuanmei 1990: 149–53; MSG 1992: 241–42). Two months later, eleven county "tyrants" (*eba*), including the most powerful of Meishan's former militarists, were publicly condemned and executed in Meishan at a mass rally of more than forty thousand people. This was followed by the execution of local leaders from the Yiguandao sworn brotherhood and of a group of alleged KMT spies and saboteurs in January 1951 (MSG 1992: 14). Nevertheless, throughout 1951, internal government circulars reported attacks on state granaries in the region and recommended additional security precautions.[7] Elderly residents of Baimapu recalled that there had been several attempted thefts at the township granary during the early 1950s.

At the same time, the CCP work teams tried to stabilize the local economy. The summer following the Liberation of Meishan again brought famine in the county, and emergency grain rations had to be delivered to rural farmers (MSG 1992: 14). The new government also abolished or reduced many of the various taxes and local surcharges levied on the public (ibid., pp. 726–27).[8] Boosting agricultural production was a high priority. In the autumn of 1950, CCP work teams began to propagandize the Four Great Tasks (*si da renwu*) among farmers: eliminate bandits, overthrow local tyrants, reduce rents, and refund extortionate rent deposits. In Baimapu, they canceled outstanding debts to private moneylenders.[9] Popular support for the Communists grew as they broadened the scope of their economic reforms. After enforcing rent reductions and deposit refunds, the work teams confiscated some of the property of large landowners and turned it over to landless and land-poor families. This land-to-the-tiller action was not part of the comprehensive Land Reform program, which followed in 1952.[10] Rather, it was a provisional redistribution that appropriated the surplus holdings of some wealthy families to alleviate the immediate burdens of the poor, thus providing them with a relatively secure subsistence base.

By all local accounts, Baimapu became a center of CCP activity during the first two years of Communist rule. Following Liberation, it was designated by the new Communist authorities as a "revolutionary vanguard district" (*geming qianfeng qu*), the seat of subcounty district administration with jurisdiction over several neighboring townships.[11] Apparently, in light of the resistance the PLA had encountered at Baimapu, authorities were concerned that they might meet with further opposition from the local population.[12] A political training school was set up in the market settlement, run by party organizers. "Activist elements" (*jiji fenzi*) from throughout the district who supported the new Communist authorities were brought there to receive instruction in the ideological principles of communism, government directives and regulations, administrative practices, and techniques of mass mobilization.

Recounting these early years of Liberation, many elderly residents of the township claimed that the local population had displayed a great deal of enthusiasm for the Communists' reform programs. Revolution had been brought to Baimapu by outsiders, but local residents joined in the construction of new relationships of power, playing their own roles in the dramas of revolutionary change.

Organicizing the Revolution: Grafting Activism onto Local Roots

The work teams focused their initial organizational efforts at the township level. As they interviewed families within the local marketing community, party workers identified potential "activists"—usually poor farmers who were likely to support the Communists. Some came forward voluntarily; others had to be courted more persistently. Later, when the work teams stepped up their efforts at mass mobilization for the class struggle of Land Reform, they encouraged, promoted, and relied on these activists to play a leading role in denouncing "local tyrants" and advocating new government policies.

Most local activists were people whose family backgrounds, it was hoped, would make them not only sympathetic to but also dependent on the new Communist authorities, if only for fear of the retribution they might suffer should forces opposed to the revolution attempt to regain power. After a period of political training and tutelage under the CCP work teams, these local activists were to assume leading roles in the new village administrations that would be created before party organizers departed. One of the early activists to gain prominence under the work teams was Jin Yuzhen, the widow from a poor family introduced in Chapter 2. Born to landless laborers, her mother had left her as an infant to become a wet nurse for a wealthy family, and Jin had spent her youth begging for food at the Baimapu market and, later, as an indentured domestic servant girl. Both her father and her husband, a Xi man from Second Bao, had been long-term contract laborers living with their employers in other townships, and her husband, recall, had starved to death only the previous year. For people such as Jin, the Communist revolution truly was a liberation:

> Not long after Liberation, I got involved in politics, trying to mobilize (*fadong*) the poor to turn over (*fanshen*) their lives. Most poor people feared the rich. At first, few dared to speak out. During speak bitterness (*shuoku*) meetings, the revolutionary cadres relied heavily on us women to voice accounts and complaints of hardships and sufferings. Because of

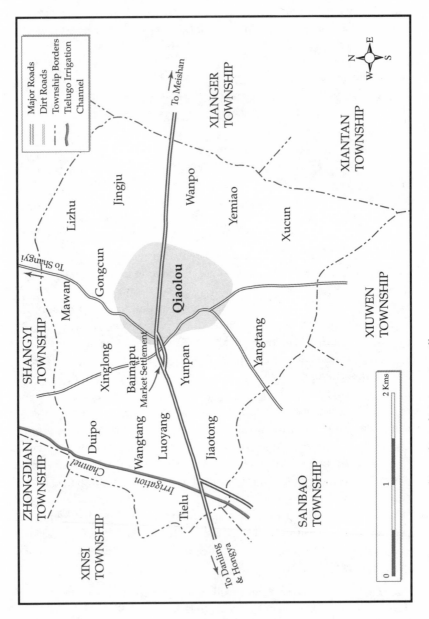

MAP 4. Baimapu township and its administrative villages, 1991

the KMT's conscription policies, there had been few men working in the fields. Since most farmers were women, our work load was heavier. The oppression we suffered at the hands of the landlords was more painful. The work teams began propagandizing for the new government. They were mainly composed of cadres from old liberated districts (*lao jiefang qu*). We had people from Shaanxi and Shandong [provinces] working here. Women and youths were the main focus of propaganda work. They tried to cultivate our support. Although we had no formal education, we were experienced in life. I joined the revolution in 1950, when I was selected as women's cadre of Yunpan [formerly First Bao]. I encouraged women to speak up against oppression in the past as well as exploitation that continued under the new order. The next year I became a full-time member of the revolutionary [township] government . . . when I was appointed deputy township head for women's affairs. I served in that post until I retired in 1979. I never took a bribe, never ate without paying, and was never criticized or purged from my position.

Yet not all those activists who emerged to take leading roles in the revolution were ideologically committed to the policies and programs outlined by the work teams (Walder 1986). A few of the early appointments made by the work teams turned out to be problematic. In later years, CCP leaders would be obliged to undertake "rectification" campaigns, which created new tensions and antagonisms with unanticipated consequences in the local political arena (see Siu 1989; Friedman, Pickowicz, and Selden 1991).

To coordinate security and economic recovery, new institutions of administrative management were established in rural townships. Recall that Republican-era state strengthening efforts had introduced offices of subcounty government at the rural district and townships levels. During the Land Reform era, state power and authority were extended even further with the establishment of administrative villages (*xingzheng cun*) within Baimapu township (see Map 4).[13] The organizational structure of the former *baojia* system provided the framework for these new villages, each of which was defined largely along the lines of a former *bao* unit.

The concept of village identity, however, was new to local residents. Living in houses dispersed across the countryside on hillsides, either alone or in small clusters, families perceived their communities in terms of exchange relations, regardless of whether these relations were mediated through earth gods, ancestral or religious associations, rotating credit societies, reciprocal labor groups, or marketing partners. The *bao* was regarded as a tax and policing unit, not as a social community. The village had similar origins, although collectivization, household registration, and redistributive accounting would later add new dimensions to social interaction among farming families. The collective village became a community of exchange, mediating between resident families and state authorities, between farmers and townspeople, between cadres and kin.

Establishing the Administrative Village

During that tense first year of Liberation, the old *baojia* system was kept in place to aid in security operations. However, work teams began organizing "peasant associations" (*nongmin xiehui*) in each rural township and, later, "branch associations" (*fenhui*) in each *bao*.[14] By September 1950, "peasant associations" had been established in every township of the county, though not yet in every *bao*.[15] They eventually became the foundation for new village administrations, and the *baojia* system was abolished (MSG 1992: 14, 234). Each *bao* was renamed as a village. Second Bao, for example, became known as Qiaolou village, after the nearby bridge and building along the Meishan road.[16] It was subdivided administratively into ten groups (*zu*) that closely paralleled the ten former *jia* units of the *bao*.

Elderly residents in Qiaolou recalled, however, that a "peasant association" was not established in their village until the early months of 1951. During the interim, as the CCP work teams moved among the local population, recruiting the support of the poor and landless, Qiaolou was placed under the authority of a "liberation chairman" (*jiefang zhuxi*) chosen by the work teams. After preliminary background investigations, the work teams selected for this post a poor farmer named Wei. Considered by many local residents to be an outsider (*waidiren*), he had resettled in the area a short time before from Shangyi (formerly Hanjiachang). Some, in fact, suspected that Wei was an underground agent of the CCP. Although his marginal status in the local web of kinship may have made him appealing to the work teams, who were anxious to avoid appointing leaders with "feudal clan loyalties," Wei was widely mistrusted by many locals (*bendiren*). Soon accused of confiscating property from local notables and keeping it for his own family gain, he was compelled by the work teams to step down.[17] Wei was replaced as liberation chairman by Xiu Xiaoping, another poor farmer from northern Qiaolou also unaffiliated with a major local descent group.

Xiu served as liberation chairman until a fire destroyed his house. No one was home at the time, which raised suspicion about the cause of the blaze. The work teams concluded, largely on the basis of circumstantial evidence, that it was a case of arson. Since it had been directed against a designated representative of new party-state authority, it was labeled a "counter-revolutionary" act. In light of the attack on Duoyue and ongoing unrest in other parts of the county, security forces were determined to identify those responsible and set an example that would deter future resistance.

Investigations soon focused on a Yan family of Catholics in northern Qiaolou. Their grandfather had owned 6 *mu* of paddy in the Baimapu area but had worked principally as an itinerant peddler, trading chickens at various rural periodic markets in the region. He had converted to Christianity when he married a woman from Meishan.[18] Religion had been a divisive issue for the family. Two sons had migrated away in search of new lives, while a third had volunteered for the KMT army, reportedly to escape hunger. Only one son remained with the parents and was raised as a Catholic, inheriting the entire 6 *mu* on his father's death. He enjoyed a reversal of fortunes and was able to rent an additional 20 *mu* from an absentee landowner, apparently through his family's religious associations.[19] He married a woman from Simeng with whom he had three sons and a daughter. However, the family's Catholicism had left them socially marginalized among local kin. They did not attend the rituals and banquets of their ancestral associations. As one of the man's sons recalled, "We were alone."

After the fire, this man's sons were among those interrogated, particularly the two eldest, who were married and in their mid-twenties. One of them recalled that he had trembled in fear after being summoned by officials. At the time the fire was said to have occurred, he had been on an errand, sent to call a village activist to a meeting. He was cleared of suspicion after both the man who had dispatched him as a messenger and the man he had been summoned to bring to the meeting testified as to his whereabouts and the official nature of his errand. His elder brother was not so fortunate. Without an alibi that could be confirmed by the authorities, he was judged responsible for the fire and was executed. Liberation chairman Xiu was said to have been so shaken by the incident that he resigned his post and retired from political life.[20]

The CCP work teams selected two other activists in Qiaolou for formal responsibilities. Like Wei and Xiu, both these men had relatively few patrilineal kin in Qiaolou. One, an educated farmer named Jun who resided in the Baimapu market settlement, was appointed clerk-accountant (*wenshu*). The other, a poor farmer from northern Qiaolou named Lin Chengying, was empowered as new chief of village security. In addition to these leading appointments, a group representative (*zu daibiao*) from each of Qiaolou's ten former *jia* units was selected to serve on a new village administrative committee. These men were reportedly chosen on the basis of their reputations for honesty, diligence, and responsibility. Some had served as leaders of their old *jia* units before Liberation, but unless they had abused their power such appointments were not held against them. One former *jia* headman had been startled to find himself reappointed to authority:

> One day, not long after Liberation, Chairman Xiu called me to a meeting. There, before representatives of more than a hundred households, he appointed me a group representative. I had to inform members of other households in my group about meetings, new instructions, and production quotas. Later, I had to assist the [CCP] work teams in gathering information about each family for the upcoming Land Reform campaign.

Group representatives were also expected to voice the concerns of their neighbors to the new authorities. Although the representatives of some sub-village groups changed frequently over the next few years, several men retained their appointments and developed influential ties with new village and township administrators.

The CCP work teams finally organized a "peasant association" in Qiaolou in early 1951, more than a year after Liberation. Many villagers came to regard the association as a foundation for local government, recalling that it offered their first sense of democracy (*minzhu*). The Land Reform campaign had, in fact, been combined with efforts to establish democratic government (*minzhu jianzheng*) in rural areas through "peasant associations" (MSG 1992: 234). The chairs of village (and township) "peasant association" served concurrently as village (or township) heads. They were nominated by these organizations and confirmed in their posts by the county government, giving the local poor an opportunity to participate in the selection of their local leaders.[21] In 1953, elections were held in which village and township heads were chosen by group representatives (ibid.). But the group representatives had been appointed (not elected), as the account above describes, and an incumbent village head could cultivate a clientele of supporters to retain his position. It was also from the ranks of the Qiaolou "peasant association" that volunteers were recruited for the new village militia, under its leader Lin Chengying.

Mobilizing the Subalterns of Patriliny

The Qiaolou "peasant association" also empowered two new positions in village administration: the director of women's affairs and the director of youth affairs. Those selected for these new posts had suffered hardships in the Old Society and were early supporters of the new Communist authorities. They were given responsibility for organizing and mobilizing women and youths, those most marginalized in the patriarchal order of the Old Society. Although they were among the first villagers inducted into the Chinese Communist Party, their influence in local affairs was based on more than their official positions alone.

Yan Guifang, for example, was selected to head up "women's work" in Qiaolou. Born to a family of poor farmers in northern Second Bao, she had spun thread as a child to help her family earn extra cash. As a teenager she helped her widowed mother by often making three trips a day to Meishan, carrying 80-pound bundles of firewood to sell at the markets there. Her elder sister had been married off as a young "little daughter-in-law" to a family in another township, but Yan was not married until she reached twenty, a year before the Communists arrived in Baimapu. Her husband was a Xi man, also from Second Bao, a match that enabled Yan to remain within the familiar social world of her natal village:

> I joined the Communist Party in 1954 and became the first party member in Qiaolou. I had been appointed as Qiaolou's first women's cadre (*funu ganbu*) in 1951, when I also served as [co]chair of the peasant association. At first I received no salary, but later I earned 5 *yuan* a month. I also spent a lot of time working as an organizer in the villages of Lizhu, Tielu, and Yunpan [in Baimapu township]. For three years I even substituted for Jin Yuzhen as assistant township head for women's affairs [while the latter was sent for training to Guanghua county in northern Sichuan]. I resigned in 1960, too tired to continue.[22] My meetings fostered human feelings (*renqing*), and many people did not want to leave after we adjourned. They would sit and talk, complaining about this problem or that, sharing their concerns on a large scale for the first time. Those meetings were like tea parties. When conflicts arose that required meditation, I would convene a big family meeting. All were encouraged to speak their hearts (*tan xin*), and in this way all views were aired and discussed. I would listen to opposing arguments and then pass my judgment as arbitrator. Any criticism that was due I passed along privately. That way nobody lost face. This was very important.

After her appointment as director of women's affairs in Qiaolou at the age of twenty-three, Yan went on to create a diffuse set of "dry kin" relations. She also developed intimate personal ties with many village families by serving as a marital matchmaker. Like many women, she worked the margins of agnatic culture, cultivating her influence across, rather than within, lines of patrilineal descent. Not only was she the first Qiaolou villager to join the Communist Party but she also eventually married one of her own daughters to the youngest son of Qiaolou's inaugural Communist Party branch secretary.

Youths, too, played a key political role during the early years of Communist rule, particularly through the militant patriotism fostered among them by the CCP work teams (Friedman, Pickowicz, and Selden 1991). Village youths were recruited and organized into an armed security force headed by Liang Jinyuan, the orphan who had been taken under the protection of Hao Caiqin's family. Liang would later join the first group of volunteers from Meishan to go off to war in Korea.[23] But at age twenty, he became head of the Qiaolou youth militia, an appointment no doubt influenced by the fact that his elder sister was married to the son of Lin Chengying, the poor farmer appointed by the work teams as chief of the new "peasant association" militia.

Instructed by the work teams on regulations concerning activity and movement in "newly liberated" areas, the youths—some no more than small children, Liang recalled—were armed with sticks, spears, or knives. They were sent out to keep watch for strangers and suspicious persons, as well as for landowners, former officials, and thugs of the Old Society.[24] Some were stationed at checkpoints along footpaths or at vantage points atop hills, while others formed patrol units. They were authorized to stop anyone, to investigate her or his errand, and to demand identification papers or travel permits. When they encountered resistance, one or two were sent running to inform local authorities while the others detained the suspect with knives or spears. According to Liang, the youths carried out their duties with "responsibility" (*zeren*) and "diligence" (*yonggong*), and did not hesitate to intimidate adults.

It as also in 1951 that a six-man Land Reform presidium (*tugai zhuxituan*) was set up in Qiaolou to prepare for the much-vaunted comprehensive redistribution campaign. Three of its members were state cadres (*guojia ganbu*), salaried outsiders affiliated with CCP work teams and the county government.[25] The other three were leading members of the new Qiaolou village administration: Lin Chengying of northern Qiaolou, the security chief and militia leader who had recently been elected chair of the "peasant association" and new village head (*cunzhang*); the village clerk-accountant Jun of Baimapu Street; and Hao Yuanan of southern Qiaolou, who had briefly succeeded liberation chairman Xiu until Lin's election victory and who subsequently became village production supervisor.

Together, these men led investigations into the political background and economic circumstances of each family in Qiaolou. Their goal was to assign class designations (*jieji chengfen*) that would determine the status—and fate—of each family in the coming Land Reform campaign. To assist them, the representatives of each subvillage group were ordered to prepare reports on every family. Members of the presidium did not visit family homes or farms to assess the extent of property holdings, nor did they summon family members for interviews. No mass meetings were convened, and people were not asked to offer assessments of their neighbors. The classification of local families, and the ascription of official class designations, was the relatively closed action of this six-member presidium, although group representatives did have some input (see also Friedman, Pickowicz, and Selden 1991: 82).

Classifying the Composition of the Old Society

Class designations were assigned to patrilineal family households. Many Qiaolou villagers, including several cadres, explained that one's class background was "inherited" (*you yichuan xing*). For decades, these political labels had great influence in determining a person's prospects for employment, education, and even marriage (see Croll 1981, 1984; Lavely 1991). They were passed down each patriline, from father to children. By superscribing patrilineal identity with class affiliation, CCP political work teams hoped to weaken agnatic solidarity between rich and poor patrilineal kin. Identification with one's family class was officially promoted at the expense of lineage, or *Qingminghui*, identity. In effect, however, the CCP created focal ancestors for new descent groups, in the persons of each patrilineal family head at the time of Land Reform. For the next quarter of a century, each individual's political status was linked in part to the class designation ascribed to her or his father or grandfather. In a sense, Land Reform displaced genealogical time and fostered in its stead the conceptualization of new descent branches based on family class identity under the new Communist property and status regime.[26]

Class assessments were based largely on a family's rising or falling economic fortunes over the three years preceding Liberation. One man, however, was widely noted in Baimapu for having come from a family "propertyless for three generations" (*sandai wuchan*). His example was extreme because most families in such a condition failed to marry or reproduce, and hence died out. But that, the work teams asserted, made the longevity of his family all the more remarkable. They had popularized his case with a phrase that alluded to the colloquially expressed ideal of "four generations under one roof" (*sidai tongtang*). Classification was also influenced by the past social conduct or political behavior of family members. Although abusive local strongmen and oppressive landlords were held individually accountable for

their actions, some degree of collective responsibility was also ascribed to
families, for all family members then received unfavorable classifications.
Determinations of status were made not only on the extent of each family's
landholdings, but also on the basis of its general "production situation"
(*shengchan qingkuan*). This term, also introduced by the CCP work teams,
was understood to mean the extent to which a family possessed the five main
agricultural tools (*wuda nongju*): draft animals, irrigation pedal wheels,
threshing tubs, winnowing machines, and hand tools. Also taken into consideration were the extent to which a family rented land (in or out), hired or
sold labor, and loaned or borrowed money, as well as the proportion of family income derived from "exploitation" (*boxue*).[27]

Generally speaking, one of five rural class designations was assigned to
each family in the village: landlords (*dizhu*), rich peasants (*funong*), middle
peasants (*zhongnong*), poor peasants (*pinnong*), and hired laborers (*gu-
gong*).[28] These classifications introduced a new language and cosmology into
local social relations. They defined the contours of stratification shaped under the Old Society while simultaneously redefining the social order, both literally and figuratively. The term "*dizhu*," for example, had been an honorific
title for local notable families, even those that did not own large amounts of
property. As a new class label, however, *dizhu* became superscribed with the
new meaning—and stigma—of "landlord."

Each family's class designation became institutionalized as a new category
of social identity and as a marker of former political status. The new status
order created at Land Reform inverted the privileges of wealth, property, and
influence that had prevailed before Liberation. Those classified as "landlords" and "rich peasants" were decried as exploiters and were subject not
only to discrimination and humiliation but also to expropriation and persecution. Work teams popularized the slogan, "Rely on poor peasants and
hired laborers, unite with middle peasants, neutralize rich peasants, and iso-
late and exterminate (*xiaomei*) the feudal system of exploitation to develop
agricultural production" (MSG 1992: 244). The interests of "middle peasants," who were between the two extremes of the deposed old elite and the
newly anointed heirs of the revolution, were to be protected in order to promote economic development.[29]

These new categories of identity were based largely on Mao Zedong's assessment of agrarian class relations in 1920s Hunan province (Mao 1975a).
Mao's treatise offered an outline of rural stratification and a distribution of
social classes: landlords, 5 percent; rich peasants, 5 percent; middle peasants,
20 percent; and poor peasants, 70 percent. Of course, the particulars of history also led to variations in land tenure patterns among different regions
and even within specific locales. Tenancy was more prevalent in the produc-

TABLE 1

Class Designations in Meishan and Qiaolou
at Land Reform, ca. 1952

| | MEISHAN COUNTY | QIAOLOU VILLAGE | |
	Percent of total families	Percent of total families	Number of families
Landlords	4.4	4.5	6
Rich Peasants	3.9	6.7	9
Middle Peasants	28.4	26.1	35
Poor Peasants	52.5	62.6	84
Hired Laborers	2.7		

SOURCE: MSG 1992: 244; Qiaolou numbers based on oral history reconstructions.

NOTE: Percentages do not total 100 due to rounding.

tive south, for example, where grain yields were higher. In North China there were fewer tenants, but ecological conditions often necessitated larger family farms. Nevertheless, Land Reform work teams in some parts of the country followed Mao's estimates much like prescriptive quotas, particularly when it came to the categories of "landlord" and "rich peasant" (Kraus 1982: 24; but cf. Selden 1993: 86).

Land Reform class assessments in Qiaolou also seem to have approximated Mao's earlier calculations (see Table 1):[30] 4.5 percent (N = 6) of village families were classified as landlords, 6.7 percent (N = 9) as rich peasants, 26.1 percent (N = 35) as middle peasants, and 62.6 percent (N = 84) as poor peasants. The distribution of classifications by surname was also noteworthy (see Table 2). Although Hao families, for example, constituted only 17.9 percent of village families, their members constituted 28.6 percent of the so-called middle peasants, 44.4 percent of the rich peasants, and 50 percent of the landlords in Qiaolou. All of the Jins, as well as most Lins and Haos (42.8 and 41.6 percent, respectively), were classified as middle peasants, while even larger majorities of Xis, Wens, Yans, and Zhens were classed as poor peasants (57.1, 64.3, 75.0, and 88.9 percent, respectively).

The earliest political appointments made by the CCP work teams had empowered families among the village poor. Yet as late as 1991, no Zhen, Wen, or Xi, and only one Yan woman had ever served in a village-level leadership position, although these families comprised almost half the "poor peasant" population of Qiaolou at Land Reform.[31] Not all prominent activists or new village cadres came from the ranks of the poor. In some cases people with politically unfavorable class designations were appointed to positions of re-

TABLE 2

Distribution of Class Designations in Qiaolou
by Surname at Land Reform, ca. 1952

	POOR PEASANTS			MIDDLE PEASANTS		
Surname	*Number of PP*	*Percent of of total PP in Qiaolou*	*Percent of PP within Surname*	*Number of MP*	*Percent of total MP in Qiaolou*	*Percent of MP within surname*
Hao	7	8.3	29.1	10	28.6	41.6
Jin	0	0	0	4	11.4	100.0
Lin	2	2.4	28.6	3	8.6	42.8
Wen	9	10.7	64.3	1	2.9	7.1
Xi	8	9.5	57.1	5	14.3	35.7
Yan	12	14.3	75.0	4	11.4	25.0
Zhen	8	9.5	88.9	1	2.9	11.1
TOTAL	46	54.7		28	80.1	

sponsibility owing to their special skills, such as literacy and accounting.[32] For example, during the late 1950s and early 1960s, a "rich peasant" named Hao Yunpo served as village accountant. As a youth he had received several years of formal schooling, and he was one of the few local men with a study name (*xueming*), symbolizing his educated status (see R. Watson 1986). This grandson of Hao Caiming was also the uncle of several Hao men who rose to prominence as leading village activists in the 1950s.

Negotiating Classification

Although most village families had no direct voice in the ascription of their class designations, they did not remain passive in the assessment process. Some influenced their classifications by participating enthusiastically in political activities directed by the work teams. Others attempted to appeal to particularistic ties of patrilineal descent, ritual kinship, affinity, or friendship with group representatives or members of the Land Reform presidium. Mitigating factors, whether personal or political, were most influential in borderline cases of classification (Friedman, Pickowicz, and Selden 1991).

Before Hao Caiqin's confrontation with strongman Hao Yuntai, which led to formal partitioning, his extended family had possessed a strong economic base that supported its more than thirty members. They had owned four

TABLE 2

(continued)

	RICH PEASANTS			LANDLORDS				
Number of RP	Percent of total RP in Qiaolou	Percent of RP within surname	Number of LL	Percent of total LL in Qiaolou	Percent of LL with surname	Number in Qiaolou with surname	Percent of total Qiaolou population
4	44.4	16.6	3	50.0	12.5	24	17.9
0	0	0	0	0	0	4	2.9
2	22.2	28.6	0	0	0	7	5.2
3	33.3	21.9	1	16.7	7.1	14	10.4
0	0	0	1	16.7	7.1	14	10.4
0	0	0	0	0	0	16	11.9
0	0	0	0	0	0	9	6.7
9	99.9		5	83.4		88	65.4

NOTE: PP = poor peasants, MP = middle peasants, RP = rich peasants, and LL = landlords.

houses, numerous hogs, and several weaving looms, as well as water buffalo and winnowing machines. Although their own landholdings amounted to only 5.2 *mu*, they rented at least 40 *mu* of additional land. Obliged to expend their grain stores and sell their hogs to ransom Hao Caiqin, family members had divided into five separate units not long before the arrival of the Communists.

The assessment of their class designation was more complicated than most. The fact that their cloth-weaving enterprise had been operated entirely by family labor was to their advantage. Because they had not hired laborers from outside the family, their activities were considered "nonexploitative" (*fei boxue*).[33] Moreover, they apparently accentuated the image of their economic decline by destroying other productive assets. As one of Hao Caiqin's grandsons, himself now an elderly grandfather, recalled with seeming nonchalance one afternoon, "The first thing we did when the Communists arrived was burn our looms."

In addition, several of Hao Caiqin's young descendants came forward and actively participated in early efforts of the CCP work teams to mobilize support for the revolution. This enthusiastic activism earned them political recognition. When local residents were sought out to "speak bitterness" at mass meetings of public denunciation of former "tyrant landlords," many had been reluctant at first, sometimes because they were uncertain whether the Communists would remain in power. There had been granary thefts,

Gowned Brothers activity, the recent "counterrevolutionary" uprising in Duoyue, and even the arson incident in Qiaolou. Yet among the descendants of Hao Caiqin the work teams found several who were particularly ardent in denouncing the most dreaded of local bullies, Hao Yuntai. Although their grievances may well have been personal, they nonetheless suited the purposes of the party work teams, who found people willing to speak up against the old elite and even against their own patrilineal kin.[34] Two of Hao Caiqin's grandsons in particular, the brothers Hao Yuandeng and Hao Yuanliang, distinguished themselves as teenagers through their revolutionary activism and were gradually brought into the widening circle of new village leaders. The younger, Hao Yuanliang (b. 1934), was appointed head of the New Democracy Youth League, a precursor to the Communist Youth League (est. 1957), which groomed local activists for eventual membership in the Communist Party (MSG 1992: 184–85).

Victimized by the "reactionary" elite of the Old Society for their refusal to serve as conscripts in the KMT army, obliged to break up their family after being forced to sell their hogs and grain to ransom their family patriarch—and, of course, now loomless—Hao Caiqin's descendants' enthusiastic support for the revolution earned them the relatively neutral classification of "middle peasants." Although their class designation did not entitle them to a share in the upcoming land redistribution, it did avoid the stigma attached to being classified as "rich peasants."

Receiving a Share of the Revolution

The first experimental site of Land Reform in the county was in neighboring Xianger township, where work began in December 1950; the campaign was not brought to Baimapu until the fourth and final "season" of Land Reform work in the spring of 1952 (MSG 1992: 15, 242–43).[35] Preparations in Baimapu had been complicated not only by the local topography but also by the fact that many families living along the market street owned farms as well as shops. In the months preceding the land redistribution, mass meetings were convened for town residents and family heads were asked to choose one of two principal occupation designations: engaging in commerce (*jingshang*) or laboring in agriculture (*wunong*). More than half, it was said, declared agricultural livelihoods, mainly because it meant direct access to grain, which was still valued as a foodstuff as well as a medium of exchange. Those who opted for agricultural designations were placed under the administrative jurisdiction of Qiaolou village, were given agricultural class designations, and took part in land redistribution.[36]

Land Reform gave the local poor new means of production with which they could subsist and perhaps even prosper. Property was expropriated from corporate associations such as lineages, temples, and the Qingfutang. Then, accompanied by armed militiamen of the village "peasant associations," local activists removed grain, silver, farm tools, furniture, animals, and other valuables from the homes of local "landlords," whose fields and houses were also confiscated when the former owner-occupants were forcibly evicted. Landless laborers, tenant families, and "poor peasant" small landholders received land and houses (or rooms in a house shared with others), as well as agricultural tools, draft animals, and winnowing machines.[37] "Landlords," in contrast, were assigned fields of the poorest quality, many of which were small, fragmented parcels that required extra labor to cultivate effectively. They were also moved into the more dilapidated houses or rooms of the village. The men among them judged to have been tyrannical (*eba*) were condemned to a more violent fate (see below), and their surviving family members were forcibly resettled in other townships. Fields owned (and cultivated) by "middle peasants" were left untouched, and some families of independent owner-cultivators continued to operate large productive farms of over 10 *mu* even after Land Reform.

Land redistribution in Qiaolou was enacted through administrative fiat. The Land Reform presidium met in closed session to allocate land to eligible families. Calculations were based on family size (or the number of mouths a family had to feed) and the total amount of land available for redistribution within each family's subvillage administrative group. Per capita allocations for the village as a whole averaged 1.4 *mu*, but actual allotments in different groups varied from 1.08 to 1.75 *mu* per family member.[38] Once plot allocations had been settled, a mass meeting was called for the entire village population, at which old land deeds were burned. The head of each family was then issued a new "land use certificate" (*tudi yongzheng*), stamped with the official seal of the "people's government" and stating the amount of land allotted. After the meeting, group representatives informed each family of which particular plots it had been assigned by the presidium. Many of the most desirable plots, it was alleged, went to families that enjoyed close associations with leading local activists and cadres.

Although Land Reform was dominated by the national assignment of class designations and redistribution of land, it was also part of a broader campaign to eradicate many physical vestiges of the Old Society. Indeed, the symbolic aspects of Land Reform, which reordered the cosmologies and identities within which people lived, were just as important as its material redistributions of property. Despite the fact that redistribution marked membership in the new social order for those who "received a share" (*de le fen*) in the revolution, its economic impact was tempered by the collectivization campaign a few years later. One might regard the Communist revolution as a geometry of theory and practice that had both material and symbolic dimensions. Along one axis would be plotted the attempts to denounce, expropriate, and destroy the prominent symbols of the former social and political order; along the other, the more constructive efforts to redefine the basis of identity and community, to reorganize the social polity into new collectivities, and to rebuild the economy. Connecting the two would be a hyperbola of selective terror and violence.

Deconstructing the Ancien Régime: The Erasure of Things Past

With a flurry of oratory, experienced and literate CCP political work teams urged local farmers to repudiate the symbols and power hierarchies of the Old Society and to arise and construct a New China. Youths, in particular, were urged to take a leading role in defying the social conventions and religious beliefs of the old order. The zealous youth guard deliberately intimidated elders, toward whom they had previously shown deferential respect. But the indignation suffered by some of the elderly paled beside their distress over the destruction of the earth god shrines.

Recall that earth gods had represented an important link between local residents and the cosmic power hierarchies of the Underworld. It was to these territorial deities that families reported their births, marriages, and deaths, prayed for rain and favorable harvests, and offered seasonal sacrifices. One day during the Land Reform campaign, local youths were summoned by the work teams to a meeting and given an impassioned lecture on the "feudal superstitions" (*fengjian mixin*) responsible for the "backwardness" of China. The youths were encouraged to go forth with an iconoclastic vengeance. They ran through the township, toppling the small statues and smashing their shrines. One man who participated in the rampage as a youth recalled it had left many of the elderly aghast. To them, he said, the destruction of the earth god shrines was an offense against Heaven, far more grievous than the public execution of the former landlords that followed. Yet to him and his friends it had been "great fun." With an aura of festive excitement, they had run through the countryside kicking over the earth gods. He reminisced that the little statues toppled with such a peculiar-sounding thud that the boys often stood them back up again to repeat the kicking, like a sport, until the statuettes finally broke apart.

Other physical symbols of the old order were also destroyed or converted to new uses. The memorial archway that had stood in the Baimapu market settlement was torn down. Many of the large banyan trees that lined the road to Meishan were removed, felled by axes and saws. Like the demolition of the earth god shrines, this was an assault on popular religious beliefs. Banyan trees were regarded as a symbol of community longevity and prosperity, and some believed them to embody mystical forces governing the fate and fortune of the market town and local residents. Their wood made poor building material, and most of it was simply burned.

The Dongyue temple was spared destruction, although the effigies of the God and Goddess of the Eastern Peak were removed and demolished. The CCP work teams first used the temple as temporary shelter for several homeless families, but this former monument to the god of "riches and honor" soon became the site of the new training school for the Baimapu revolutionary vanguard district.[39] The property of local lineages was also confiscated. Their lands were reallocated to the poor, and their cemeteries were opened to nonpatrilineal kin. The Wen ancestral hall became home to several poor families in need of housing. The Xi hall was converted to a granary, as was the Hao hall, which also served for a while as the village offices. The Qingfutang vegetarian hall was also disbanded and its property redistributed. Its residential compound was divided among five families (twenty-two people) in need of decent shelter.

The Guan Ye temple, which had housed the former township offices, the lockup, and the ritual theater for the Gowned Brothers, was physically dismantled. It had become a "polluted" symbol of oppression in the Old Society and was removed from the landscape. Not all traces of its presence were erased, however, for the mudbricks of its walls were reused to build a new government granary on roughly the same site. Several decoratively engraved stone bases that had once supported roof pillars of the temple were also salvaged. These were placed at the gate of the state granary, as if to "superscribe" yet again the symbolism of the powerful Guan Di with new state authority.

The township offices were moved into the tall mansion built by the retired KMT tax collector, the man who had used guns to win election to county assembly. His family, like those of other wealthy local notables, was evicted. Many of the poor families allotted rooms in the former homes of landlords eventually dismantled their share and carried away the materials to build a new home elsewhere in the village. Some did so to defuse growing personal conflicts with other families assigned to share the household, others for fear of ghosts after the mass execution of the "tyrant landlords."[40] As a result, the monumental *siheyuan* homes of the former local notables all but disappeared from the landscape.

The erasure of things past culminated in the dramatic mass execution of the "tyrant landlords" and other local "bullies" of the Old Society. Public executions have long been used by state authorities in China, under imperial as well as both the Nationalist and Communist governments, as a vivid deterrent to dissent and crime. Most residents of Baimapu township, however, had never before witnessed such acts, at least not on the scale on which they now witnessed them in southern Qiaolou.

The Ritual Spectacle of Public Execution

One day in the midst of Land Reform, the entire township population was summoned to a mandatory mass meeting atop Xi Upper Slope, where the Battle of Baimapu had been fought a few years earlier. As they arrived, they found a group of fifty to sixty bound prisoners assembled under the armed guard of the PLA. Moving closer and speaking with others who had arrived earlier, nervous murmurs grew among the crowd as people realized that the gathered prisoners were the once-powerful and most-feared township strongmen of the Old Society. Among them were not only landlords of the area but also prominent leaders of the local Gowned Brothers, many former *bao* heads, Baimapu's KMT official, several former township heads and deputies, former militia bosses, and conscription patrols leaders, including the once dreaded Hao Yuntai himself.

Three short years before, these men had been the wealthiest and most influential in the township. Since then they had been the targets of ritualistic class struggle sessions, humiliation, and/or beatings. They were accused of having lived parasitically off rents, usurious interest on loans, and exploitative mercantile business, or of having abused their power as local authorities by embezzling public funds, engaging in extortion and racketeering, and inflicting violent retribution on their opponents. Now dispossessed of their homes, property, and official positions, they were publicly condemned in one final, terrifying pageantry of revolutionary power. Then each was forced to kneel and was shot with a single bullet.

Of all the revolutionary iconoclasm of Land Reform, this mass execution had the most profound effect on popular consciousness. Although the elderly had been deeply distressed by the insolent behavior of local youths and their destruction of the earth god shrines and banyan trees, the violent elimination of these "class enemies" sent an unequivocal message to young and old alike. "'A revolution is not a dinner party,'" villagers recalled that the CCP work teams had explained to them, quoting Mao. But to many, the executions were startlingly excessive, jolting them into a realization of what "class struggle" ultimately entailed. Some, who harbored deep grievances against former local notables, supported these punitive measures, but others pitied the condemned and their families. A few were undoubtedly relieved that the power coming out of the barrel of the gun was not directed against them.[41]

One afternoon in 1991, lingering reservations about the executions nearly forty years earlier surfaced during an interview I had with an elderly farmer. Present with us at the time were two party members, one from a state (provincial) work unit, the other a retired village cadre. The old farmer had just finished his own account of the executions and the shock they had given the village. He paused for a moment and shook his head as he looked at the ground. "Things were very complicated [back] then," he murmured softly.

Immediately both party cadres, seated on each side of him, began to lecture him on the necessity of violent class struggle in the course of revolution. "It was necessary to overthrow the old political order," his fellow villager explained. "We had to clean up local society and start building anew."

But the old farmer continued to shake his head. "There were not so many bandits around here. But [the Communists] killed many people."

At this point, perhaps owing in part to my presence, the state cadre interrupted. "You had served as a head of a *jia* unit! You should be grateful they didn't struggle *you* or kill *you*!"

"*Zhei hua bu yinggai shuo le*," the old man muttered softly, almost to himself. "You should not say this sort of thing. You [sic] executed them, but they were human beings."

"That was class struggle!" the state cadre retorted. "Just be happy they did not go after you!"

"I did things openly!" the old farmer protested. "They had no reason to touch me. But still they killed many people. No matter what, those men were people. They had families. They had children. You Communists always talk about education, but you just killed them."

Establishing a New Order

When referring to the Land Reform era, Qiaolou villagers frequently used the terms *jianguo* ("to establish the state") and *jianzheng* ("to establish government"). These terms, each a verb-object construction, denoted a time of new beginnings, of new origins. They marked the repudiation of the Old Society and the establishment of a new order, a New China. Land Reform represented a major watershed on the local landscape, fundamentally altering conceptions of time and space and transforming the ways rural farmers conceived of their relationships to the land as well as to each other.

The CCP work teams introduced a new rhetoric of revolution and a new cosmology of class power. Many of the symbols and beliefs of local popular religions were attacked as "feudal superstition." Earth god shrines were demolished, and temples and ancestral halls were either torn down or converted to other uses. Patrilineal family identity was superscribed by class affiliation, and the work teams initiated new rituals of class struggle to replace the rituals of solidarity formerly practiced by popular associations, which they disbanded or suppressed. Family heads at the time of Liberation became new focal ancestors from whom descendants inherited their class identity, which took on renewed relevance during the Cultural Revolution, when notions of bloodline class purity and pollution were popularized. "By freezing life in a single frame, fate was sealed in perpetuity" (Friedman, Pickowicz, and Selden 1991). "Speak bitterness" meetings and more violent class struggle sessions offered a dramatic forum at which new forms of consciousness were shaped via collective participation in ritualized practice. Old land contracts were burned, and new documentation was issued bearing the seal of the people's government. Local notables were redefined as tyrannical landlords and publicly executed en masse, while their surviving family members were resettled in other townships and their grand homes dismantled. Land Reform removed from the local landscape the monuments and symbolic markers of the Old Society, literally clearing the ground for the construction of a new territorial community, the collective village.

During the Republican era, Second Bao had been an administrative unit of taxation and conscription that encompassed specific households dispersed in various *jia* units across the countryside. But socially, many families living to the north and south of the Meishan road had little direct interaction with each other. Some did not even know the names or surnames of those in other parts of the *bao*. Most of their social and economic interaction was structured through communities of exchange based on relations of kinship, affinity, friendship, or other idioms of voluntary association—relations that were mediated through the township's periodic market, a territorial exchange community of a higher order.

Communist organizers began their political work among rural farmers at the township level and then extended their organizational efforts from market towns out into the countryside. They established new institutions for government oversight and management, creating new administrative villages and new criteria for local leadership. The orchestrated violence of Land Reform provided a ritual showcase for the power of the new Communist authorities, and hence for the force that stood behind their newly anointed local agents.

CHAPTER 4

Getting Organized

Struggling with Collectivism

> Apart from their other characteristics, the outstanding thing about
> China's 600 million people is that they are "poor and blank." . . . On a
> clean sheet of paper free of any mark, the freshest and most beautiful
> words can be written, the newest and most beautiful pictures can be
> painted.
>
> —MAO ZEDONG, *"Introducing a Cooperative"*

> Lifting a rock only to drop it on one's own foot.
>
> —CHINESE FOLK SAYING

Pearl married into a Baimapu family in 1943, just one month shy of her fifteenth birthday. She had been born in Taihe, a busy market town on the west
bank of the Minjiang near the northern border of Meishan county, and grew
up poor. Her father, a water seller on the town streets, had a job of low status and little income. He died when Pearl was still very young, leaving his
widow to care for Pearl and two younger siblings. As an infant, Pearl recalled,
she had suckled at her mother's breast but was never allowed to drink the
milk. Instead, her mother forced her to spit it into a small bamboo container;
she would then sell the milk to a wealthy old woman in the town. To feed
Pearl, her mother would put a bit of cooked rice between her cheek and
gums, work up some saliva, and slip it into the baby's mouth. Occasionally,
she would boil some rice porridge, place it in a small cloth pouch, and offer
Pearl a corner on which to suckle.

Her mother could not afford many of the customary betrothal gifts when
Pearl married, and used the bridewealth to buy her daughter's dowry—
a bed, a reed sleeping mat, and a table. Pearl's husband was nine years her senior, and they began "conjugal relations" immediately after marriage, although she did not conceive her first child until she reached menarche four
years later. Her father-in-law was also a recent settler in Baimapu, having
bought 10 *mu* of land and gone into business as a meat seller. But he was a

notorious gambler and lost most of the land. On the very morning of Pearl's wedding, he had pawned the family house on Baimapu Street. He died not long afterward, and Pearl's widowed mother-in-law took over management of the family.

To meet their debts she tried to conserve grain, scooping out the insides of sweet potatoes and filling them with rice for their daily meals. On the little land that remained to them, they cultivated rice, beans, sweet potatoes, and cotton. Pearl's mother-in-law spun thread every evening, working well past midnight by the dim light of a small, open-flame oil lamp. Sometimes she also wove cloth to sell to merchants and tailors in their market settlement. Pearl often carted goods for Baimapu merchants to and from Meishan. On days when she could not find such work, she would walk down to the county markets with a bundle of firewood, trading it for sweets and cakes that she and her husband could resell from a small stall in front of their home on Baimapu Street.

Although Pearl had been poor, her liberation was more personal than economic. Her husband was a man of violent temper, a trait she claimed he inherited from his father. "After Liberation, he did not dare to beat me anymore," she recalled. Following one battering, she found the courage to approach party political workers. "I went and told the leaders. They had *him* beaten up. After that, he never hit me again. But still, we would speak three sentences and argue two."

At Land Reform, the family had opted for a commercial rather than an agricultural designation. Pearl's husband was not fond of field labor, and the family forfeited the few holdings that remained to them. Soon afterward, the government began a new cooperativization campaign, promoting the formation of agricultural, commercial, and credit cooperatives that would help economic recovery and development. In 1953, party-state authorities imposed a monopoly on the purchase and sale of grain. As townspeople without land, Pearl and her husband's family were designated as "urban residents" in a new, national household registration system through which grain rations were distributed. A job was arranged for her husband at a factory in Emei, a city roughly 80 kilometers south of Meishan, leaving the family household in relative domestic harmony. Yet they had been too poor to warrant inclusion in the new "Cooperative Store" being organized among Baimapu merchant families. Instead, they continued to make a living as petty peddlers, selling cigarettes from a makeshift tabletop—a plank atop two benches that they would set in front of their door.

"I had to pay 3 *yuan* just to set up that simple table," Pearl recalled. "We had no capital to do anything else. We worked on our own and did not belong to any organization. We did not have any money, so the cooperatives did not want us. People who had money hired others, like me, to cart goods for them to Meishan." Sometimes, Pearl would take bigger jobs, pulling carts loaded with agricultural goods, bamboo, or other local products on the three-day walk to Chengdu, making one trip with her infant daughter wrapped on her back in a cloth bundle. There she would use her savings and wages to purchase return cartloads of cigarettes and matches, or fancy biscuits and cakes not readily available in Meishan or Baima. "That is how I earned money to buy rice to feed my family."

With collectivization in 1958, Pearl and many of the other market town poor were reclassified as "peasants" and administratively assigned to Qiaolou, the new collective village that surrounded their half of the market town. "If you had money, you had to give it to the collective when you joined. If you did not have any money, they took things [e.g., goods, tables, stools] from your home. If you had neither, they did not want you. You had to 'go down to the countryside' and become a 'peasant.'" Yet families like Pearl's lacked the tools and experience for farming, and were generally not welcomed by other members of the collective village, seasoned farmers who looked upon the uninvited newcomers as a burden. "We had no money, no tools, and no knowledge of farming," Pearl recalled. "Some of us got permission from the [Qiaolou] leaders to go to Chengdu for a few days to earn some money. We hauled a cart loaded with several thousand catties of thick tree trunks. . . . We used the money to buy some tools."

Pearl was befriended by the elderly widow of an executed landlord, who headed another socially marginalized household in the village. The old woman taught her how to till the land better, although Pearl and other "street farmers" (*jienong*) still faced prejudice from those who saw them as a drain on collective resources. The experiences of the town poor over the next quarter of a century were emblematic of many social contradictions created by rural collectivism in China. The great mass mobilization campaigns of the Maoist era tried to harness the productive potential of the Chinese people, only to foster deepening schisms among the population and keep most rural inhabitants virtually bound in poverty. Class designations had redefined the formal status hierarchy of New China. Yet in the mid-1950s, a new administrative measure, the national "household registration" (*hukou*) system, divided the population into rural "peasants" and urban "residents," with profound ramifications for family economic security, prospects for mobility, and quality of life. Although Land Reform had cleared ground for the construction of new communities based on collective organizations, the social canvas upon which Mao painted his words and pictures of revolutionary transformation was not a tabula rasa.

The Maoist revolution attempted to undermine the autonomy of individual families and to subordinate particularistic interests to those of the collective. Even the administrative household (*hu*), "between state and family," became a technology of power, promoted and supported as a collective economic unit of consumption, production, reproduction, and resource management (Judd 1994: 164–211). Marketing exchange, popular associations, and sworn brotherhoods were disbanded or disrupted and replaced with new redistributive hierarchies. The struggle with collectivism reshaped alliances and antagonisms among local families as new exchange communities took form around administrative channels and positions of bureaucratic control. Heralded as a "Great Leap Forward," collectivization "mobilized" the labor of hundreds of millions of Chinese, but at great environmental and human costs. Its successes, as well as its failures, created the foundations for a nascent collective village identity.

Orchestrating Socialist Transformation

The years between Land Reform and collectivization were described by most Qiaolou villagers and Baimapu townspeople alike as the best in memory. Debts had been annulled, property redistributed, and prices stabilized. With the threat of conscription eliminated and restrictions on travel relaxed, rural marketing activity rose sharply. For the first time in years, the ranks of itinerant peddlers swelled with large numbers of men eager to buy, sell, or trade agricultural produce and consumer goods. There were ample money-making opportunities, and with the violence of class struggle apparently behind them, many people recalled feeling optimistic about the future.

The 1950s were a decade of new organizational initiatives. Voluntary cooperatives were set up among farmers as well as town merchants, and new sources of credit were opened. The cooperativization movement was heralded as an attempt to boost rural incomes and to enhance rural-urban exchange. What farmers were not told was that it was also intended to lay the foundations for the subsequent collectivization campaign.[1] When land was appropriated under the new people's commune system, farmers became, in effect, agricultural laborers, administratively confined to village collectives through the new household registration system that regulated the distribution of foodstuffs as well as occupational and even physical mobility. State authorities monopolized control of production and exchange between rural and urban areas, channeling resources to support an ambitious industrialization program. But collectivization created a bifurcation of town and countryside, as members of rural and urban collectivities came to live, work, marry, and reproduce in largely mutually exclusive administrative domains. Nowhere was this more apparent than in the great famine at the end of the decade, which hit farmers in collective villages much harder than the urban "residents" of Baimapu town.

The institutional foundations of growing rural-urban inequalities under collectivism lay in the national household registration system instituted in the mid-1950s (Cheng and Selden 1994).[2] This *hukou* (literally, "door-mouth") system became the basis for centralized state procurement and re-distribution of staple foodstuffs. Urban "resident households" (*jumin hu*) received state-controlled rations for key commodities as well as preferential access to education, health care, and employment in salaried or wage-labor jobs that promised retirement pensions. "Peasant households" (*nongmin hu*), in contrast, were expected to deliver government-mandated production quotas of grain and other staples to state purchasing stations, and to provide for their own subsistence with what remained of their harvests.

This new administrative institution assured that most of China's popula-tion would remain in the countryside, dependent on their agricultural liveli-hoods as hereditary "peasants." Unlike class designations, which were in-herited patrilineally and which attempted to divide descent group solidarity, household registration status was passed from mother to children. Under collectivism, physical mobility was tightly restricted and the vast majority of all residential transfers involved women changing homes at marriage. Thus in China's predominantly virilocal society, any children born to a "peas-ant" woman married to an urban "resident" were registered as members of their mother's rural collective and were ultimately obliged to return there. Yet an urban woman who married a "peasant" man was expected to live with his family in the countryside, and her household registration was thus trans-ferred to his rural collective. Even "peasant" men willing to marry uxorilo-cally into urban families had little hope of obtaining a change in registration. Urbanites could easily transfer their registration to the countryside, but it was extremely difficult for "peasants" to acquire urban registration.[3] Mar-riages between "peasants" and urban "residents" were rare throughout the collective era, reflecting the imbalance of opportunities and privileges in this new status hierarchy.

There was nothing novel in the fact that China's socialist development was predicated on the extraction of grain and other resources from the coun-tryside; such is the political economy of all state systems. Yet the mass cam-paigns to collectivize the population were conducted in a heady ideological atmosphere. Under the militant egalitarianism of the Great Leap Forward in the late 1950s, misguided production quotas, inflated output statistics, and mismanaged labor, production techniques, and transport led to one of the largest famines in history. By the early 1960s, material incentives and mar-

ket reforms had been introduced to ease the crisis. The commune system was
scaled back and reorganized, as the "battle lines" of socialism were retrenched
to encourage economic autonomy and family initiative. Although these measures had widespread popular support, some regarded them as a retreat from
communism and a step toward capitalist restoration. Debate among top party
leaders escalated into a fierce struggle for power, culminating in the return
of class violence during the Cultural Revolution (1966–76). During this period, a new group of political allies gained control of the village leadership in
Qiaolou, under the banner of militant radicalism.

Supported by allies and kin, these cadres consolidated their dominance
during the 1970s. Buoyed by the Study Dazhai campaign to strengthen the
role of "production brigades" in the management of rural life, they created
new institutions of collective village enterprise and diversified into nonagricultural activities. This gave both Qiaolou, as a collective unit, and Qiaolou
families, collectively, a source of income and revenue independent of state
administrative allocations or procurement payments. It also enabled village
cadres to enhance their own power and authority, even after the death of
Mao in 1976 and the subsequent reforms that abolished the commune system, restored a market economy, and initiated local elections (see Chapter 5).

Cooperativizing the Countryside

With great fanfare, the Three Great Cooperatives (*san da hezuo*) campaign
was launched in Baimapu in the early 1950s. Farmers and townspeople recalled that they had been promised it would bring prosperity by boosting
production, promoting wider market integration, and opening new credit
sources for entrepreneurial activities. But the cooperative organizations into
which they were organized also provided new institutions of control and influence for state officials and local cadres. A township branch of the state-run
Supply and Marketing Cooperative (SMC) was set up; its staff purchased
agricultural products from local farmers at set prices and sold them seed, fertilizer, pesticides, and other agricultural supplies. A credit cooperative was
also established through the SMC to offer low-interest loans of cash or seed
grain to farmers and small-business proprietors.[4] Agricultural cooperativization began with voluntarily recruited mutual aid teams of several families
each, which, along with those families still farming independently, were supervised through new village administrative institutions.

Recall that, in the early 1950s, Qiaolou had been divided administratively
into ten subvillage groups (*zu*), based largely on the former *baojia* organization. Shortly after Land Reform, to help coordinate production activities and

grain tax collection, these were reorganized into two new main subvillage groups, each comprised of five renamed small groups (*xiaozu*).[5] Those living north of the Meishan road were monitored by Lin Chengying, the formal "village head." Hao Yuanliang, the twenty-year-old youth leader, was placed in charge of the main group to the south. A production supervisory committee was also formed, comprising an elected representative from each of the two new main groups, plus a chairman. Two "middle peasants" were selected as subvillage administrative group representatives, both of whom had experience in large extended family economies: a Jin man from southern Qiaolou, and a Yan man from the north. The committee was chaired by Hao Yuandeng, the elder brother of Hao Yuanliang. Both these grandsons of Hao Caiqin had been prominent activists during Land Reform, and together they established Qiaolou's first multifamily cooperative labor team, or "mutual aid group."

Mutual aid groups (*huzhu zu*), or MAGs, were similar in many respects to the labor exchange (*tiaogong*) relationships practiced by many farm families. Several families, often patrilineal kin, cooperated during peak labor seasons to assist one another in plowing, seeding, irrigating, transplanting, harvesting, and processing crops. Each retained independent ownership of its land, draft animals, tools, and other means of production, but careful tallies were recorded of the balance of labor shared.[6] While many mutual aid groups in Qiaolou were, in fact, organized among families already sharing labor exchange relations, in some cases MAGs attempted to create new patterns of mutual assistance where none had existed previously.[7] Often, mutual aid groups were formed among families living or farming land in the same general vicinity, although considerations of affect, friendship, or kinship were more important than residential proximity.

The first MAG in Meishan county had been established in Baimapu's Jingju village, in late 1951; directed by an experienced state cadre, it was reported to be a great success.[8] In early 1952, the brothers Hao Yuandeng and Hao Yuanliang convinced several close patrilineal relatives to join them in Qiaolou's first, model mutual aid group. Headed by Hao Yuandeng, the elder of the two brothers, this MAG consisted of five Hao families from southern Qiaolou: three "middle peasants" (including Hao Qisan, the former Hao lineage master), one "poor peasant" family (that of Land Reform presidium member Hao Yuanan), and the family of educated "rich peasant" Hao Yunpo, for a total of more than twenty able-bodied adult laborers. Demonstrating that small-scale cooperation could lower production and labor costs while boosting output, the Hao brothers actively promoted mutual aid groups as a solution for labor-deficient households. Few villagers were impressed, however, noting that the Haos had carefully selected families of kin who not only shared amicable relations but also enjoyed ample cash reserves, sizable amounts of land and numbers of draft animals, and a plentiful supply of labor.

A few months later, a second mutual aid group was established in Qiaolou. It, too, was organized in the south by a "middle peasant," Jin Yuting, a relatively prosperous farmer and one of the two village production supervisors. Unlike the Haos in their "model" MAG, Jin organized families that were dispersed residentially over a wider area and that faced frequent shortfalls in cash, grain, and labor. Participating families in his mutual aid group averaged only two able-bodied adult laborers each. Jin's effort was watched more closely by local farmers and became the subject of much discussion at harvest time, when his group produced over a ton of rice more than did the model run by Hao Yuandeng.[9] The following season, more families began to organize themselves in mutual aid groups, and over the next few years they experimented with different configurations of membership.

At first, these cooperative groupings were small and seasonal. Some broke up in failure, but families were encouraged to try again, often by teaming up with successful organizers who moved from group to group. Gradually, however, mutual aid groups were expanded into progressively larger communities of cooperative exchange.[10] Larger numbers of families were organized into single groups, which began to engage in more permanent, year-round (*changnian*) activities. Some also began to experiment with workpoints (*gongfen*), a system of labor accounting and remuneration that became a hallmark of the collective era.[11] By 1954, roughly 80 percent of Meishan farmers had been organized into mutual aid groups; some villages were already experimenting with larger cooperative institutions with more centralized management (MSG 1992: 247, 441–42).

Cooperativization in northern Qiaolou, however, had not gone smoothly. Lin Chengying had encountered many "management difficulties" (*guanli wenti*), often a euphemism for interfamily conflicts. In an attempt to reduce tensions, the northern subvillage administrative group was partitioned in 1955 into eastern and western sections, each with a separate production supervisor (both Yan men). This proved effective, and southern Qiaolou was similarly partitioned, with Jin Yuting and Hao Yunpo, the "rich peasant" veteran of the "model" Hao mutual aid group, as the two production supervisors (see Figure 5).

In the second half of 1955, however, village cadres received instructions from government superiors to "join the groups" (*lianzu*).[12] Various MAGs in northern and southern Qiaolou were amalgamated to form two separate but parallel subvillage production groups whose activities would be coordinated jointly by a single village administration.[13] While harvests had improved

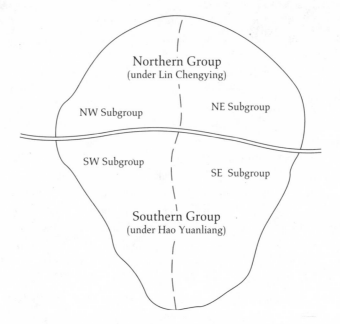

FIGURE 5.　Administrative divisions in Qiaolou during cooperativization, ca. 1955.

over the years following Liberation, rates of growth had slowed as agricultural production came under centralized management (MSG 1992: 247). CCP leaders grew increasingly concerned that agricultural procurements would not keep pace with the needs of the Soviet-style, heavy-industry-oriented first Five Year Plan. In midsummer of 1955, Mao called for a "high tide" of socialist transformation, leading to a surge in the establishment of rural collectives designed to increase agricultural production to meet state procurement needs.[14]

Leaders such as Mao were also concerned about reports of growing polarizations of wealth in the countryside. Some families had prospered—particularly "middle peasants" with 10 *mu* or more as well as their own water buffalo, hogs, winnowing machines, and other key production assets. A few smallholders, however, had declined economically. Selden (1993: 87) has argued that a nationwide survey of sixteen thousand households in 1954 suggested that while "rich peasants" had gained a nearly two to one advantage over "poor peasants" in terms of farm size and family income, polarizations were not as acute as Mao contended. In Baimapu, people recalled instances of "poor peasant" families that had been obliged to borrow grain, mortgage property, or even sell land they had acquired at Land Reform just a few years earlier.

Nevertheless, party-state authorities ordered a reassessment of rural class status. Except for "landlords" and "rich peasants," whose classifications remained unaffected, all farm families were divided into wealthy (*fuyu*) and nonwealthy (*fei fuyu*) households. The former were reclassified as either new or old "upper-middle peasants," while the latter, who had not prospered as much as their neighbors since Land Reform, were classified as either "poor peasants," "new lower-middle peasants," or "old lower-middle peasants" (MSG 1992: 17, 247).[15] These newly defined "poor and lower-middle peasants" (*pin xiazhong nong*) were officially considered the "red classes" (Chan, Madsen, and Unger 1992: 22). By redefining rural class status in this way, it was hoped that those with more experience and skill in managing larger family economies could be recruited and promoted as politically trustworthy local cadres for the impending "socialist transformation" of agriculture. That effort gained ground in Qiaolou in 1956, when two agricultural cooperatives were formally inaugurated in the village, one to the north of the Meishan road and one to the south.

Collectivizing the Administrative Village

The first agricultural cooperatives in Meishan, like the first mutual aid groups a few years earlier, were established in Baimapu township in January 1954, but it was another two years before Qiaolou farmers, and almost all other rural cultivators in the county, were brought into such organizations (MSG 1992: 247, 442).[16] Formally referred to as "semisocialist elementary-stage agricultural producers' cooperatives," these new co-ops were nominally voluntary. But cadres began to pressure families that resisted incorporation, conducting long "educational" sessions with them and even resorting to fines.[17] Farmers were assigned shares based on the productive assets (land, animals, tools) they had contributed to their cooperative. They labored collectively with other cooperative members and were assigned to various tasks by co-op managers. Remuneration was based partly on shares of assets contributed and partly on contributions of labor, as measured in workpoints. Families continued to hold formal ownership rights to the land, draft animals, and large tools (Riskin 1987: 68; Selden 1993: 93–95), but they no longer controlled how such productive assets or their hours of labor were deployed.[18] Village cadres coordinated planting, irrigation, and harvest, assigned tasks, and managed revenues in an unprecedentedly centralized manner.

With the establishment of the cooperatives in 1956, village cadres began to receive pay for their administrative duties. Cooperativization meant bureaucratization, and hence new requirements for accounting, meetings, planning, and recordkeeping. "Poor peasant" Lin Chengying was appointed by county authorities as the inaugural secretary of the Qiaolou Communist Party branch. He served concurrently as head of the northern cooperative and was referred to as "chief cooperative head" (*zheng shezhang*). Hao Yuanliang, the newly reclassified "lower-middle peasant" youth activist who had led southern Qiaolou during the years of the mutual aid groups, was also admitted to the Communist Party and appointed village director (*cun zhuren*). Two years later he was named deputy party branch secretary of Qiaolou and placed in charge of the village Communist Youth League, to recruit and train future cadres. His elder brother, Hao Yuandeng, who since Land Reform had chaired the production supervisory committee, was promoted to head of the southern cooperative. He, too, acquired party membership and was given the title of "deputy cooperative head" (*fu shezhang*). A "poor peasant" from the northern cooperative was appointed head of the Qiaolou militia, but after his death a few years later, "lower-middle peasant" Hao Yuandeng took over control of village riflemen. Other positions in the expanded village administration included a "poor peasant" as treasurer (*caijin*) and a "rich peasant" as accountant (*kuaiji*). A "lower-middle peasant" from northern Qiaolou was appointed grain storage supervisor (*baoguan*), assisted by two "poor peasant" deputies (one for each cooperative). Yan Guifang retained her post as director of women's affairs (*funu zhuren*), the only village administrative office ever to be held by a woman.

The autumn rice harvest of 1957 was disappointing, dropping 3 percent countywide over that of the previous year (MSG 1992: 442). Qiaolou cadres were directed by authorities to press ahead and merge the two cooperatives into a single unit of production management. This campaign to "join the cooperatives" (*lianshe*) established a new "socialist advanced-stage agricultural producers' cooperative."[19] In such "collective villages" (*jiti cun* or *jiti nongzhuang*), as they were also called, productive assets that had been invested by families were expropriated as collective property; no compensation was given for them. Families were, however, issued a small amount (0.1 *mu*) of dry land as so-called private plots (*ziliudi*), on which they were permitted to grow vegetables and animal fodder for their own use (MSG 1992: 442).[20] Until this point, "socialist transformation" had attempted to harness rather than to undermine more productive and prosperous families. Collectivization, however, sharpened the contradictions between the interests of "poor and lower-middle peasants" and those of their wealthier neighbors. Remuneration based on shares of assets contributed was abolished, replaced by remuneration based on workpoints alone. But the exchange value of a single workpoint was not determined until a comprehensive accounting was made of collective village income at year's end, when net revenues were divided by the total number of workpoints accumulated by all members of the collective. Only then were farmers paid.

Combined with the new, national household registration system that effectively confined agriculturalists to the countryside, this new production regime imposed collective responsibility for state procurement levies on Qiaolou farmers, linking the economic security of every family to the collective village. Popular response was less enthusiastic than it had been for the mutual aid groups. Many resented the loss of family autonomy. The expropriation of property was met with confusion and disbelief. Most "poor peasant" smallholders who had first received farms at Land Reform felt they had lost what they had been given just a few years earlier. The collectives were administrative units intended to boost productivity, output, and procurement for state needs. But as village cadres assumed more exclusively administrative duties and labored less alongside their kin and neighbors, cynicism grew. Farmers in Meishan began to tell each other, "Now that land has been returned to the public (*gong*), the collective puts out the labor. Let's relax and be free" (MSG 1992: 248).

Resistance to the "socialist transformation of agriculture," initiated a few years earlier in other parts of China, had led to declining grain output. State development plans called for heavy extraction of agricultural surplus through rural collectives, but party leaders had been anxious to avoid the disastrous consequences of collectivization in the Soviet Union. Moreover, the changing tenor of relations between the PRC and the USSR, following Khrushchev's 1956 denunciation of Stalin's autocratic leadership style and personality cult, put the future of Soviet aid in question. Popular uprisings in Poland and Hungary had made CCP leaders increasingly uncomfortable with the blooming "Hundred Flowers" of criticism Mao had solicited in 1957, and they launched a repressive "Anti-Rightist" campaign that had profound consequences well beyond its original intent. At the same time, party leaders debated the pace at which they should proceed.[21] Mao and other proponents of accelerating the collectivization drive prevailed.

In December 1957, about the time when Qiaolou's twin cooperatives were being united in a single collective village, the government announced a new mass mobilization campaign. This visionary "Great Leap Forward," championed by Mao, called for the Chinese people to overtake England's level of industrialization within fifteen years. To attain such fantastic results would require a revolutionary transformation in economic organization and public consciousness. It came in the form of a fanatic idealism that put "politics in command" (*zhengzhi guashua*) and promoted militant egalitarianism, experimentation, determined struggle, and selfless commitment to the collective cause.

Communalizing Rural Life

In the early summer of 1958, the Great Leap Forward was propagandized throughout the Meishan countryside by traveling song and dance troupes. Farmers enjoyed the excitement such performances brought during the lull between transplanting and harvesting. After several critical weeks of exhausting labor, rice saplings had been safely replanted in flooded paddies. "*Guan yangmer!*" farmers called to each other in greeting, indicating they had finished transplanting and were looking forward to some rest and relaxation. Normally, this was a time when friends called each other to teashops for drink, conversation, or card games. But the color and noise of the propaganda teams were soon followed by a barrage of mass meetings and organizational sessions. Laborers were mobilized for large-scale public works projects, or to work at the hundreds of small furnaces constructed in the countryside to melt down "iron and steel" (*gangtie*) objects for the new national industrialization effort. "Hao Yuanliang was calling meetings all the time!" one man exclaimed. "A year has 365 days and we must have had 200 days of meetings. Everything was a blur. I could not keep it all clear back then, much less recall now what they said."

That autumn, county authorities announced that Chairman Mao had endorsed a new "people's commune" system that would unite industry, agriculture, commerce, education, and the military to mobilize the productive potential of the countryside. In early September 1958, Meishan's first commune was set up, a massive unit of centrally organized production, distribution, and consumption that encompassed five rural townships, including Xianger, which bordered Baimapu to the east. By the end of the month, the entire rural population of the county—more than 440,000 people in forty rural towns and townships—had been communalized in eleven such units (MSG 1992: 253).[22] Qiaolou was amalgamated with more than forty other collective villages in west-central Meishan to form the Shangyi Greater Commune (Shangyi Dagongshe). Headquartered in a rural town roughly 7 kilometers north of Baimapu, this commune encompassed three former market townships: Shangyi, Baimapu, and Zhongdian (see Map 2).

Communalization promoted militant egalitarianism and a work ethic of "battle" (*zhandou*) against the material constraints of nature and the ideological fetters of old beliefs (MSG 1992: 252). "Fight bitterly for one winter" (*kuzhan yidong*), people were told; "Climb to Heaven in a single step" (*yibu dengtian*). The people's commune system also imposed a regimented milita-ristic organization on production, exchange, and consumption activities. At first, communes were divided administratively into "managerial districts" and "production teams."[23] Public canteens were set up to foster a commen-sality of collective identity, and organized into dining "regiments," "bat-talions," and "companies." Markets were abolished, as were townspeople's wages and farmers' private plots.[24]

During the Great Leap, Baimapu was a managerial district (*guanli qu*), or what local residents called a "fulcrum" (*zhidian*), within the Shangyi Greater Commune. Designated as the "basic accounting unit" of communal life, the former township became the basis of local collective economy (MSG 1992: 253). Under the direction of commune leaders in Shangyi, cadre managers in Baimapu assigned production quotas and allocated food rations among roughly fifteen hundred families in sixteen production teams, which orga-nized labor assignments. In the Qiaolou team, families were organized into two dining battalions (*ying*), each of which consisted of a couple of mess companies (*lian*).[25] Party Secretary Lin was "battalion commander" in the north, where people stored food, cooked, and ate at the former Xi ancestral hall. Deputy secretary Hao Yunaliang served as commander of the southern Qiaolou dining battalion, which was set up in the former Hao lineage hall.[26] Hao Yuandeng became grain storage supervisor for the Qiaolou team.

Even by late 1958, it had become clear to some that serious problems were developing under the Great Leap. Teams had turned over all their grain to managers of subcommune districts, who reallocated it to dining battalions. But at some collective canteens, stocked with grain from the recent harvest, people had been encouraged to eat their fill, and supplies dwindled.[27] More-over, much of the forest cover of the county had been cleared for fuel to use in the "iron and steel" furnaces and for the canteens. Undeterred, Mao and his associates pushed for renewed efforts, introduced new cropping tech-niques intended to boost production, and continued to mobilize mass-labor crews for public works projects.

Contributing to the Leap

During the Great Leap Forward, Qiaolou farmers were organized into work crews and dispatched to construction sites near and far. A new irrigation ca-nal over 30 meters deep was dug through the western Baimapu countryside, bringing water from the Minjiang through the hills southwest of Chengdu. It also gave local farmers a sense of connection to one of the most celebrated technological achievements of Chinese history, the ancient water control station at Dujiangyan.[28] Many Qiaolou men were also sent to work building the Chengdu-Kunming railway, another feat of engineering through some of China's most difficult terrain, between Sichuan and Yunnan provinces. Although most worked only on sections of the railroad within the county, they identified with the overall project, which strengthened the integration of the Southwest within the national economy. During 1958 and 1959, many village men were assigned to a series of such construction projects, building reservoirs, flood levies, or bridges, or working in the coal mines of Emei, in the steel mills of Hongya, or with road crews on the Sichuan-Tibetan frontier.

Men recalled with patriotic pride their participation in the construction of railways and water control systems, monuments to "New China" that transformed the landscape and fostered a stronger sense of membership in a national collectivity. Despite the heavy labor, most had been pleased for an opportunity to travel and to escape the tedium of "digging mud" (*wa niba*), as farmers described their livelihood. On some projects, they were housed in tent camps for weeks or months and fed generous meals at state-run canteens. In other cases, they lived among local families, paying for their meals with cash and ration coupons provided by state cadre supervisors. Many were nostalgic about the friendships they had formed on such crews and the hours spent exchanging accounts of their experiences.

Women, however, looked back at those years quite differently. Most had remained in Qiaolou, caring for the elderly and the very young—and "digging mud." More and more men were called away on work crews, until at one point only three able-bodied males remained, all supervisors of agricultural work.[29] As one woman recalled:

> I was working very hard during those years as a farmer, a household head, and a mother. My husband had been sent [elsewhere] as a worker, so I was required to perform double duties as a commune member (*sheyuan*) and a household head (*huzhu*). I had to attend many meetings, and then make up for the lost work by doing household chores in the evenings or late at night. In agriculture, each team member had to dig 4 *fen* [0.4 *mu*] each day. I would get up before dawn to dig 2 *fen* and to thresh some soya before the heat of the day set in. After sunrise, I would return home and have breakfast, do some chores, and begin attending meetings. I would finish the remaining 2 *fen* of my work assignment later. . . . I had lots of trouble with [the team treasurer]. He was suspicious of me and accused me of lying about my work. He said that a woman could not do so much work. He said I was using the cover

of darkness to steal workpoints (*tou gongfen*). The team had to assign someone to watch me work.

Throughout the collective era, the workpoint system undervalued the labor of women by at least 20 to 30 percent, and arguably much more. An able-bodied male laborer could generally earn up to ten workpoints a day, whereas his female counterpart could earn only seven or eight at most. Moreover, as suggested in the account above, women received no labor credit for the time-consuming tasks of cooking, cleaning, laundry, and childrearing (see Andors 1975; M. Wolf 1985).[30]

State authorities attempted to provide replacement laborers by reassigning some urban "residents" to rural production teams as "peasants."[31] In 1958, the first group of Baimapu townspeople were "sent down" to Qiaolou. Most, like Pearl, were reluctant converts to agriculture and resented their loss of urban household status and its benefits. Others, however, answered Chairman Mao's call for "volunteer farmers" (*zhiyuan nong*) with a revolutionary zeal, likening themselves to those who had volunteered to fight in the Korean War a few years earlier. Shopkeeping families that voluntarily left the commercial collective to make a contribution for New China were awarded small metal busts of Chairman Mao. But then many of them, too, were called away:

> In 1958, I gave up my *jumin* [urban resident] registration and volunteered to become a peasant in Qiaolou. . . . I still resided with my natal family in our house on Baimapu Street, but I worked in the fields. Then the leaders called on me to work on [a] section of the Cheng-Kun railway. A large group of us volunteer farmers left [Qiaolou] right in the middle of the fall rice harvest, even before we had finished bringing in the crop.

With many recent transfers similarly reassigned to outside work projects almost as soon as they arrived, those who remained in Qiaolou found themselves in a critical labor season with roughly half the work force absent.

Leaping into Famine

Harvests in the county that year barely reached half their intended targets, and output still hovered at levels attained under the cooperatives in 1956. In 1959, county officials set new grain production targets of 5,000 million *jin* (2.5 million metric tons), a fabulously extravagant number considering that the best harvest in county history (in 1983) had totaled less than 400,000

metric tons (7.9 million *jin*).[32] But "greater, faster, better" was the call put out
to the country. Although that year's harvest was in fact very poor, procurement targets for 1960 were raised another 34 percent (MSG 1992: 251–54,
505).[33] By January 1960, problems had become too serious to deny or to hide.
Grain supplies in the countryside were virtually exhausted, and many communal dining halls were closed. There was widespread hunger and edema,
and many women suffered prolapse of the uterus. By March it was apparent
that people were dying. The provincial first party secretary of Sichuan made
repeated visits to solve the "Meishan problem." The 1960 rice harvest was
roughly half the poor harvest of 1957; a single *mu* of paddy in the county
yielded only 105 to 132 kilograms of rice, down even from the 156 kilograms
on the eve of Liberation (ibid., pp. 255, 443, 505).

Mismanagement during the Great Leap Forward had been encouraged by
an atmosphere of fanatic idealism. The repressive Anti-Rightist campaign
had coerced most critics into silence. Because cadres and kin were told that
"high yields in fields depend on great boldness in people" (MSG 1992: 252)
and that true revolutionary spirit could overcome all obstacles, any lack of
enthusiasm or admission of failure was politically dangerous. Production difficulties were sometimes not reported or were actively covered up, and output figures were deliberately falsified to exaggerate harvests.[34] Misled by in-
accurate statistics, state authorities increased grain procurement quotas, further exacerbating conditions in areas already beset by shortages.

Bernstein (1984) has argued that excessive state procurement of grain was
a leading cause of the Great Leap famine, an assessment also shared by local
residents in Baimapu:

> [The authorities] will tell you that there was no grain shortage here. In
> a way, they are correct. The famine was human-made (*renzaode*). We
> had grain, but the state took it away. They redistributed only a little of
> it back to [local *jumin*]. Most of it went to feed the cities. [In 1959, *ju-
> min* in Baimapu] had monthly grain rations of only 18 *jin* [9 kg].

By 1961, monthly rations for Baimapu *jumin* were cut even further, to only
9 *jin* (4.5 kg) per person, well below the 27 *jin* officially considered "grain
deficient" (Oi 1989: 47). If such assertions by local residents were accurate,
annual per capita grain rations for Baimapu *jumin* at the height of the famine were roughly 108 *jin* a year, a dramatic drop from the national average
of 614 *jin* in 1957 (ibid., p. 33).

The plight of farmers, who produced rather than received government-
allocated grain rations, was much worse than that of townspeople. State demands took precedence over "peasant" subsistence needs:

At first, we began eating rice porridge all the time to stretch our grain supply. But still there was not enough grain. Later, sweet potatoes, the old staple food of the poor, became common fare. But then there was not even enough labor to dig up all the sweet potatoes, because everyone had been sent outside to work. Some families had only 80 *jin* of grain to last the whole year [i.e., about 3 kg a month]. People began eating tree bark, grass, and whatever else they could find. . . . In some cities, urban residents received subsidies and the situation was tolerable. But in rural areas, things were difficult.

Farmers who had "spoken bitterness" against their former landlords less than a decade before now had to "eat bitterness" under the new Communist regime.

In 1960, men began to return to Qiaolou as construction projects were suspended. That year, a new group of Baimapu *jumin* was involuntarily "sent down" to Qiaolou, stretching collective resources even further. What little grain had not been procured to alleviate problems in urban areas was kept under close guard and carefully rationed out in team canteens. Families were prohibited from cooking in their homes. If smoke were seen coming from a chimney, the team militia would come to smash the family's stove.

The Ebb Tide of Collectivism

The crisis precipitated by the Great Leap did not ease until the early 1960s. In 1961, the state government announced a series of reforms to revitalize the economy.[35] The country's large and unwieldy communes were broken up into smaller units. China had twenty-six thousand communes at the start of the Leap in 1958; by 1963 the number had nearly tripled as the original units were partitioned into smaller communes (Riskin 1987: 170). In Meishan, small communes (*xiao gongshe*) were reorganized around former rural townships.[36] The Shangyi Greater Commune was broken up, and Baimapu became a separate commune. Its periodic market was also restored on a limited scale, convening once a week. Later, a second day was added. Grain procurement quotas were cut back significantly and fixed for three years. Workpoint assessments were modified to recognize different abilities. Those who surpassed their production quotas received bonuses. Private plots were restored.

Production teams were also reduced in size, and thus increased in number. Qiaolou was redesignated a production brigade (*shengchan dadui*), and new production teams were established at the subvillage level. Qiaolou bri-

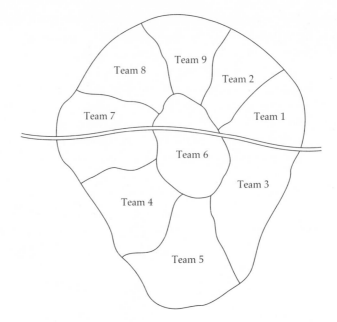

FIGURE 6.   Qiaolou brigade and its production teams after the
Great Leap Forward, ca. 1963.

gade was originally comprised of four production teams, based on the east-
west administrative subdivisions of the earlier northern and southern cooperatives.[37] For a short time, each new subvillage team maintained separate
mess regiments. Soon, however, Qiaolou brigade was reorganized into a total of nine production teams, and the canteens were closed. The boundaries
of these teams approximated those of the former *baojia* units of the Old Society and of the early administrative groups of the 1950s (see Figure 6).

Although collective management continued, redistributive accounting
was turned over to the new subvillage production teams, whose cadres also
assumed control over labor assignments, workpoints, grain allocations, and
cash remunerations. Teams also acquired formal collective ownership rights
to productive property, including land and tools.[38] New cadre posts were also
set up within each production team, including a team leader, deputy team
leader, accountant, storage supervisor, and workpoint recorder (*jifenyuan*).
All "surplus" (i.e., above-quota) grain was to remain within teams, rather
than be distributed throughout the brigade or commune. "Differences" between teams, and even between households, were to be permitted in order to
encourage flexible entrepreneurial initiative. Between 1962 and 1965, average per capita subsistence grain allocations for "peasants" in Meishan rose
from 112 kg to almost 240 kg (MSG 1992: 447).

Farmers were assured that these reforms were guaranteed for thirty years. But this retrenchment from radical collectivism was opposed by other party members, both top leaders such as Mao and local cadres in some areas, who argued that it would encourage petty capitalism. Within a few years, many of these directives were reversed. Debate ensued between advocates of mobilizational collectivism and those who espoused market entrepreneurialism, with contending party-leadership factions struggling to affix responsibility for the failure of the Leap. Attention focused on local rural cadres who had managed basic-level production and distribution. Some were alleged to have used their positions for personal profit, or even to have embezzled collective funds. The divergent interests of different party-leadership factions converged in agreement that the situation required rectification.

In 1964, posters were pasted up along Baimapu Street summoning all brigade cadres to a mandatory meeting at the commune. They were instructed to bring along a bedroll, which suggested to many that new turmoil was coming. The meeting was conducted behind closed doors and lasted several days. In the stores and teahouses of the market town, anxious shopkeepers and farmers exchanged rumors. Having enjoyed several years of strong economic recovery, they reassured one another that at least this new campaign would be different from the Leap, in which the public had been involved from the outset.

Cleaning Up Cadres

When the meeting finally adjourned, news spread quickly that a fifteen-member work team of state cadres had arrived from Meishan to investigate local conditions. They would be auditing the books of the commune, brigades, and production teams in search of irregularities. This new "Four Cleanups" campaign aimed at rooting out corruption and bureaucratism among rural cadres was part of a broader "Socialist Education Movement" (Baum and Teiwes 1968).[39] In Qiaolou, it led to a dramatic turnover in brigade administration and to the public humiliation of several brigade cadres, although both the brigade party secretary and his deputy retained their posts.

During the mass meetings that followed, the revolutionary rhetoric of class struggle was revived. New "poor and lower-middle peasant associations" were set up as a forum for the campaign (MSG 1992: 259). At their meetings, CCP work teams alleged that "hidden capitalist roaders" and "revisionists" had sabotaged collectivist efforts.[40] In Qiaolou, investigators soon focused on the brigade accountant. Hao Yunpo's "rich peasant" classification had been outweighed by the importance of his schooling and his close ties to the Hao brothers. Now, however, auditors discovered inconsistencies in brigade accounts. Recalling the incident nearly thirty years later, Hao Yunpo insisted that the discrepancy amount only to "several tens of *yuan*." But it was sufficient evidence for the agenda of political workers:

> I had only a few years of education. I am not a high school graduate. Those were big numbers I had to deal with back then, and I made a few errors in my arithmetic. I cannot deny that. It is the truth. But they made me step down as accountant. They said I had embezzled the money. They put a dunce cap on my head and paraded me along Baimapu Street like a criminal.

Many others in Qiaolou expressed their belief that Hao Yunpo had indeed been guilty of nothing more than muddled math. But at the time, the stigma of his class label made him a prominent and vulnerable target. "A rich peasant handling the brigade's accounts!" people were told. "No wonder catastrophe occurred!" As replacement accountant, the work teams selected a young man named Jun Yueqing, a "poor peasant" who had shown promise as a Youth League member under Deputy Secretary Hao Yuanliang.[41]

Yet there was still the matter of brigade finances. The tallies on the books were not only incorrect; they totaled far more than the cash investigators counted in the till. Several thousand *yuan* were reportedly missing from the brigade cash holdings.[42] Further inquiries revealed that the brigade treasurer, a "poor peasant" from northern Qiaolou, was an avid gambler rumored to have lost a large sum of money over the past few years. The work teams summarily dismissed him from his post and fined him to recover the money.[43] Thereafter, the new brigade accountant also kept the treasury. A new women's cadre was appointed as well. The discontent caused by the Leap had led to deteriorating relations between families, and some held Yan Guifang responsible, suggesting that tensions among women, the principal agricultural workers, had impeded production. The purge of brigade cadres included even Hao Yuandeng, the powerful "lower-middle peasant" who since collectivization had held the posts of brigade head, security chief, and storage supervisor. The work teams held him accountable for failing to supervise properly the cadres under him. He was removed as brigade head and replaced by his younger brother, Deputy Party Secretary Hao Yuanliang. The work teams entrusted control of brigade guns to "poor peasant" Liang Jinyuan, the Korea veteran recent demobilized from the PLA and returned to Qiaolou. The post of brigade storage supervisor was abolished, and communes and brigades were stopped from appropriating production team grain for their own needs (MSG 1992: 257).[44]

Opposing the Capitalist Road

During the mid-1960s, the power struggle within the CCP leadership in-
tensified, culminating with the Cultural Revolution in 1966. In the years
that followed, supporters of mobilizational collectivism violently purged
"revisionist" cadres who advocated market reforms and material incentives.
Chairman Mao called on a new generation of youths to rebel against what he
portrayed as an entrenched bureaucracy of "hidden capitalist roaders" and
to attack the symbols of their authority. Encouraged to "Destroy the Four
Olds," young Red Guards unleashed a new wave of violent iconoclasm
against thought, culture, customs, and practices of the "feudal" past—and
against anyone who opposed Mao.[45] In Qiaolou, militant collectivists reas-
serted their influence over affairs in the brigade, once again employing a rhetoric of class struggle and loyalty to Chairman Mao.

To foster cultural revolutionary consciousness, place names were changed
to promote new identities. The streets of Meishan, for example, were given
names such as Revolution Street, Resist Imperialism Street, Fanshen Street,
and the like (MSG 1992: 790). Most production brigades in the county were
also renamed, many as Red Star, East Wind, or Vanguard (ibid., pp. 294–99).
Qiaolou became known as "Wenwu," a term that denoted qualities of literary (*wen*) and martial (*wu*) statecraft.[46] In the context of the Cultural Revolution, *wen* referred to being well-versed in "Mao Zedong Thought," while
wu implied a militant, radical posturing. In fact, it was during those years
that Wenwu acquired a reputation well beyond the confines of Baimapu
commune as a center of militant radicalism. Its leadership was associated
with the extremist faction (*jipai*) of the commune. As one man from a politically marginalized "poor peasant" family in Wenwu put it, "Even breaking wind was not permitted!"

Some of the early targets of local Red Guard "struggle sessions" were
those nonmembers of the "red classes" who had been criticized during the
recent Four Cleanups campaign. As the former brigade accountant, "rich
peasant" Hao Yunpo, put it, "It was enough that [during the Four Cleanups]
they 'struggled' you. Then in the Cultural Revolution they wanted to rough
you up a bit!" The "middle peasant" who had served briefly as co-op storage
supervisor before the Leap and, since the early 1960s, as a team accountant,
recalled how an angry crowd of Red Guards interrogated him about money
that was alleged to have disappeared from the team's cash box:

> I came home one night and they were waiting for me, inside our [*sihe-
> yuan*] courtyard, just in front of the main hall. There must have been
> several tens of people. They wanted to "struggle" me. They forced me

to my knees and bent me forward, putting a "stone pillow" [a large flat
rock] atop my head. "Where is the missing money?" they demanded.
I did not know anything about it. But people gossip. They repeat things
they hear, even if they do not know whether they are true or false.
Team members had told [the Red Guards] different things. But they
had appointed themselves to this "duty" (*renwu*), this investigation.
They were determined to find a hidden culprit. First they "struggled"
me, then [years] later they still had to call on me to serve as team leader.
It really infuriates you! They told me, "Chairman Mao says you have
a duty to the country!" "Serve the People!" *Aiya! Wo de ma!*

Teenagers and young adults once again emerged as a potent militant force
in local politics. The Cultural Revolution gave a new generation of youths,
the heirs of Liberation, an opportunity to demonstrate their own loyalty to
Chairman Mao. Deputy Party Secretary Hao Yuanliang, who had been a
militant youth himself, had cultivated such sentiments as head of the brigade
Youth League. Many of those forced to endure criticism or abuse at the hands
of local Red Guards, however, saw their persecutors as the unwitting agents
of adult machinations. "You cannot blame them," reflected one victim of their
abuse. "Children don't understand things."

The tense political atmosphere of the Cultural Revolution heightened
other contradictions among families, and conflicts erupted even without in-
citement by Red Guards. With the renewed emphasis on class struggle, independent entrepreneurial activities were denounced by government authorities as "capitalist," and the size of private plots was reduced by half to "cut
the tail of capitalism." New policing measures were imposed to suppress the
communities of exchange that had once again formed around the local market. Farmers were required to obtain permission from brigade cadres before
venturing up to the Baimapu commune settlement. Even "street farmers"
such as Pearl, who lived along Baimapu Street but were registered as "peasants" in Wenwu, were prohibited from visiting neighbors in the town. Violators faced punitive deductions of workpoints or even fines, which were difficult for cash-poor farmers to pay.[47]

Reluctant "Peasants" Rebel

Among those most dissatisfied with collectivism were the street farmers
(*jienong*) of Baimapu. These families occupied a rather anomalous position
in the rural people's commune system. They lived in homes along Baimapu
Street but were administratively registered as "peasant households" in ad-

jacent production brigades. Their neighbors with urban "resident" registrations worked at wage-paying jobs in the commune's Cooperative Store, Credit Cooperative, or Supply and Marketing Cooperative, and were issued food rations by the commercial collective. But street farmers labored largely for subsistence grain in their agricultural collectives.

When Qiaolou's nine production teams were established under the post-Leap reforms, the brigade's street farmers were all assigned to Team 7, where they comprised at least half of its households. Recall that many of these reluctant "peasants" had little experience with agriculture. Many of their teammates looked upon them with disdain, and some refused to help them learn skills or even criticized them as a burden. Divisiveness hampered production activities, particularly after Cultural Revolution radicalism rescinded much of the economic autonomy families had enjoyed under the reforms. Output began to fall, and with it team revenues, family incomes, and subsistence supplies. By the late 1960s, year-end redistributions gave team members only about Y0.20 for each full day's labor (or Y0.02 per workpoint). Even for a farmer with (an unlikely) 365 days' worth of full-credit labor, this amounted to an annual income of only about Y73, roughly one-third the average of other production teams in the brigade.[48] Moreover, grain shortages obliged many team families to eat more sweet potatoes, which they called "pig feed" (*zhushi*). Anxiously, some began to compare the situation to the hunger of the Great Leap.

As grain production continued to stagnate, many of the team's families were obliged to borrow grain privately from members of other teams and brigades.[49] The grain crisis of Team 7 was disproportionately hard on farm families residing in the countryside. The street farmers living along Baimapu Street had more ready access to the local cash nexus and were able to arrange grain loans more easily. A few reportedly even acted as unofficial grain brokers, buying extra rice which they then loaned out (with interest) to less fortunate team families. This led to further acrimony against street farmers and more arguments between team families.

The street farmers of Team 7 had found that on market days, twice a week, they could earn as much as several *yuan* of cash. They set up makeshift tables or stalls and peddled merchandise from their homes along Baimapu Street. This was a violation of commune rules, which strictly separated agricultural and commercial activities. There were altercations and shouting matches as cadres attempted to enforce greater discipline among the street farmers. The latter apparently began what amounted to a work slowdown that was just shy of open defiance. At times, the brigade militia had to be deployed to compel them to go out to the fields.

Then rumors began to circulate that grain was missing from the team's storeroom. Street farmers alleged that team cadres embezzled cash and grain. Speculation was fueled by the sudden flight of the production team leader to Xinjiang, in China's far northwest.[50] Commune authorities took the unusual step of appointing Zhen Jiming, a Baimapu *jumin* who was also a demobilized Korea veteran, as the new leader of Team 7. They assumed that the new leader's organizational experience in the army would help improve conditions in the ailing team and enforce labor discipline. He had served in Korea alongside Liang Jinyuan, who now commanded the Wenwu militia. For their part, brigade leaders hoped that Zhen Jiming's residence in the commune town would better enable him to police the activities of the team's street farmers, ensuring that they went to work in the fields and were not distracted by the temptations of "capitalist roading" along Baimapu Street.

Team members, however, claimed that their new leader's lack of experience in agriculture and weak relationships with team families only made matters worse. Subsequently, two party secretaries from the Baimapu commune took over temporary management of the team. One even arranged an interest-free loan with which to purchase fertilizer and supplemental grain, in an effort to assure each team member of an annual ration of at least 350 *jin* of rice, roughly the level deemed subsistence-sufficient. Yet conditions continued to falter. At one point, the Meishan county party secretary himself came to Wenwu with a work team to supervise planting in Team 7, and local commune officials dispatched their own office staff to assist in the harvest. Nevertheless, these measures proved generally ineffective. Authorities finally decided to disband the team in 1971, and reassigned its members.[51] Thereafter, Wenwu brigade had eight production teams instead of nine, an administrative configuration it retained through the 1990s.

The crisis in "Old Team 7" had grown out of the structural anomalies of the collective system. It expressed the dissatisfaction of administratively created "peasants" toward their forced encapsulation in cash-poor agricultural collectives, and their relatively bleak prospects for social and economic mobility compared with their urban counterparts and neighbors. The team's dismemberment resolved the immediate crisis, but the incident had lingering consequences. At its height, the conflict had pitted street farmers against other farm families in the team. But decades later, it was remembered by many of the street farmers as a victory against corrupt cadres (*fubai ganbu*). The unorganized character of their resistance prevented authorities from targeting ringleaders with fines, punishment, or other sanctions. The incident became a major embarrassment to local cadres, many of whom denied that it ever happened, and it no doubt contributed to subsequent efforts by Wenwu cadres to strengthen brigade-level management.

Ascending Radicals

The militant radicalism of the Cultural Revolution provided the means for an emerging group of allied families to consolidate their dominance in Wenwu. In 1968, at the height of the Cultural Revolution and in the midst of the growing crisis in "Old Team 7," Brigade Party Secretary Lin Chengying stepped down from his post, reportedly for reasons of "poor health." A bad leg, it was said, had made walking to the brigade office increasingly difficult for him. Unable to keep up with the physical demands of the frequent meetings, he began to stay at home.[52] The timing of his retirement coincided with several major developments in the county, including an effort to increase the direct involvement of cadres in production work, the mobilization of the PLA to suppress factional violence, and a reorganization of rural administration.

In the late 1960s, local party committees throughout China were being abolished and replaced by provisional "revolutionary committees" (*geming weiyuanhui*). Organized by the PLA to restore order, maintain production, and select new cadres for a reorganized brigade leadership, these committees were to unite representatives of military authority, party cadres, and mass organizations to combat bureaucratic elitism and the entrenched self-interests of administrative incumbents (Hinton 1983: 541; MSG 1992: 264; Harding 1993: 197). When Party Secretary Lin resigned, Deputy Secretary Hao Yuanliang, then in his early thirties, assumed leadership in Wenwu. His move was supported by his affine, Liang Jinyuan, the PLA veteran and brigade militia chief. After the Korean War, Liang had been assigned to flood relief work in North China, and later as a supervisor in coal mines in Sichuan and road crews on the Tibetan frontier, returning to the village following his demobilization in the early 1960s.

As a "poor peasant" orphan who had suffered from the persecution of landlords and an honored war veteran with years of experience in military discipline and organization, Liang had excellent political credentials. He had also earned a reputation as a tough security chief who was not reluctant to enforce regulations with physical incentives. The street farmers had nicknamed him "Liang Jieshi," punning his name off that of KMT leader Jiang Jieshi (Chiang Kai-shek).[53] Although Liang did not become a formal member of the Wenwu revolutionary committee, he was nevertheless influential in shaping its formation. His political alliance with Hao Yuanliang had very personal foundations. As teenagers, they had evaded the KMT conscription patrols together, and Liang had remained a loyal friend to Hao Caiqin's family ever since that rainy night when they had saved him from discovery and capture. Liang's elder brother, recall, had married a Hao woman from the senior branch of the local Hao lineage. During the Cultural Revolution, his nephew [eBS] became leader of the Wenwu Red Guards.[54] Liang's sister was married to the eldest son of Lin Chengying, which protected Lin from abusive criticism or harassment.

Hao Yuanliang had been a prominent youth activist at Land Reform, and as a "lower middle peasant" he had subsequently gained a reputation as a fervent supporter of Maoist collectivism. Under his leadership, the brigade Communist Youth League came to adopt its militant radical posturing. Potential detractors found it difficult to challenge such a powerful incumbent without rendering themselves vulnerable to accusations of disloyalty to the Chairman. Hao pressed his advantage and strengthened his influence over the management of Wenwu. He orchestrated the appointment of his elder brother Hao Yuandeng, who had been dismissed during the Four Cleanups, to the brigade revolutionary committee, along with his "poor peasant" protégé, the young brigade accountant Jun Yueqing appointed by the Four Cleanups work team. For three years, these three men governed Wenwu with militant emulation of Mao Zedong Thought, supported by Liang Jinyuan as security chief.

As party organizations and offices of bureaucratic management were reestablished in the early 1970s, brigade administration was reexpanded. In 1971, Hao Yuanliang was formally confirmed by county authorities as new brigade party secretary. He immediately reappointed his brother, Hao Yuandeng, as brigade head. He also nominated a young nephew of his predecessor Lin Chengying as the new deputy party secretary of Wenwu. The young Lin had a senior high school education and had married a Hao woman from Team 3 in 1965.[55] He was first placed in charge of youth organization. But when Liang Jinyuan resigned his post as brigade security chief following the death of his wife, young Lin was also entrusted with command of the brigade militia.[56] The women's cadre appointed during the Four Cleanups also rejoined the brigade administration. These militant advocates of Maoist collectivism dominated the management of production and exchange in Wenwu well beyond the death of Mao in 1976.

"Studying Dazhai"

During the decade of the Cultural Revolution, the influence of "radical leftists" led to renewed efforts to strengthen rural collectives (Zweig 1989, 1991). The post-Leap reforms had encouraged strong economic recovery but had also led to growing differentiation in income and living standards as families regained a limited amount of autonomy from collective management. In the mid-1960s, prompted by U.S. bombings of North Vietnam in the wake of the Gulf of Tonkin incident, Mao called for a massive shift in state investment to a "third line" of key industries in the mountainous hinterland of Southwest China (Naughton 1991; Lieberthal 1993: 131). In Sichuan's Meishan county, rural party cadres were urged to pursue strategies of local self-reliance by "Studying Dazhai" (MSG 1992: 23, 268–70), a North China production brigade that had become a model of revolutionary determination and egalitarian commitment.[57] This campaign promoted Mao Zedong Thought, class struggle, mass mobilizations of labor, and a spirit of plain living and collective struggle.

The Dazhai model advocated brigade-level management, and income and subsistence security were again made dependent on collective efforts. In many instances, production teams lost their autonomy as moralistic incentives were introduced in support of more egalitarian redistributions across teams (Whyte 1969; Unger 1985). Workpoints, for example, were no longer based on the difficulty of task or the strength and skill of the laborer, but rather on attitude, commitment, and effort in work. Under a system of "self-reporting and public evaluation" (*zibao minping*), farmers submitted oral assessments of how many workpoints they felt they deserved each day, which were then appraised and criticized by co-workers. Such practices led to a general leveling of income within collectives. Amid renewed rhetoric of class struggle, conservative cadres were replaced by more radical leaders. Restrictions were tightened on family and personal consumption, and "capitalist influences" were again attacked.

As the Study Dazhai campaign peaked in the mid-1970s, other "radical" policies were enforced.[58] The Shangyi Greater Commune was revived, and marketing activities were again suppressed. In 1975, rural markets in Meishan convened only once a week, all on Sunday. Two years later, they were permitted only twice a month, on the first and fifteenth days (MSG 1992: 424). Travel to markets beyond the borders of one's own commune required official authorization. Private plots were retrenched, and families were forced to give up independent entrepreneurial activities. Restrictions were tightened even on house construction and repairs.[59] When the Shangyi Greater Commune was in operation, residents of the Baimapu area had to walk several hours just to file such petitions or to register a marriage.

During the 1970s, tens of thousands of rural laborers in Meishan were once again mobilized for public works projects, particularly those relating to water control (MSG 1992: 268–70). In the lowlands, flood levees were raised along the banks of the Minjiang, reducing the threat of floods and facilitating the consolidation of fields and introduction of mechanization. Reservoirs were built in the western highlands of the county, and new irrigation stations and water distribution channels were created to pump water throughout the countryside. Prior to this, almost 85 percent of the paddy in the county had a single production season, being converted after each year's harvest to winter water fields (*dongshuitian*) that would hold water for spring transplanting. The expansion of centralized irrigation management enabled farmers to convert almost 90 percent of those fields to two- or three-season paddies.

In Wenwu, for example, a network of irrigation channels was dug to distribute water from the deep trench excavated in the western part of Baimapu during the Great Leap. This enabled cadres to free up land that had previously been used as winter water fields. A second season of rice production was introduced, with a new harvest in the spring. At first, farmers applauded the new double rice crop, which increased their income and their food supply. They were less enthusiastic, however, when the government ordered them to introduce a third growing season of winter wheat. Many had never grown wheat and did not use flour products in their diets. They viewed the introduction of wheat as an unfair burden of no benefit to them and feared that it would deplete soil fertility. They were relieved when triple cropping was abandoned, but then dismayed to learn that the second rice crop was being dropped in favor of retaining wheat.[60]

In their study of Dazhai, brigade leaders in Wenwu also introduced chemical fertilizers and pesticides, as well as new strains of hybrid rice and chemically treated seed. Rice yields doubled or even tripled, although the costs of such innovations led to a mixed response among farmers.[61] From 1958 to 1968, county grain yields had increased at an average annual rate of 0.6 percent. During the decade of Dazhai study, that rate rose to almost 5 percent (MSG 1992: 270). Incomes, however, remained relatively stagnant under the forced egalitarian ethos of Dazhai emulation. Brigade cadres withheld a greater portion of collective revenues to cover the costs of new agricultural inputs and to build investment and welfare funds. Renewed labor demands were imposed on brigade families. As one farmer recalled, "Life is not all labor, but we had to work every day. Even in the off-season (*nongxian*) they would drudge up something for us to do. If you didn't work on this, you had to work on that. We had no leisure time." Moreover, it was no longer enough merely to complete one's assignment. Now one was also expected to display a revolutionary commitment to work tasks and the collective good. "You could not rest," asserted another villager. "But neither could you show a lack of spirit."

To promote brigade self-reliance, Party Secretary Hao Yuanliang attempted to diversity production activities in Wenwu. New cash crops such as cotton and tobacco were introduced to boost collective revenues but were abandoned after a few years. Roughly 25 percent of arable land in the brigade was taken out of grain production, but the new crops were of inferior quality and brought few returns from their sale to the state Supply and Marketing Cooperative. In fact, despite the impressive statistical gains in grain production in the 1970s, by the time the Study Dazhai campaign wound down in 1976, many areas of Sichuan—including Baimapu—were facing grain shortages. Once again agriculture output had been harnessed to industrialization efforts. But this time the problem lay not so much in greater state procurement quotas as in the growing appropriation of agricultural proceeds by local commune and brigade cadres to fund new rural enterprises.

China's rural industrial revolution gained great momentum in the 1970s, although it had historical antecedents in the Great Leap, if not earlier. Mao had endorsed collective rural industries as a solution to the poverty and surplus labor of "peasants" confined to the countryside by the household registration system. There had been more than seven hundred rural enterprises in Meishan in the mid-1960s, but half had been closed during the early years of the Cultural Revolution in an effort to "cut the tail of capitalism." By the peak of the Dazhai campaign in 1975, the number had grown again to more than eight hundred (MSG 1992: 571). In Wenwu, the brigade leadership diverted agricultural revenues into a new capital accumulation fund, which they used to finance experimental nonagricultural collective enterprises. Although many of their early attempts ended in failure, the Hao brothers persisted in their efforts to diversify the brigade economy. Their eventual success was awarded official recognition in the 1980s, when the collective village became a showcase for rural development.

Village Collectivism and the Maoist State

Mao had championed mobilizational collectivism as a strategy of economic modernization that would transform China's "poor and blank" peasantry. Collectivism did revolutionize China's "mode of production," but it also generated its own contradictions and unintended consequences. Organizational initiatives during the early 1950s created the administrative foundations for new managerial regimes under the people's commune system. The mandatory grain procurement system, household registration, collective accounting, workpoints, and other technologies of power forced farmers into dependency on their rural collectives. New forms of moral, material, and coercive incentives were introduced to effect compliance (Madsen 1984; Oi 1989; Zweig 1989).

Under Communist rule, state and local polities became deeply intermeshed, and state control over the countryside reached unprecedented proportions (Unger 1989; cf. Shue 1988). Recall that, during the Republican era, state strengthening initiatives had extended the formal offices of government from the county level to the level of rural townships. Land Reform established the administrative village of Qiaolou, based largely on the earlier *baojia* organization. The household registration system effectively confined "peasants" to the collective village, while the suppression of rural marketing under the people's commune system destroyed their economic autonomy. During the Maoist era of mobilizational collectivism, brigade cadres, team leaders, and individual families often struggled covertly against one another to control labor, grain, and cash. But the Dazhai campaign strengthened the organization of the brigade as a centralized economic unit of production, redistribution, and consumption.

Lest state power be caricatured as overly determinstic, it is important to note that the new institutions of collectivism offered opportunities for both families and individual people to pursue their own strategies of mobility or empowerment. "The structure of power was also a network of familial relations" (Friedman, Pickowicz, and Selden 1991: 283). Kinship, affinity, friendship, and other forms of social organization continued to provide the basis for interfamily associations and alliances, and were of great importance to the structuring of power and status among local families. The new institutions of managerial authority created in communes, brigades, and teams enabled local cadres to attain an unprecedented degree of compliance. Under collectivism, brigade party leaders in Wenwu became key intermediaries between state cadres and "peasant" laborers. They brokered the flow of labor and material goods at this key level of the state administrative system. Implementation of state directives was shaped not only by particular circumstances but also by particular interests. The actions of local cadres profoundly influenced how kin and neighbors experienced, remembered, and interpreted the Communist revolution.

Under the compulsory egalitarian ethos of the collective era, when constraints were imposed on consumption practices, individual expressions of family status were highly noteworthy and often focused on major life rituals such as marriages. Regulations stipulated that wedding expenditures, for example, were to be kept low. Bridewealth and other betrothal gifts were denounced by Communist authorities as "feudal" customs. In fact, few families had the cash or grain to finance either gifts or wedding banquets. Marriages during the collective era were colloquially referred to as "sweet potato weddings" (*hongshu hunyin*), symbolizing their meagerness. In a sample of forty-three marriages during the collective era, the average wedding banquet hosted six tables. Most frequently, there were only one or two tables of diners (four to eight people), usually immediate family members.

The overall average was skewed by two large wedding feasts, both hosted by close relatives of leading brigade party cadres. The first, following the Four Cleanups campaign in the relatively prosperous post-Leap reform years, involved the nephew of then party secretary Lin Chengying, who married a Hao woman from Team 3. The Lins hosted a banquet of twenty tables (some 160 guests), while the bride's family fed ten tables at its own feast. Ironically, the grandest wedding of the entire collective era, with twenty-five tables of guests, took place in 1969, at the height of the radical phase of the Cultural Revolution. The groom was Hao Yuanqian, a close cousin [FeBS] of Hao Yuanliang, who had taken over leadership of Wenwu only a year earlier, and the wedding was hosted in the large tile-roofed *siheyuan* compound that the two men shared with their families.[62] Hao Yuanqian was the only son of the eldest of Hao Caiqin's five sons and represented the senior branch of Hao Caiqin's family descent group (see Figure 1). He had two "dry fathers" (*gandie*): the "rich peasant" and former brigade accountant Hao Yunpo, and a nephew of his grandmother, a Zhen man in neighboring Minzhu (Yangtang) brigade. When the couple had become engaged in 1966, the Haos had presented their affines with an engagement payment (*dinghun fei*) of Y400, and *caili* betrothal gifts worth more than Y200. These were impressive presentations, considering that the average per-capita income among farmers in the county was roughly Y70 at the time.[63] While families in Team 7 were struggling to meet their subsistence needs, Hao Yuanliang, the new brigade party leader, helped host a feast for two hundred guests.

In the 1990s, farmers looked back on the collective era as a period of drudgery and poverty. During the 1960s and 1970s, they had little cash and few opportunities for mobility, and even worried sometimes about their subsistence security. Land Reform and the voluntary cooperatives of the early 1950s gave the CCP wide popularity among rural cultivators. But when visions of communal abundance, so beautifully depicted by party political workers, materialized in hunger and death, many lost faith with collectivism. Over the next two decades, they became increasingly disillusioned with their forced confinement and compliance in discriminatory relations of state-guided production, procurement, and redistribution. Yet despite its failings, collectivism created organizational foundations for corporate village enterprise, which brought such a dramatic rise in family incomes and living standards in the post-Mao era.

CHAPTER 5

Village as Enterprise

Corporate Community Management in the Deng Era

Prosperity lies in industriousness.

—QIAOLOU VILLAGE COMPACT

In the spring of 1991, a delegation of state representatives from Chengdu arrived in Qiaolou for a "study tour." Village cadres, as well as several township officials, all dressed in clean Sun Yat-sen tunics ("Mao jackets"), waited to greet them as the cars and vans pulled into the walled village administrative compound (see Map 5). After introductions and presentations of namecards, the visitors were ushered upstairs to a reception hall on the top floor of the three-story Brigade Building, which has a commanding view of the surrounding countryside. Hot water for tea was brought in kettles and thermoses, not by the wife of the village head, who usually served it to village office staff, but by young former soldiers, smartly dressed, who glided into the room silently, served tea, and retired quickly.

The meeting started with formal welcomes, perfunctory praise for the correct reform policies endorsed by the Third Plenum of 1978, and self-deprecating apologies for the "backward" conditions of life in the village. A senior member of the county government, who earlier in the day had received the delegation in Meishan and who now accompanied them to Qiaolou, explained that the visitors had wanted a firsthand look at the village enterprises established since the advent of the post-Mao reforms. "Qiaolou village," he told the group, "is a *hao tou cun*"—a fine leading example of entrepreneurial initiative combined with commitment to collectivist principles.

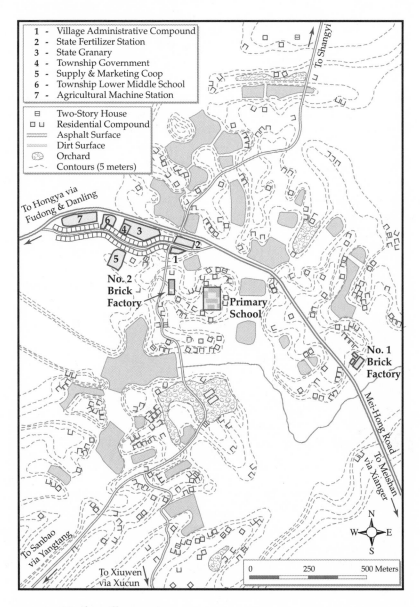

MAP 5. Qiaolou village, 1991

The head of the Chengdu delegation expressed gratitude for an opportunity to learn from what had been accomplished in Qiaolou, noting that the village enjoyed a good reputation among provincial leaders as well. The village party secretary then recited a long list of demographic and economic statistics as evidence of income growth, rising living standards, and subsidized collective benefits made possible through village-owned and -operated enterprises. Junior delegates on the study tour listened earnestly, dutifully recording information in their notebooks.

Following this introduction, the visitors were led on a tour of the village. They were taken first to the distillery, also located within the administrative compound, walking past parked trucks belonging to the village transport team. Next, they were escorted to the No. 2 Brick Factory, located a few hundred meters south of the compound and visible from the balconies of the Brigade Building. From there, they were led along a dirt road out to the southern village orchard, atop Xi Upper Slope. Along the way, their attention was directed to the variety of crops being cultivated in terraced beds and hilltop plots alongside the road, and to the impressive two-story house of the elected village head. A few years earlier, they were told, an American university professor had visited the village and been taken to the rooftop of the house, from which he (reportedly) remarked that the view was "damn beautiful."

After a brief rest at the orchard, a favorite site for photo opportunities, some of the more senior members of the study tour returned with an escort to the village offices. A few of the visitors, however, were taken to see a "typical" family home—in this case an impressive fired-brick "three-cornered compound" with a ceramic tiled gateway that led into a walled courtyard surfaced with cement. Before returning to join their colleagues at the village offices, they were also shown the smaller and more modest home of the village party secretary, located nearby.

Back at the village administrative compound, the visitors were given a banquet in the reception hall. The feast was catered by the proprietor of a small restaurant in the Baimapu market settlement, a patrilineal cousin of the Qiaolou party secretary and the man widely regarded as the best chef in the area. A young former army cook—a son of former Party Secretary Lin Chengying and the chef assigned to our research team's "mess regiment" while I was in Qiaolou—waited tables and introduced each dish. Toasts were drunk with alcohol from the village distillery. The feast, which included such Meishan specialities as Dongpu Pork, concluded with fresh oranges from the village orchard. Afterward, cigarettes were offered to the hosts, although another village official smoked with the guests as a "representative" of Secretary Hao Yuanliang, a nonsmoker.

As the visitors approached their cars and vans for the trip back to Chengdu, which could take five hours or more if traffic were congested, sacks of oranges were brought forward by orchard workers. Some were presented as gifts to the guests, many of whom also purchased additional fruit at discount prices. Village workers on hand were delighted to sell the urbanites a few bags of sweet potatoes as well, although some found the request humorously peculiar. Most no longer ate such crops. The old staple food of the poor, so common even at wedding banquets of the Maoist era, was now generally fed to hogs.

During my stay in Qiaolou, a number of villagers privately complained about the costs of hosting such study tours. They contended that discount orange sales, so commonly offered to the many visiting delegations, hurt enterprise revenues and, ultimately, family incomes. Some noted with apparent cynicism that such visits tended to peak during the period immediately following the orange harvest. A few, well versed in the rhetorical polemics of the old mass campaigns, criticized banquets for VIP delegations as "wasteful and extravagant." Village leaders, however, justified such practices as important to developing commercial and political relationships. Each visiting delegation offered potential new contacts that could help Qiaolou leaders negotiate new business transactions, receive credit or investment capital, and qualify for technical assistance.

After all, the use of assets from one enterprise to support another, to fund village administrative costs, or to pay for infrastructure construction, social welfare benefits, and tax subsidies was what had made Qiaolou a success. Since the early 1980s, the village had been managed as a corporate group. It owned a variety of collective enterprises, the operations of which were directed by village cadres. Under the Study Dazhai campaign in the 1970s, the brigade leadership had begun an initiative to diversify into nonagricultural enterprise. Revenues were reinvested in new ventures, but brigade cadres maintained direct control over these new collective assets. With the post-Mao reforms, and the renaming of revolutionary Wenwu back to Qiaolou, agriculture was contracted out to individual family households, but these brigade-owned enterprises were not. In many parts of China, rural collectives lost their economic and political significance in the 1980s. Rural cadres often found their authority and responsibilities reduced to the unpopular roles of tax collectors and birth-planning monitors. In Qiaolou, however, the collective (*jiti*) thrived at the village level for more than a decade after Mao.

The contrast to the situation in some other locales was profound, as the party secretary of a periurban village on the outskirts of the county seat lamented during a study tour for a busload of fellow villagers he had brought to Qiaolou:

> Since the redistribution of land, our village collective has become an empty shell (*kong ke*). Everyone wants to grow vegetables for the county markets. No one wants to grow grain anymore. Many are unwilling to pay their local administrative levies (*tiliu*) to the village. They say, "The collective has disbanded! What is in it for me?" We have no money for

social benefits, no subsidies for children's schooling, and no welfare net for our "five guarantee households."[1] The Party is of no use anymore. We only collect taxes and mediate disputes.

Although agriculture had also been decollectivized in Qiaolou, village cadres shifted other collectively owned assets out of agriculture and into new investments in commercial and industrial enterprises. Managing Qiaolou much like a corporation, and employing rhetoric and practices evocative of corporatist political organizations, they tried to cultivate a basis for collective identity that focused on the village as a commercial enterprise.

Decollectivizing Agriculture

Agricultural decollectivization, referred to by some as China's "Second Land Reform," so dramatically altered relationships among villagers, townspeople, and administrators that it has become a symbol of the general post-Mao reforms program. The devolution of land (*tudi xiafang*)—or the granting of control over its use, exchange, and profits to families through household contracting—became an historical moment in popular consciousness, a watershed event noted in every person's life history. In fact, the redistribution of land to family households was but one aspect of a more comprehensive package of economic and political reforms approved by the post-Mao party leadership under Deng Xiaoping.

Following a series of key meetings in Beijing during the late 1970s and early 1980s, the CCP announced several major policy changes. Party history was reassessed. "Leftist" excesses, such as those during the Great Leap Forward and the Cultural Revolution, were criticized and repudiated. Class designations and discriminatory political labels were abolished, and many of those who had been persecuted as "rightists" or "capitalist roaders" were rehabilitated, if only posthumously. Material bonuses were offered to workers who exceeded production quotas, price controls were eased, rural periodic markets were restored, and restrictions were relaxed on independent entrepreneurial activity and travel. Agricultural production was contracted out (*chengbao*) to individual families, collective property was redistributed or sold off, and the state rationing system was scaled back. Efforts were made to promote a younger and better-educated generation of cadres, and the control of party authorities over economic matters and civil administration was reduced. Local elections were even introduced, and villagers were permitted a voice in the selection of their representative officials.

In the Baimapu area as Mao's designated heir, Hua Guofeng, renewed calls to "Learn from Dazhai," the Shangyi Greater Commune of the Great Leap period was revived yet again in 1977. Sale or trade of agricultural subsidiary products was suppressed by special work teams, in an attempt to consolidate collective control of commerce (MSG 1992: 27). Three years later, however, after Deng had replaced Hua, the Baimapu commune regained its autonomy. Moreover, production teams, including those in Qiaolou, reintroduced material incentives and contracted farming to subteam work groups.[2] Nevertheless, full agricultural decollectivization came relatively late in Qiaolou. In 1981, roughly one-third of all production teams in China had already redistributed land and assigned contract production quotas to individual family households (Chan, Madsen, and Unger 1992). By May 1983, a few months before such reforms were enacted in Qiaolou, those numbers had risen to over 90 percent nationwide (Riskin 1987: 200).

In Qiaolou, the redistribution of land was complicated and time consuming. Brigade and team cadres prepared by numbering and measuring each parcel of land, wet paddy and dry field alike, and assessing its quality on a scale of three grades. The actual reallotments were carried out, under the close scrutiny of village families, after the fall rice harvest of 1983, during the brief off-season before winter wheat was planted. Each of Qiaolou's eight production teams undertook household contracting separately. Brigade leaders supervised the process, occasionally intervening in disputes over particular plots or over the boundaries within subdivided plots.

Land was redistributed on a per capita basis. The class labels of the Maoist era were not taken into consideration.[3] On average, each family received roughly 1.1 to 1.2 *mu* of paddy for each "mouth" (or registered household member). Actual per capita allotments, however, ranged from 1.0 to 1.3 *mu*, based on the population to land ratio in particular teams.[4] Moreover, team leaders were given discretion to follow one of two redistribution procedures. A few adopted a method that assigned fixed and equal per capita state procurement quotas to each family.[5] In this manner, its advocates maintained, the "burden" (*fudan*) each person bore for the state would be equal, and fields would be redistributed on the basis of their production capacity rather than their area alone. The alternative—namely, allotting equal amounts of land to each team member—would, they argued, impose unequal burdens on different families. One family might obtain plots of more marginal quality, which could reduce that family's surplus after fulfilling its state procurement quotas, whereas another family might have the good fortune to receive the most productive parcels and thus attain an unfair advantage.

Instead, under the first method of redistribution, a complicated series of procedures was followed in the name of equity. Family heads (or their representatives) drew lots for specific numbered parcels, the size and quality of which were reviewed by team cadres. Adjustments were then made for families that drew plots with a production capacity that either exceeded or failed to meet their procurement quotas. Many plots were subdivided in the process, while others were exchanged between families. As a result, per capita allocations of land in teams employing this first method varied from 1.0 to 1.2 *mu*. Family holdings were often more fragmented than under the second method, but each family in such teams did end up shouldering equal per capita state procurement obligations. This first method led to many conflicts, however. Brigade cadres were called in to mediate numerous disputes. Some people, dissatisfied with their fields, complained that team cadres manipulated the procedure to favor relatives or friends, who, they alleged, obtained more productive plots closer to their homes or to water sources.[6]

Because of these difficulties, most team leaders adopted the alternative of allocating equal-sized per-capita allotments of land. Lots were drawn, subdivisions were made for equity, and different procurement quotas were assigned to each family household based on the total area and quality of its specific plots. As one former team leader explained, "It is easier to adjust procurement quotas than land allotments. Quotas are written paper. Land is more tangible." To avoid confrontations in which farmers who had drawn prime paddies would be obliged by local cadres to exchange them for less preferred plots, it was far easier and more popular to assess state obligations flexibly, on the basis of land that farmers had drawn for with their own hands.

With the decollectivization of agriculture, individual families acquired more autonomy in their production and consumption activities. Beyond the "duty" of meeting their procurement quotas, and a state agricultural tax (usually deducted from their procurement payments, along with local administrative surcharges [*tiliu*]), farmers were relatively free to cultivate whatever crops they desired.[7] No longer did local cadres direct who labored where, when, at what, with whom, and how well. Nor did they determine how farm labor would be remunerated. Such decisions were now made within individual families, which once again became the basic managerial units of agricultural production. Moreover, with the restoration of rural markets, farmers were largely free to sell surplus produce anywhere they chose, and at negotiated prices.

Exercising Property Rights

Agricultural decollectivization, however, was not unambiguous privatization (cf. Kelliher 1992). Responsibility contracts issued to family households granted them fifteen-year use rights to the plots they had drawn.[8] Families did not own land, nor could they buy or sell it.[9] Yet both land itself and the procurement obligations that accompanied it were popularly regarded as part of family property (*jiachan*), like other assets and liabilities. Sons had recognized rights of succession to contracts signed by their fathers (as did daughters, although their claims were not universally recognized in practice). Land and procurement quotas were also included in family division negotiations. In fact, the process of agricultural decollectivization itself was commonly discussed in terms of "dividing" (*fen*) team assets and distributing "shares" among member families.

Land, however, officially remained under the formal ownership of production teams and, ultimately, the state.[10] Latent state property rights were manifest periodically, and sometimes dramatically, in claims of eminent domain when land was appropriated for roads or reservoirs (Jing 1996). Production teams' claims to contracted land were expressed more routinely, in adjustments (*tiaozheng*) of family allotments made every five years.[11] Despite such state and production team property rights over land, individual families attempted to exert greater rights of their own, seeking strategies that advanced their own interests while still complying with official authority.

Those who were unhappy with state-imposed procurement quotas, particularly for wheat, often carefully calculated their agricultural inputs so as to produce only what was necessary to meet their obligations to the government. Families obliged to surrender land during a periodic adjustment sometimes offered to return to the team specific parcels of less value. Others, as already noted, exchanged land or transferred use rights (temporarily) to others through subcontracting (*zhuanbao*). Those who expanded cultivation into formerly barren hills (*huangshan*) received special lifetime usufruct rights to the new plots they opened, and the crops they grew on such reclaimed land were exempt from procurement quotas.

Tensions between the formal status of land ownership and the particularistic claims of individual families were also evident in betrothal patterns and negotiations. When a Qiaolou woman married, the land that had previously been allotted to her natal family as her per capita allocation remained with her natal family until the next periodic adjustment. Families preparing for the marriage of a daughter often sought to delay the wedding until after an approaching redistribution, so as to retain control over her allotment for another five years. Prospective affines, for their part, pressed for earlier marriages so as to become eligible for additional land with which to offset the burden of another mouth (or two) to feed. Until a bride was actually issued an allotment in the next periodic land adjustment at her husband's locale, she could either continue to work the share of land allocated for her to her natal family by herself, or she could subcontract it to her father or brothers.[12]

Agricultural decollectivization also entailed the redistribution of other collective property formerly held by production teams. For example, Qiaolou's eight teams possessed a total of forty-eight water buffalo, which were distributed to team families on a shareholding basis.[13] Most hand tools in each team went to the poor, who could not afford to purchase their own implements, while larger, wealthier, or better-connected families obtained most of the winnowing machines, which many leased for profit.

In January 1984, a few months after team decollectivization in Qiaolou, the rural people's commune system was abolished. Communes were redesignated as townships, and brigades as villages. Former teams, now to be called "villager small groups" (*cunmin xiaozu*), had few administrative functions other than population registration, tax and fee collection, and irrigation coordination.[14] In some ways, these groups were more like the *baojia* units of the Republican decades than the production teams of the Maoist era. The village, however, resembled the collective brigade far more than the old *bao* unit on which it had been administratively based. Under the post-Mao reforms, the collective (*jiti*) came to symbolize a powerful new form of economic and political management: the corporate village.

Walking on Two Legs

Party Secretary Hao Yuanliang had reportedly resisted the decollectivization of agriculture, delaying the enactment of reform in Qiaolou for several years. He warned that the abandonment of redistributive socialism in favor of a privatized market economy would lead to polarizations in wealth and, ultimately, to social and political instability. It was even rumored that Hao had forestalled the implementation of household responsibility contracting in Qiaolou until party superiors in the county government gave him explicit orders to enact the new official policies.

Hao told his brigade cadres that it was necessary to provide a safety net for families that might be adversely affected by the decollectivization of agriculture. He proposed that before contracting out land use to individual family households, Qiaolou should first diversify its economic base by establishing new nonagricultural enterprises. These would be collectively owned by the brigade and would remain under the management of its administrative committee. Only once they established a new industrial sector would they proceed with land redistribution. In this way they would "walk on two legs," as Mao had urged since the Great Leap Forward. Regardless of how individual families fared in the developing Baimapu market economy, each would still be assured access to wage labor and various collective benefits. At the same time, the brigade leadership could maintain a degree of control over economic activity in Qiaolou, creating a new property base that would enhance the autonomy of the collective village as a corporate group.

Throughout their political careers, the Hao brothers Yuandeng and Yuanliang had reputations as militant collectivists. From their childhood in the large joint family of their grandfather Hao Caiqin to their youthful activism in organizing Qiaolou's first mutual aid group and their command of the Wenwu revolutionary committee, they had been advocates of diversified collective economies of scale. Moreover, their diligent study of Dazhai during the 1970s had included several attempts to establish brigade-run enterprises.

One of the earliest of these efforts, a rudimentary seed oil press, had been abandoned as impractical. Its rather makeshift technology—a wooden beam battering seeds in a metal drum—required too much labor to be cost effective. The first sustained success came with the brigade construction team, established in 1974. Most of its revenues were remitted to a brigade capital accumulation fund, which was then used to finance other collective enterprise ventures.[15] In October 1976, Sichuan provincial chief Zhao Ziyang led a delegation on a tour of Meishan county (MSG 1992: 27), reportedly visiting Baimapu commune. That same year, Wenwu made several major investments in new brigade-run enterprises.

A three-story guesthouse and canteen were built on a former public graveyard at the eastern end of the Baimapu Street. The Hao brothers anticipated that Zhao's visit to the commune would be followed by political pilgrimages of lower-ranking delegations, which they hoped to provide with rooms and meals. Unfortunately, the expected clientele never materialized, and the guesthouse closed in the early 1980s. Its tall edifice, still referred to as the "Brigade Building" (*dadui lou*), was converted to administrative offices, meeting halls, and storage space, and remained a prominent local landmark. Also in 1976, the brigade purchased a full-size tractor and established an agricultural machine repair station (*jixiu zhan*) in a walled compound surrounding the Brigade Building (see Map 5). This enterprise drew on the skills of demobilized soldiers who had worked with machinery in the army, and on the talents of "sent-down youths" from Meishan and Chengdu who were then living in the brigade.[16] It proved too successful, however, and closed in 1978 after Baimapu authorities "called up" the technicians to work at the commune machine station. But the brigade was left with its tractor.

The location of Qiaolou, situated astride an intercounty asphalt road with major rail and highway links at Meishan, encouraged investment in transport activities. Although the small terraced paddies and fields of the Baimapu countryside made agricultural mechanization impractical, tractors were important vehicles of transport, a growing sector of the economy.[17] In 1974, the brigade had authorized the purchase of a smaller, wagon-bedded hand tractor to haul materials for the construction team. Both this tractor and the full-sized one purchased two years later were also used to cart grain from Qiaolou production teams to the Baimapu state granary. Without them, farmers were obliged to carry such materials by shoulder pole or push cart, or to hire transport contractors. The tractors were later used to ship to the county railway depot tangerines and oranges from a brigade orchard, also established in 1976.

Harvesting the Fruits of Collective Labor

Using funds from Qiaolou's brigade capital accumulation account, roughly three thousand tangerine saplings were purchased from a nearby brigade that had pioneered citrus cultivation in Baimapu commune. They were transplanted to some 50 *mu* of land in southern Qiaolou, at the site of the Battle of Baimapu. These saplings formed the core of an experimental collective orchard managed by Brigade Head Hao Yuandeng. The orchard occupied a previously uncultivated barren hill (*huangshan*) atop Xi Upper Slope, where the borders of three production teams in southern Qiaolou meet (see Map 5).[18] The brigade paid an annual cash rent (*zu*) to each of these teams, which team leaders either dispersed among team families or applied toward team production costs, such as fertilizer. A special quota of jobs on the orchard staff was set aside for members of these three teams. This practice of "land for jobs" (*tudi gong*) was common in both rural collective enterprises and state industrial development (Walder 1986; Oi 1989). After decollectivization, families in these three teams were also given several kilograms of oranges each year as their share (*fen*) of the enterprise.

For three years, the orchard staff tended the saplings with care, spraying them with pesticides purchased by the brigade and fertilizing them with manure from more than a dozen hogs raised expressly for that purpose. In 1980, the young trees fruited and were carefully transplanted again, over a wider area. Sales of tangerines brought new cash revenues to the brigade, but a decision was made to graft roughly half the trees into larger and more profitable oranges. The same year, the orchard was expanded onto Yan Grave Hill in northern Qiaolou, which was planted entirely with more expensive orange saplings, rather than the cheaper and less widely marketable tangerines.

The orchard took in its first major harvest in 1982. Rather than redistributing profits among brigade families, or even to members of the orchard staff, all earnings were reinvested in the purchase of grafts and saplings of large navel oranges, for which there was great market demand. By the mid-1980s, Qiaolou oranges were being shipped as far away as Gansu, Beijing, and Heilongjiang, consistently bringing in valuable cash earnings that made the orchard one of the brigade's key "backbone" enterprises.[19] Several consignments were even exported to Japan and the Soviet Union, providing a rare source of foreign exchange. Expansion of the orchard continued. By 1990, it had more than 8,500 fruit-bearing trees covering over 100 *mu* of formerly barren hills. Annual gross earnings totaled nearly Y80,000, but the high costs of shipping, new chemical fertilizers, and pesticides reportedly reduced net revenues to roughly Y30,000.

The success of the brigade orchard fueled other collective enterprise development efforts in Qiaolou, as Secretary Hao Yuanliang attempted to tap lucrative niches in reemerging markets. Constrained by limited capital, little technological expertise, and few material resources, he sought to establish other relatively low-cost, labor-intensive enterprises that would make Qiaolou more self-reliant as a collective economic unit while also providing job security for brigade families, collectively. In 1979, he proposed establishing a factory to produce kiln-fired bricks for construction projects. For years, the only brick factory in the area had been in nearby Xianger, and it had enjoyed a very profitable business that included many state contracts.[20] Setting up a similar industry in Qiaolou would help further diversify the brigade economy as agriculture was decollectivized.

As with the orchard, the brigade capital accumulation fund was used as a source of investment capital. But the brick factory required more substantial financing, so each registered household in the brigade was obliged to purchase a Y100 mandatory share (*gufen*) in the enterprise. For those who lacked ready cash to purchase a share outright, the brigade leadership ordered Y100 withheld from their year-end production team redistribution. In this way every family became a shareholder in the new enterprise. Those willing to forego dividends on their share were eligible to have a family member employed in a wage-paying job at the factory.[21]

The compulsory sale of shares generated more than Y30,000 toward the construction costs of the new brick factory. Secretary Hao also obtained a Y230,000 loan from the state Agricultural Bank. The relationships he had developed with county leaders during his long incumbency as brigade party secretary were influential in obtaining such credit. Moreover, the status of the brick factory as a collective enterprise qualified it for certain privileges not extended to privately contracted enterprises, such as a one-year tax exemption and no strict limit on the size of its labor force. County authorities applauded Hao Yuanliang for his determination to keep to the collective path (*jiti daolu*) and awarded him several lucrative contracts to supply bricks for government projects.

Following a Red Brick Road

Built at the eastern base of Big Xi Hill, not far from the former site of Qiao-lou's namesake Bridge Building (Qiaolouzi; see Map 3), the brick factory became operational in 1982. The timing was fortuitous, for it opened just as a post-Mao housing boom was getting under way in the region. The brick factory quickly became the principal supplier for families throughout the township that undertook new housing starts. Within a year it had produced more than nine million bricks, with profits of more than Y80,000 (MSG 1992: 572). This success enabled the Qiaolou leadership to repay its bank loan within three years, establishing a good credit rating that was helpful later in securing new loans for subsequent enterprise initiatives. It also brought a rapid rise in family incomes, much of which was invested in home renovation.[22] Yet a large percentage of factory profits was remitted to the brigade's capital accumulation fund to finance further industrial development, including a second brick factory that opened in 1984.

The brick factories were fired by coal brought in directly from mines in neighboring Emei and Renshou counties. Qiaolou's own tractors proved insufficient for such transport needs, obliging brigade leaders to hire outside contractors to truck in consignments of coal. In 1983, Secretary Hao authorized purchase of an "East is Red" lorry, and soon thereafter a second, and then a third. A few years later, Qiaolou acquired a "Chengdu Brand" light flatbed truck as well. The transport team not only eliminated dependence on coal truck contractors but also gave new leverage to Qiaolou leaders, who sometimes loaned or rented out trucks and drivers to the township government or to state work units.

The No. 2 Brick Factory was established with investment capital of Y600,000, derived entirely from Qiaolou's other enterprises. The new factory was built at the base of a small hill in southern Qiaolou, in close proximity to the Brigade Building and the Baimapu market settlement.[23] Although the facility enjoyed an excellent location, accessible by truck along a dirt road that ran through southern Qiaolou to the site, it proved less profitable than the "No. 1 Brick." Unlike the rich, claylike soil near the first factory, the soil behind the second factory was permeated with tiny stones that rendered it less suitable for firing. Many bricks cracked or exploded in the kiln, and those that survived were generally of marginal quality and thus had to be sold at discount prices, mainly to families looking to save money on home renovations.

Poor product quality proved a serious handicap for the new enterprise, yet production continued even as the quality of soil deteriorated with deeper excavation. Secretary Hao, who closely monitored management of the No. 2 Brick Factory, as he did all collective village enterprises, pushed for a return on capital investment in the new facility. He directed revenues from the No. 1 Brick Factory and the brigade orchard to subsidize production costs at the "No. 2 Brick." With more effective marketing, it was hoped, products could still be sold. However, while the No. 1 Brick sustained a regular clientele that included state contracts, sales agents for the No. 2 Brick found themselves obliged to constantly seek out new clients because so many previous customers had been dissatisfied. In fact, during the late 1980s, production at the No. 2 Brick was suspended for nearly a year, after the backlog of unsold bricks surpassed the factory's storage capacity.

The relaxed political atmosphere of the early 1980s permitted a rise in consumer spending and celebratory activities that helped to revive and stimulate the market economy. New house building was accompanied by festive banqueting, as were major life events, ritual observances, and market-day visiting. Alcohol had long been an important aspect of Chinese food culture, ritual practice, and popular medicine, and it was in high demand at local markets during the 1980s. In 1985, Qiaolou opened its own collectively owned and operated village distillery, with revenues from the No. 1 Brick Factory as the sole source of investment funds. Its sorghum-based spirits won official awards of recognition and were, for a time, a highly marketable consumer product in the township.

The distillery was built in the walled administrative compound at the eastern end of Baimapu Street, where the Brigade Building and a storage house were located. The former brigade machine repair station had been based there as well, and vehicles of the transport team were parked within this compound, the gate of which was locked and guarded at night.[24] Sorghum, imported by rail from North China to Meishan and then hauled to Qiaolou by the transport team, was used to produce two strong, clear alcohols: a standard *baijiu*, and a higher quality *qujiu*. Secretary Hao's well-established ties with county authorities were instrumental in this venture as well. Distillation required government licensing, and many private petitioners waited years for authorization. But Qiaolou quickly received an official permit for its collectively operated (*jiti ban*) enterprise. The county government also arranged for technical specialists from a state research institute in Chengdu to provide assistance in designing the facility and its products, and for the distillery staff to contact potential sorghum suppliers in other parts of China.

The distillery began very successfully and returned an early profit. Within two years of opening, its fiery "Meishan Qujiu" won county awards of excellence. In 1988 it again received similar recognition, as well as a "Silver Cup Award" at provincial competition in Leshan city. By the late 1980s, however, alcohol supply overtook the demand on local and regional markets. The apparent success enjoyed by many early distilleries attracted other investors and entrepreneurs, and the number of distilleries in Sichuan grew dramatically, as did the proportion of unlicensed operations. State authorities began to police rural distilleries more strictly, particularly after 1989, closing unlicensed facilities and even revoking permits. Qiaolou escaped this crackdown and its facility was relicensed, but by 1990 the distillery had nevertheless accumulated a large backlog of unsold *qujiu* spirits. With market demand and prices having fallen significantly, the enterprise faced serious financial difficulties.

Rather than selling at a loss, Hao Yuanliang directed the distillery staff to retain the large overstock in storage until prices recovered. The distillery labor force was downsized from over a dozen workers to only five, and production shifted to a more common, plain alcohol (*baijiu*) that was cheaper to produce and more affordable to local consumers. In the meantime, funds from other collective assets, such as the No. 1 Brick Factory and the orchard, were used to support operations at the ailing enterprise. As when the No. 2 Brick Factory had faced financial problems, corporate management practices of cross-asset subsidization were employed to sustain production.

Administering the Corporate Village

The post-Mao reforms had profound implications for political organization in Qiaolou. Restrictions were eased on independent rural marketing activities, and agricultural decollectivization abandoned workpoints in favor of incentive-based household procurement contracts. Individual farm families gained considerable autonomy from their production teams as team property was divided up and redistributed.[25] Yet while teams faded in significance, in Qiaolou the brigade rose to unprecedented prominence. Brigade assets remained largely under centralized collective control. Only two small grain-processing machines owned by the brigade were contracted out to individual households.

In January 1984, rural people's communes throughout Meishan were officially abolished. Nevertheless, Qiaolou residents continued to refer to "the brigade" and "brigade leaders" well into the 1990s, owing largely to the strength of collective village enterprises, the corporate management style of village leaders, and the continued incumbency of former brigade cadres in the new village administration. In contrast to many villages, where the cadre responsibility system, local elections, and other political reforms of the post-Mao era led to a turnover in local leadership, most village positions in Qiaolou continued to be held by former brigade leaders who had come to power with Hao Yuanliang during the Cultural Revolution.

The political reforms introduced in the 1980s were intended to promote a younger, better-educated, more professional and specialized generation of cadre leaders. Administrative staffs were reduced in size, and local officials gained greater autonomy as the economic and political functions of government were separated (White 1990). In Qiaolou, a new, streamlined village council (*cunmin weiyuanhui*) was elected, technically separate from the village party committee. It was staffed with four elected positions: village head, accountant, security chief, and women's cadre.[26] For the first time, villagers would themselves cast votes for village administrators in local elections.[27] A slate of five candidates was nominated by the village party committee, and the top four vote-winners were elected to the new village council.

Every three years, since 1983, area residents have gathered at the Baimapu township administrative compound to cast their ballots in local elections. During the Maoist era, brigade cadres were appointed to their posts by the party secretary and confirmed by the brigade party committee. Although most production team leaders in Qiaolou were sometimes elected by fellow team members during the Maoist era, the electoral reforms of the 1980s represented a move toward democratization at the village level. Regardless of their former class designations or political labels, all men and women aged sixteen or older gained a voice in the selection of village administrators. However, not all eligible voters always cast ballots. Some abstain, while others designate a relative as a proxy (*daipiao*) to vote on their behalf.[28]

Each voter was given a ballot printed with the names of village council nominees and instructed to circle the candidates of her or his choice and to cross out the names of others. Voters were permitted to cross out as many candidates as they wished, but ballots with more than four names circled were disqualified. The names of the four winning candidates were publicly announced and posted along Baimapu Street, along with election results from other villages in the township. The number of votes won by each candidate was not revealed, nor were the names or vote tallies of write-in candidates.[29]

In the first elections of 1983, incumbent members of the brigade leadership nominated themselves to the slate of candidates for the new village council. The only new candidate on the ballot was Hao Mingchao, then in his early thirties, a former "rich peasant" Red Guard who had been to see Mao at one of the mass rallies in Tiananmen Square. He was widely perceived as a replacement for his uncle, former brigade head Hao Yuandeng, who had died earlier that year. This young man was from the senior branch of the Hao descent group in Qiaolou, which consisted of descendants of eldest sons of eldest sons. He assumed the new post of village head (*cunzhang*) after the elections. When production team property was redistributed during the decollectivization of agriculture, this same young man was allocated the former Hao ancestral hall, which had survived the Maoist era as a team meeting and storage hall. Many of his patrilineal uncles, however, were outraged when he subsequently dismantled the hall and sold off its mudbricks and roof tiles for a handsome profit. He was voted out of office at the next elections, in 1986, and the post of village head went to a party member obviously nominated as an intended replacement.[30] With the exceptions of this instance and the replacement of the women's cadre in 1989, there was no real contestation in village elections.[31]

Elected officers of the village council continued to work under the supervision of the party secretary, whose post remained outside the civil electoral reforms. But developments in the 1980s led to reshuffling in the Qiaolou party branch leadership as well. Recall that when Hao Yuanliang succeeded Lin Chengying as brigade secretary, he nominated a nephew [yBS] of Lin, a young affine, as his deputy. When this man later amassed a sizable gambling debt, he was dismissed by Hao from his party post. Hao then nominated his own nephew, the son of his late elder brother Hao Yuandeng, as deputy and heir-apparent. A graduate of the township junior high school, the young Hao Mingwei was then groomed to succeed his uncle. He was extensively involved in interactions with county authorities, served as a manager at both the No. 1 Brick Factory and the distillery, and accompanied older village cadres on business trips as far away as Heilongjiang province in Northeast China.

Hao Yuanliang, who had come to office during the Cultural Revolution, continued to control the administration of Qiaolou. His influence over reshaping the village leadership under the reforms, when state authorities granted more administrative autonomy to local cadres, enabled him to confirm his close allies by popular elections. Together, he and the village council appointed the staff of enterprise management committees (*qiye guanli weiyuanhui*) for each of Qiaolou's collective village enterprises. Although enterprise management staff were responsible for the daily operation of their facilities, production planning and fiscal allocations were coordinated by the village council.

During the 1980s, the authority of Qiaolou village cadres became less dependent on their status as designated agents of the party-state and more firmly based on the powers they exercised as executive officers in the management hierarchy of a village corporation. Qiaolou emerged from the Maoist era as a coherent institutional entity. Its leaders enjoyed an unprecedented degree of administrative autonomy and controlled an independent property base owned by the village as a corporate group. Village cadres tried to cultivate a sense of solidarity underlying their newly defined community. They portrayed themselves as representatives of the corporate village community as an interest group. In practice as well as rhetoric, Qiaolou cadres in the post-Mao era based the legitimacy of their local dominance on their success as managers of the interests of the village collective, and of the interests of Qiaolou villagers, collectively.

Promoting Imagery of Corporate Solidarity

The village enterprise initiative undertaken by Hao Yuanliang achieved widely noted success. It was publicly praised by government officials, and many residents in other parts of the county had heard of Qiaolou even if they were not familiar with details of its industrialization project. Publicly, Qiaolou's managers cultivated an image of prosperity vis-à-vis the corporate village, attributing their achievements to the virtues of rural socialist development and their determination "to keep to the collective path." Their efforts were rewarded politically in the late 1980s, when Qiaolou became a showcase of village enterprise development.[32] It repeatedly received official acclaim from county and provincial authorities as an "advanced civilized village" (*xianjin wenming cun*).[33] Study delegations visited the village and its enterprises, and a PLA filmmaker considered doing a documentary on Qiaolou.

For such visitors, village officials often recited a list of impressive statistics as evidence of their accomplishments. For example, average per capita income in the village more than doubled in the 1980s.[34] More than 90 percent of the homes were converted to fired brick and tile-roofed houses. Nearly all Qiaolou families had their own private wells, most of which were operated by electrical pumps. Many families also constructed biogas pits to harness methane for cooking and lighting. In addition, a wide range of consumer goods became common in most family homes, from bicycles, electrical fans, and washing machines to radio-cassette players, televisions, and even a few VCRs. Funerals and tombstones also became larger and more elaborate in recent years, as did the size and cost of weddings and dowries, although such trends were not part of the litany of achievements touted by village officials.[35]

The corporate village also provided its residents with collective benefits and services. Revenues from village enterprises, for example, were used to finance health, education, and social welfare subsidies. Free basic health care was provided to all villagers through the former brigade "barefoot doctor" (a PLA veteran and former production team leader), who was given a salaried post running a small village pharmacy. Funds were also set aside to cover unanticipated family expenses from emergency hospitalization. Village leaders built a large new primary school with enterprise proceeds and hired several supplemental (*minban*) teachers to assist the regular state-assigned (*guoban*) core faculty. This became the "central primary school" for the entire township, with competitive admissions, but all Qiaolou children were permitted to attend free of charge.[36] Profits from collective village enterprises were also used for infrastructure improvements, such as upgrading irrigation channels and resurfacing village paths and roads, and to support elderly "five guarantee households." The village also had electricity wired to every village home, although individual families paid their own use fees.

Enterprise revenues paid village administrative expenses and cadre salaries as well. This enabled Qiaolou authorities to avoid imposing local levies (*tiliu*), so widely unpopular in rural China, to fund their operating expenses.[37] While Qiaolou families, like those in other Baimapu villages, were assessed similar fees by the township government, proceeds from collective village enterprises were used to pay (or to subsidize partial payment of) such local township taxes. Remarkably, Qiaolou also maintained full compliance with the single child family policy throughout the 1980s, through a combination of incentives and sanctions relating to village enterprise employment.[38] Such accomplishments attracted attention and praise from government and party superiors, on whom these achievements also reflected favorably. Qiaolou's success had been attained at minimal financial cost to the state. It also generated new tax receipts for local state authorities under the fiscal reform system (Oi 1992). This strengthened Secretary Hao's political standing with county officials, both earning Hao favorable cadre performance ratings and helping him sustain his long incumbency.[39]

Many of the visiting delegations that came to tour Qiaolou were fêted in a reception hall on the top floor of the Brigade Building. The southward orientation of the building gave its balconies a commanding view of the No. 2 Brick Factory and its surrounding fields and hills while the walls of the hall itself were adorned with numerous banners and framed awards, among them a "village compact" (*cungui minyue*) drafted in neat handwritten calligraphy and hung in a protective glass frame. Resembling the "big character posters" (*dazibao*) popularized during political campaigns of the Maoist era, this document had been promulgated by the village council in 1990. It contained a list of proclamations about the norms of proper behavior among villagers, their responsibilities and obligations, and regulations concerning public order (see Appendix).

The village compact represented a community creed, or social charter, to which all resident members of the corporate village were expected to adhere. It was similar in many respects to community compacts popularized in model villages during the early 1980s. Concerned that the post-Mao reforms might generate divisive forces in the countryside, political authorities promoted such compacts in an attempt to create "ethical" communities based on a "new moral order" (Anagnost 1992).[40] These credos rephrased social conflict in terms of interpersonal relations rather than class antagonisms and thus helped village cadres redefine the basis of their legitimacy in more populist terms.

Qiaolou cadres frequently spoke of the village as "one big family" (*yi da jiating*). Such an analogy might seem like a superficial euphemism for the complex web of kinship and marital ties that links village families. But the evocation of this kinship idiom suggested the extended family as a metaphor for the corporate village community. The term "big family" (*da jiating*) was the vernacular phrase used to refer to complex extended forms of family organization, such as the large joint family of Hao Caiqin in the 1940s, which were based on corporate shareholding principles. Shareholding also became an important aspect of corporate village organization in post-Mao Qiaolou.

Shareholding in the Corporate Village

The notion of the village as a corporate group was strengthened through the use of shareholding practices. Shareholding, recall, had been a well-established organizational principle of many corporations and popular associations (Sangren 1984; Cohen 1993b).[41] The greater economic and political autonomy ceded to rural areas under the post-Mao reforms enabled Qiaolou cadres to pursue local practices that broadly conformed with politically approved economic strategies, such as the development of new "shareholding cooperatives" officially promoted by national authorities during the 1980s (Selden 1993; see also Yang Minchuan 1994). Yet the significance of shareholding, and the meaning of shareholding rights, were framed by the interaction of local families and the perceptions that developed about village administrative management.

Recall that each family in Qiaolou had been obliged to purchase at least one hundred-*yuan* share when the brigade leadership announced its initiative to establish the first brick factory. Shares had been restricted to Qiaolou families, as resident members of the collective, and to a few well-connected relatives in neighboring brigades. But Qiaolou shareholders were not offered dividends; rather, they were promised employment in collective village enterprise. Shareholding rights thus came to be regarded primarily as labor rights in the corporate village.[42] Although the sale of shares raised over Y30,000 in venture capital for the new brick factory, that single facility alone could not support a labor force with representatives from every shareholding family. Some received jobs at the orchard, while others were obliged to wait until the distillery and the No. 2 Brick Factory opened a few years later and offered more employment opportunities.

As shareholders in the village corporation, each family enjoyed the right to have at least one family member employed in a Qiaolou enterprise. Families also enjoyed succession rights to enterprise employment. They were permitted to substitute one family member for another on enterprise payrolls, but not necessarily at the same job or even at the same enterprise. Of course, some positions were more desirable than others, particularly those that paid well, required less physical labor, or involved office work or even travel. Village enterprise jobs might be divided into three general categories of employment, although levels of income were linked to productivity and profits at specific enterprises.[43]

One occupational cohort essentially entailed physical labor at piece-rate remuneration. Workers in this category were mainly the male clay-diggers at the brick factories, who often worked in terms of two or three, digging soil out of the hills and carting it to the mixing pit and mechanical brick press. This was a job that demanded strength and stamina because workers were paid based on the number of cartloads of clay they could deliver to the mixing pit in a day. Clay-diggers received Y0.10 for each cart they delivered for processing. Digging teams hauled an average of twenty to thirty carts a day, earning roughly Y60–90 a month.[44] Most clay-diggers were men from shareholding families outside the village, although a few Qiaolou men, mainly from poorer and less influential families, were also employed in this capacity. The low social status of such jobs was reflected in the occupational designation of clay-digger (*wa ni*), a self-deprecating local euphemism for farming.

The vast majority of village enterprise laborers earned basic monthly wages based on a modified workpoint system, supplemented by bonuses usually (but not always) paid when their enterprise was running at a profit. Unlike workpoints of the Study Dazhai era, those used in corporate Qiaolou were graded to reward skilled experience and job seniority. Basic wages varied by specific job (with machine operators, for example, earning slightly more than those who stacked bricks for drying, firing, or storage) or by enterprise (with truck drivers earning much more than orchard workers), but remuneration was linked to enterprise productivity and profits. If workers at an enterprise failed to meet their production and marketing quotas, they lost bonus payments and sometimes had their wages withheld entirely.

The third occupational category consisted of enterprise management staff, most of whom worked in offices and generally enjoyed stable incomes.[45] Although their wages were officially (or ostensibly) based on workpoints and enterprise productivity, in practice office staff earned what were, in effect, steady monthly salaries, sometimes upward of Y100. Management staff rarely lost wages or bonuses even when their enterprises were operating at a loss.[46] Moreover, their work environment was far more relaxed and less rigorous than any other. They generally were not penalized, as other workers were, for tardiness or absence. Their work load could be quite heavy at times, and they shouldered the responsibility for enterprise efficiency and labor relations, but many and much of their workdays were spent in relaxed conversation over tea and tobacco. Staff jobs also provided business contacts and practical experience for aspiring entrepreneurs. Irregular privileges such as these made enterprise management posts among the most sought-after in the village.

The executive authority and financial remuneration enjoyed by managerial staff had little to do with their formal shareholding status. Managers, like workers, were equal shareholders in the village corporation. The patterns of dominance that emerged with the development of managerial corporatism in Qiaolou were based on familial ties and personal relationships that dated back to the Maoist era or, in some cases, earlier. Distributing wage labor and social benefits to all village families, the "dividends" of shareholding in the corporate village mitigated against the more extreme polarizations of wealth seen in some parts of rural China since the early 1980s. But the contours of privilege were nevertheless discernable in the staffing of management positions, and perceptions of favoritism led to growing alienation among families that felt more marginalized in the corporate hierarchy.

Managing Elites

The allocation of jobs in Qiaolou enterprises was controlled by Secretary Hao Yuanliang and the village council, and by the enterprise management committees they appointed. Most staff positions and other highly desirable jobs have been held by members of families with well-established ties to the party secretary and the village cadres allied with him. Such relationships have enabled Qiaolou leaders to consolidate their control over collectively owned village assets and to pursue their development agenda. As an administrative tactic, this has encouraged the formation of a local managerial elite with growing status, wealth, and influence both in Qiaolou and beyond.

Consider, for example, that while Hao families comprised roughly 22 percent of the village population in 1990, they were disproportionately represented in positions of enterprise management. Of Qiaolou's enterprise office staff of forty, nineteen (48 percent) were Haos, while another eleven (28 percent) were marital affines of Haos. Of the ten remaining positions, half were held by people with close personal and political ties to Secretary Hao, some of whom had served terms as brigade cadres during the Maoist era (see Table 3). Moreover, nearly all families that employed two or more members in collective village enterprises belonged to this group of close cadres and kin.

The creation of the brigade orchard in 1976 entailed a major commitment of collective assets, and management of that enterprise remained closely controlled by cadre leaders in subsequent years. After the death of Hao Yuandeng in 1983, he was replaced as orchard manager by Qiaolou's new security chief. The dispersed character of the orchard's main assets, namely, thousands of trees, meant that security against pilfering or crop theft was a major concern. This man, married to a Hao woman from a neighboring village, had been brought into the brigade leadership by the Hao brothers during the 1970s, and continued to serve as a member of the elected village council. Most of the other orchard staff also had close ties with Secretary Hao. Both the accountant and the storage supervisor were his close patrilineal relatives, and the treasurer was Liang Jinyuan.

The orchard employed a full-time labor force of twenty-three men and women drawn from families of various surnames in each of the village's former production teams. All were required to have a lower middle school education, but this stipulation apparently did not apply to orchard management staff, many of whom had only a few years of primary school. Wages for orchard workers were relatively low (roughly Y50 a month in 1990, plus annual bonuses of Y60–70 at harvest time), but so, too, were the demands of

TABLE 3

Qiaolou Village Enterprise Management Committees, 1991

Enterprise	Staff position	Relationship to party secretary or other noteworthy status
No. 1 Brick Factory	Factory head	village head; party member
	Assistant factory head (production)	nephew; former village head; party member
	Assistant factory head (finances)	daughter-in-law; party member
	Accountant	affine of early Land Reform activist
	Treasurer	son of former women's cadre, who was the first villager to join CCP
	Storage supervisor	nephew; party member
	Purchasing and sales agent	nephew
No. 2 Brick Factory	Factory head	brother of state cadre
	Assistant factory head (production)	nephew of former women's cadre, who was the first villager to join CCP
	Assistant factory head (finances)	party member
	Accountant	nephew; son of township credit-cooperative director
	Treasurer	nephew
	Storage supervisor	cousin; party member
	Purchasing and sales agent	son of former team leader
	Pharmacist	PLA veteran; former team leader
	Tea water attendant	wife of village head
Orchard	(Former orchard head)	(brother, now deceased)
	Orchard head	security chief; party member; affine of current party secretary
	Assistant orchard head	—
	Accountant	cousin
	Treasurer	PLA Korea veteran; party member; former team leader and brigade security chief; lifelong friend of current party secretary
	Storage supervisor	uncle; former brigade accountant
Transport Team	Director	[Current party secretary]
	Accountant	uncle; former brigade treasurer
	Driver 1	son

TABLE 3

(*continued*)

Enterprise	Staff position	Relationship to party secretary or other noteworthy status
	Driver 2	nephew
	Driver 3	nephew of former party secretary; affine of current party secretary; party member and former deputy party secretary
	Driver 4	son of former women's cadre
	Driver 5	neighbor
Distillery	Distillery head	nephew; party member; current deputy party secretary
	Assistant distillery head (production)	neighbor; party member; affine of current party secretary
	Accountant	cousin
	Storage supervisor	cousin
	Treasurer	cousin; brother of former team leader and military policeman
	Purchasing and sales agent	affine of village accountant, who was longtime ally of current party secretary

such jobs, which most of the year entailed only occasional pruning, fertilizing, or pesticide spraying. However, from the time each year that fruit began to ripen on the trees until the collective harvest was completed, each worker (or one of her or his family members) was expected to live in one of twenty-one crop-watching huts strategically placed throughout the orchard.

Among the most coveted jobs in the village labor force were those of truck drivers. Driving could be arduous and sometimes hazardous. Almost every Qiaolou driver has been involved in a serious accident, although most have escaped with minimal injuries.[47] But such jobs also offered opportunities for profitable independent entrepreneurial activities while away from the village. One of the wealthiest men in Qiaolou was also one of its first drivers, a young man who was the only (adopted) child of Hao Yuanliang.[48] His monthly income, by his own assertion, was well over Y300, a figure that approached the average annual per capita income in Qiaolou at the time.[49] Four of Qiaolou's five drivers were children or close relatives of leading brigade cadres of the Maoist era; the fifth was a young neighbor of the party secretary and a distant relative of the latter's grandmother. The transport team was managed directly by Secretary Hao, whose elderly uncle (a former brigade treasurer) served as its accountant.

In 1990, Qiaolou's brick factories represented the most substantial capital investment for the village and were its largest enterprises. The factory head of the No. 1 Brick was the new village head. Three of the six other staff members were nephews of Secretary Hao, a fourth was his daughter-in-law, and two more were relatives of "old revolutionary" activists of the Land Reform era. The managerial staff of the No. 2 Brick Factory included two nephews of the party secretary, a cousin, a nephew of Qiaolou's first party member, and a former production team leader from the Maoist era. The factory was headed by a close political ally of Secretary Hao, a man whose brother had become a cadre in the county government.[50]

Employment at the distillery was also considered highly desirable, and highly selective. Basic wages for production workers there rose from Y45 a month in 1985 to Y70 a month by 1990, and with supplemental bonuses sometimes reached Y100. There were also numerous fringe benefits to distillery employment, such as hot baths and access to fermented sorghum, which was said to make excellent fertilizer as well as hog feed.[51] All four permanent distillery workers were closely related to the village political elite under Hao Yuanliang.[52] Two were his nephews, another was related to him by marriage, and the fourth was a nephew of Liang Jinyuan. Of its six management staff, four (the factory head, accountant, treasurer, and storage supervisor) were close patrilineal kinsmen of the party secretary. The deputy manager was a young party member with close personal ties to Secretary Hao, who was also his neighbor. The purchasing agent was related by marriage to the village accountant, a political ally of Hao since the early 1960s. The rather privileged character of distillery employment was widely recognized in Qiaolou. Although many young people aspired to jobs there, most believed their hopes were unrealistic. As one brick factory worker put it, "We all would like to transfer our jobs to the distillery, but we cannot. That is run by the Hao family (*Hao jia bande*)."

The "Civilized Village" and Its Discontents

Mobilizing a variety of material, political, social, and symbolic resources, Qiaolou's brigade leaders created a new foundation for the village collective in the post-Mao era. Under the reforms, as Zweig (1997) put it, "power grew out of the barrel of a smokestack." Managing the village-as-enterprise, Secretary Hao and his allies brought substantial material benefits to local families. Their "civilized village" provided them with a new basis of legitimacy at just the time when many rural cadres were being replaced. But corporatization also sharpened some antagonisms, old and new, as many villagers came to feel relatively marginalized from the preferential access to resources enjoyed by a few families. During the 1980s, there were few viable alternatives to farming, so exclusive wage-labor jobs in Qiaolou enterprises were the envy of many in other villages of the township. Yet by the 1990s, rapid commercialization of the local economy had opened new strategies of mobility outside the village corporation. Discontent grew among those who were frustrated with relatively low-paying jobs, or who believed they lacked the social influence and family connections to win promotion to coveted managerial positions.

Qiaolou's managerial elite tried to foster a new sense of community centered on the corporate village. They distributed benefits to family shareholders regardless of former class designations, and their public rhetoric encouraged an imagery of solidarity in contrast to the class struggle of the past. Invoking metaphors of family, village leaders attempted to cultivate a new collective consciousness of the corporate village as a social community as well as a political and economic institution. They styled themselves as elected representatives of their fellow villagers as an interest group and thus promoted an ideology of harmony. As one leading village councilman and long-time brigade party cadre asserted, Qiaolou was "free of contradictions."

Yet patterns of dominance based on control of corporate resources often contribute to the development of relatively rigid social hierarchies in which mobility is restricted (R. Watson 1990). Qiaolou's managerial elite, and Secretary Hao in particular, retained tight control over collective assets in the village, exerting their property rights in decisions about the use and transfer of enterprise assets and the disposition of revenues from enterprise operations.[53] Many villagers expressed dissatisfaction with the closed character of the corporate hierarchy and with what they saw as an imbalanced distribution of benefits. When changing market conditions led to a drop in village revenues and a downsizing of the enterprise labor force, the sense of alienation grew stronger.

When the pie, so to speak, was relatively large and benefits were distributed plentifully, village managers had few critics. But as profits fell and perquisites were disbursed more selectively, the façade of solidarity fell. Disgruntled villagers complained of favoritism and nepotism in hiring practices and management staffing. Popular sentiment grew against what many perceived as unfair privileges being taken by some families of the managerial elite. When I asked an elderly man, whose home was one of several that still prominently displayed portraits of Mao Zedong, what the poster meant to him, he replied: "Under Chairman Mao we commoners were all poor, but at least the cadres were honest. No one dared to engage in corruption."[54] Perhaps most significantly, others had come to see the families of Qiaolou's new managerial elite as a distinct group. "They are like a [political] party," claimed one man from a less affluent village family. "They have their own organization and discipline. Yet they take care of themselves before they take care of others."

Assertions such as this suggest that a new sense of class consciousness was taking form in Qiaolou as some villagers began to see the interests of their families as being in opposition to those of the local elite group of cadres and kin. During the 1980s, as the cash-poor Baimapu market began to recover, even lower-paid wage-labor jobs in Qiaolou enterprises contributed to significant growth in family incomes. Aside from agriculture, villagers had few other avenues of mobility.[55] Local retail trade was controlled largely by *jumin* families in the township settlement, who had privileged access to wholesale suppliers through the former commune Cooperative Store. By the 1990s, however, expanding market opportunities presented disaffected families with new possibilities for a "road out" (*chu lu*), an exit from dependency on—and subordinate status within—the village collective.

Many of those who had come to feel marginalized in the organization and distribution of benefits in corporate Qiaolou, or impatient to make their own fortunes, began to diversify their family economic activities into the marketplace. Street farmers reopened shops in the front rooms of their homes. By the mid-1990s, families from other villages in the township were renting store space and businesses in Baimapu. Some traded consumer goods they would bring in from Meishan or even Chengdu. Others opened small eateries, offering new dishes such as mutton or dog. A few set up garment shops or hairdressing salons. At first, Secretary Hao and his deputies actively attempted to dissuade villagers from independent entrepreneurial ventures in the marketplace. They publicly criticized families whose fields fell into weedy disorder for lack of attention. They also remonstrated against the volatile uncertainty of markets, against the dishonest practices that were prevalent in trade, and against the shirking of moral responsibilities to the village collective. But when Qiaolou's brick factories finally exhausted their clay supplies and were forced to close, many of those who were laid off had little choice but to seek other avenues of mobility and sources of security.

Meanwhile, Hao Yuanliang and his cadres struggled to mobilize new resources to invest in new collective assets and to shift factory operations to new product lines. They promised massive rehirings once the proposed new factories were operational, but for those left scrambling to find new means of support, such reassurances offered little solace. It remains to be seen whether managerial corporatism will be a sustainable enterprise in Qiaolou. Retrenchment strategies have created further schisms in the village collective, schisms that threaten to render the spirit of corporate community illusory. The very social relationships, political alliances, and material incentives that Qiaolou's cadres and kin used to make their village enterprise a success have also led to alienation among other village families. The "civilized village" imposed constraints on its constituency, demanding compliance and discipline from a client labor force. The quest of the discontented for individual autonomy and economic independence may yet lead to new constestations for control over collectively owned village assets, and hence to new patterns of dominance.

Late one night, two elderly grandfathers were philosophizing on life over cups of warm *baijiu*. "Socialist state," one of them mused. "Now that's a fine sounding name."

   "Yeah," his companion nodded heavily. "But do you live upstairs or downstairs?"

Farmers carry polished rice back to their homes after a visit to a grain processing hut in the Baimapu market town settlement. The three-story Qiaolou Brigade Building rises in the background (1991).

Peanuts dry in the sun in front of the homes of Qiaolou "street farmers" along the eastern end of the Baimapu town settlement (1990).

Wa niba ("digging mud"): A Qiaolou farmer turns his family's contracted fields in preparation for planting the fall rice crop (photo by Anastasia Karakasidou, 1991).

Workers at the village orchard in southern Qiaolou measure, crate, and weigh oranges in preparation for shipment (1990).

Qiaolou distillery workers preparing a batch of fermented sorghum for distillation (1990).

Machine operators at the No. 2 Brick Factory load new bricks onto carts bound for the drying grounds. After being mixed, pressed and cut, bricks are sun-dried in preparation for firing (1990).

Some families save on the costs of house construction and renovation by building with mudbricks. After a paddy is drained of excess water, the soil is pressed firm with a cement roller. Lines are then cut to mark the length and width of the blocks, which are then flipped on their side and left to dry in the sun (1991).

Ancestors are commemorated at death anniversaries, festivals, and major life course rituals such as weddings. Here, packets of "spirit money," carefully wrapped in preparation for burning, are addressed to the dead, both male and female (1990).

Above: A bride's dowry being transported to the groom's family home by hired tractor (1991).

Opposite, above: A cabinet, part of a bride's dowry, is carried through the Baimapu settlement en route to the groom's family home. Staff members of the Qiaolou No. 2 Brick Factory watch from their office, on the left (photo by Anastasia Karakasidou, 1991).

Opposite, below: Fall rice harvest. Women cut stalks while men thresh the grain into large wooden tubs. The Qiaolou No. 2 Brick Factory rises in the background (1990).

Rice is prepared for banquet guests on a makeshift stove, fashioned from mudbricks, at a family wedding (1990).

CHAPTER 6

A Topography of the Present

Shaping a Village Landscape in the Late Twentieth Century

Ladies and gentlemen, don't feel let down:
We know this ending makes some people frown.
We had in mind a sort of golden myth
Then found the finish had been tampered with.

—BERTOLT BRECHT, *The Good Person of Szechwan*

When the Sichuan Academy of Social Sciences minivan that took our research team to Qiaolou approached the Baimapu settlement, I mistook the small, single-street rural market town for the village itself. It was not my first trip to Sichuan, nor my initial visit to Meishan, and I was aware of the dispersed residence patterns that characterized many villages on the Chengdu plain. Even to the uninitiated observer, such patterns were discernable from the air, provided one's plane broke through the basin's thick haze and cloud cover before touching down on the runway.

But coming up the road from Meishan, one of my colleagues had directed my attention to the sprawling grounds of the Qiaolou No. 1 Brick Factory. Then, as we drove up into the eastern end of the settlement, the village distillery and the No. 2 Brick were pointed out to me. Painted on a nearby wall, faded white characters a meter high proclaimed, "In Agriculture, Study Dazhai!" A moment later we pulled through the open iron gate of the Qiaolou administrative compound and parked next to the village trucks in front of the Brigade Building. "*Dao le*," my escorts announced. "We're here."

The prominence of these landmarks, situated in such close proximity to the small strip of houses clustered on a gentle hillock, led me to assume that the settlement was Qiaolou village. My misperceptions were reinforced a short time later when I was introduced to several "Qiaolou villagers" living in homes along the settlement street. "No, no," I was embarrassed to hear my hosts finally correct me. "This is Baimapu, the township [seat]." "So, where's Qiaolou village?" I recall asking. They looked at me with what I took to be confusion, and one man said, with a sweep of his hand, "Here." I suddenly feared that I was going to have a hard time with the local dialect.

Fortunately, my nerves soon subsided and I came to understand the conceptual parameters of the village. As the head of our research team explained to me, "In other parts of China there are mostly natural villages (*ziran cun*). Sichuan has many administrative villages (*xingzheng cun*)." Yet as I was slowly to learn, the Qiaolou of the ethnographic present was only the most recent "monoumentalization" of time and place to appear on the local landscape. The "rains" of power have transformed the local topography over the years, eroding some structures while preserving others. Amid the sediments of memory, however, clear sentiments toward the soil remain, even as new monuments have been built upon the landscape, reshaping perceptions of community and difference, power and status.

By historicizing Qiaolou, this study has questioned some of the assumptions implicit in notions of village communities. Although other villages have much longer histories, they, too, are landscapes framed by human agency. Like Qiaolou, their contours of privilege are formed and altered by patterns of exchange and punctuated by watershed events of monumental importance.

Communities of Interest and Emotion

Sichuan, of course, is better known in Western academic literature for communities of a different order. Working in the rural market town of Gaodianzi on the plain just south of Chengdu during the 1940s, G. William Skinner (1964–65) applied the models of central place theory to patterns of exchange, arguing that rural social structure was based on "standard marketing communities." Others, such as Phillip Huang (1985), have countered that in rural North China "natural villages" rather than market towns were the basic unit of social community. Even when North China farmers went to market, they tended to associate with neighbors from their own village. Nevertheless, contemporaneous but independent observations by Treudley (1971) in "Chungho," a market town near Gaodianzi, supported Skinner's assertions about the centrality of periodic markets as organizational foci for social, economic, and ritual activities in rural Sichuan. On the Chengdu plain, and in its outlying hills, there were no village settlements between rural market towns. One might find two, three, or even four houses clustered together in some places, but family homes and farms were generally dispersed throughout the countryside. Yet even in the Pearl River Delta of the Southeast Coast, a region generally noted for its strong, lineage-based village communities, rural residents had their "social and political horizons expanded" on periodic market days (Siu 1989: 15).

Skinner's landscape was framed by the spatial and temporal models of economic geography. His study was rich in detail and broad in scope, but its perspective generally privileged rural periodic market towns as *the* fundamental organizational nexus for interaction and exchange. It looked from rural market towns toward urban centers, situating the standard marketing community at the base of a rural-urban continuum, as the lowest level in a hierarchy of markets stretching all the way to the imperial capital and global trading ports. Even though, as Skinner noted, economic centers did not always correspond to their political counterparts, the importance of this "network" to state elite extraction of rural surplus was evidenced both in Republican-era state strengthening efforts and in Communist management of the people's commune system. Yet like other systems models, Skinner's was a framework that expanded upon itself, subordinating alternative relations of exchange that were organized around forums other than standard market towns.

Prasenjit Duara (1988a), for example, argued that, marketing relations notwithstanding, China's rural-urban continuum was based on a shared "cultural nexus" of meaningful symbols and norms embedded in hierarchical social organizations and informal family ties. For Duara, who drew on observations from North China, community integration was located in mind rather than in space. His study drew attention to the way that local elites operated as cultural brokers, mediating the projection of state authority over (and the extraction of surplus from) rural inhabitants through a variety of popular associations. Duara's perspective highlighted the importance of culture in the legitimation of state power (see also A. Wolf 1974). Temples to Guan Di, Dongyue, and even Guanyin feature prominently in landscapes of his genre. Myron Cohen's work (1990) suggested that ancestral associations, too, provided a forum for the organization of interests and identity in North China, although lineage groups were generally weaker in the north than in regions of the south.

In early-twentieth-century Baimapu, descent group development attained a degree of complexity intermediate between the extremes often represented in ethnographic accounts from north and south China, respectively (but see also Strauch 1983). The presence of local corporate lineages was marked by ancestral halls, cemeteries, written genealogies, collective rituals, and trust properties. But these relatively young descent groups had modest holdings compared to better-established and wealthier "lineage communities" such as those of the Lower Yangzi (Jiangnan) or southeast coastal regions. They apparently did not control local settlement rights as powerful lineages did in areas where land reclamation efforts were more capital- and labor-intensive and more centrally organized. Nevertheless, from a local perspective, the *citang* (ancestral halls) of Baimapu's lineages conveyed an "imposing territorial presence" (Siu 1989: 15) on the landscape, particularly for those families who did not share membership in such organizations.

By and large, ancestral associations (*Qingminghui*) rather than lineages per se had been the principal medium of patrilineal alliance among Baimapu families, and the main focus of agnatic community. Patterns of affiliation resembled the principles of asymmetrical segmentation modeled by Maurice Freedman (1958, 1966) and the "nested hierarchies" of "higher order" organizational dynamics described by Skinner (1964–65), Kuhn (1980), Duara (1988a), and Siu (1989). But the segmentary structure of Chinese lineage organization represents a view from above, a perspective framed by sometimes creative literary sources (Faure 1989). At the local level, patterns of affiliation were constructed through individual family participation in activities of ritual exchange, a process better described by the metaphor of fusion than by that of fission. While rhetorical claims of common identity were expressed in terms of segmentary affiliation (as in the nested hierarchies of *fen, da, zong,* and *dazong* ancestral halls), communities of interest cut across ties of patrilineal kinship (R. Watson 1981, 1985).

The Communist revolution attacked "feudal clan loyalties," expropriating lineage properties and disbanding ancestral associations. Yet many observers have noted a renaissance of lineage organizing in post-Mao China, particularly in coastal regions where residents have ties to overseas emigrés and foreign remittances. Potter and Potter (1990), in fact, have argued that collectivization in single surname villages helped to preserve notions of local lineage identity throughout the Maoist era. Other accounts, however, have suggested that affinal ties and particularistic relationships were often more important than patrilineal solidarity in the social organization of power in single lineage villages (Chan, Madsen, and Unger 1992) as well as "multi-surname" villages (Judd 1994; Yan 1996). Although patrilineal identity was more commonly shaped by participation in ancestral associations than by membership in lineages, agnatic solidarity was a phenomenon of a different order, more limited in scope and more particularistic in its development.

The genealogy of power in Qiaolou suggests that agnatic solidarity among selective patrilineal kin was a critical element in the local political arena throughout the twentieth century, but so, too, were other modes of alliance, such as marriage, ritual kinship, and personal friendship. The particularly close relationships that developed among a core group of cadres and kin during the Maoist years were instrumental in orchestrating Qiaolou's industrializing during the reform era. Village leaders invoked the metaphor of "extended family" (*da jiating*) in their corporate community building efforts. In the early 1990s, the popularly elected village head held a largely ritual position of authority compared to the managerial power exercised by the party secretary. But recall that the man nominated to become the first elected village head of the reform era was a young (former) "rich peasant" from the senior branch family of the Hao descent group. The disproportionately high number of Hao men staffing positions of enterprise management also suggested that some families emerged from the Maoist period with a strong sense of patrilineal solidarity. At the Qingming festival of 1991, Hao graves—both those at the Hao ancestral cemetery and those at the nearby burial site for the descent branch of Hao Caiqin—were generally better tended than others in Qiaolou.

Violence, Bureaucracy, and Authority

Helen Siu's rich ethnography of the Pearl River Delta (1989) has shown that, the presence of strong lineages notwithstanding, property and politics in the early twentieth century were controlled by local elites through their participation in a variety of popular associations, academies, guilds, and temples, as well as their command of rural administrative positions and security forces. Similar patterns of local elite dominance were apparent in Baimapu, although on a smaller scope and scale. Land ownership was only one dimension of social stratification, and not necessarily the most important. Far more significant was the ability of each family to mobilize resources, whether economic, political, social, or symbolic (Esherick and Rankin 1990). Yet violence became increasingly common in local political arenas during the early twentieth century. As institutions of state government were extended into the countryside below the county level, the agents of state authority acquired growing powers to compel compliance among the local population.

The Chinese Communists brought revolution to most areas of China, grafting it onto local roots by mobilizing activists to their cause. Although women played critical roles in early organizational efforts, it was mostly militant young males who rose to positions of power in the revolutionary order (Friedman, Pickowicz, and Selden 1991), men such as Hao Yuanliang and Liang Jinyuan. They continued a process of rural militarization that had begun more than a century earlier, institutionalizing military organization in the production brigades and dining battalions of the people's commune system. The Communist revolution also pushed political violence to new heights, through class struggle, the execution of "tyrants," and the suppression of "counterrevolutionaries." Yet the violence of Land Reform also had cultural dimensions, attacking the symbols as well as the agents of authority from the Old Society in order to clear ground for the construction of new administrative communities. The legacies of a century of sporadic but pervasive violence, coupled with frontierlike market conditions and loosened state control, were also apparent in the 1990s, with the rise of new "sworn brotherhoods" and entrepreneurial cartels whose members are not averse to using threats or violence itself in their commercial activities (see also Blok 1974).

The institutionalization of Communist rule in the 1950s introduced new technologies of power and bureaucratic control. The creation of the administrative village of Qiaolou epitomized many aspects of such change. Its history was one of local family relationships and state bureaucratic regulation, punctuated by periodic militancy and directed violence. Collectivism transformed the character of interfamily relations, severely restricting property rights and linking each family's subsistence security and economic prosperity to broader administrative units of production and consumption. State monopolization of the trade and transport of grain and other key foodstuffs, coupled with the household registration system, was soon followed by the suppression of rural marketing and the curtailment of unauthorized travel under the communes. These administrative actions truncated the social worlds of villagers and disrupted popular channels of interaction and exchange. State authorities gained unprecedented influence over the lives of local residents, but largely through local activists who aligned themselves with the Communists for their own particular reasons. Cadres of the village collective, under both Maoism and the Deng-era reforms, were empowered with new technologies of discipline and compliance (see Foucault 1995).

The social organization of power under Maoist collectivism had a strong clientelistic character. Although villages were no more "isolated" than they were "natural," access to key resources such as grain, credit, cash, job opportunities, and education was tightly restricted through the new administrative agencies of the party-state. Basic-level rural cadres controlled positions that mediated the flow of goods, personnel, and services across the reified boundaries of agricultural collectives. Whereas Oi (1989) saw village cadres of the Maoist era as patrons, I would characterize them as brokers because most of the resources they distributed were controlled, ultimately, by state officials. However, the basis of local cadre power underwent important transformations in the wake of the post-Mao reforms. As Qiaolou cadres developed a new corporate property base under their own control, they became the managers of collectively owned and operated village enterprises, and local patrons in their own right. In this sense, conditions in Qiaolou resembled those generally found in areas with high levels of both industrialization and collectivization.

Although the basis of local cadre power during the Maoist era lay largely in the clientelistic relationships that they brokered between state authorities and village families, cadres were, nonetheless, agents of state authority. Siu (1989) has suggested that the legitimacy of rural cadres was based solely on their affiliations with the Communist party-state. This may well have been the case for those assigned to posts at the subcounty district or commune levels. But more locally textured village studies, such as those by Friedman, Pickowicz, and Selden (1991) or Chan, Madsen, and Unger (1992), have shown that basic-level cadres shared a world of socialization with kin and neighbors.

Qiaolou cadres employed the symbols, rhetoric, and sometimes the coercive force of party-state power. Yet their local authority—or power legitimized—was based more on effective production management and judicious distribution of resources than on distant patrons of power. Indeed, collective villages were the economic foundations of state power. Agricultural procurement fueled urban industrialization. In the eyes of party-state superiors, the legitimacy of local cadres lay in their ability to effect compliance with government directives concerning production, distribution, exchange, consumption, and reproduction. To local kin and neighbors, the legitimacy of cadre managers was based on family subsistence security and economic prosperity. Under the reforms, Qiaolou's cadres rhetorically promoted the notion of village family in their community building efforts—efforts that tended to reduce social experience to a generic collective expression that they controlled and that masked the tensions and antagonisms implicit in village management.

Collectivism, Corporatism, and the Local State

The foundations of the managerial corporatist regime in Qiaolou lay in the organizational initiatives of the collective era. Yet as party-state authorities withdrew from active intervention in economic affairs and devolved greater administrative autonomy to local cadres, a space was created for the construction of a new corporate village community. I have adopted the notion of "corporatism" to characterize the social organization of economy and polity in Qiaolou under the reforms. The term has been used by several other ob-

servers, and often with markedly different meanings. In the case of Qiaolou, however, I would suggest that corporatism, in its various guises, is a particularly useful device with which to explore the implications and legacies of
Maoist collectivism.

Since the early 1980s, Qiaolou village has been organized and managed
much like a business corporation, in a manner not unlike that described by
Oi (1990). Under what others might prefer to term a process of "corporatization" (see Chan 1993: 36n17), the village became, in effect, a diversified
economic enterprise with a distinct identity and considerable independence.
Daily operations and production responsibility at its collectively owned brick
factories, distillery, orchard, transport team, and refinery were managed
with reasonable autonomy, but village administrators practiced cross-asset
subsidization and other common strategies of corporate management. Notions of shareholding were an important component in popular acceptance or
legitimation of such arrangements (Yang Minchuan 1994). Under the new
civil laws adopted in the 1980s, the corporate village as a collective enterprise
could be considered a "legal person" (Gray and Zheng 1986: 723). In a sense,
the village itself might be regarded as a composite enterprise of a higher
order. Managerial strategies pursued by its local elites were rooted in interests and concerns beyond the short-term profitability of particular production lines.

The work of Oi (1992, 1995), Walder (1995), Lin (1995), and others has
shown that some local governments have taken on many of the hallmarks of
business corporations. Fiscal reforms of the post-Mao era imposed stronger
hard-budget constraints over county and subcounty administrative offices
than they had hitherto known. A fiscal responsibility system was introduced
that imposed tax quotas on township and village cadres but permitted them
to retain any surplus revenues collected. The reforms also empowered local
cadres to raise additional levies based on particular needs. In some cases, collective enterprises were leased out, their profits taxed, and the revenues invested in local health, education, or capital construction; in other cases, local government authorities themselves became deeply involved in enterprise management. Where industrialization was carried out under collective
ownership, cadres retained considerable administrative and economic power
and resident workers developed a stronger sense of identity with their locale
(Wang et al. 1995).

Qiaolou's new village cadres were not, technically speaking, officials of
state government. State cadres—such as those in the county and township
governments, the Supply and Marketing Cooperative, the middle school, or
the granary—had salaried ranks, enjoyed retirement benefits, and were often reassigned to posts in different places over the course of their careers.

They "ate state grain" (*chi guojia liang*), whereas village cadres remained among their kin and "ate their own grain" (*chi ziji liang*). Yet local cadres were nonetheless agents of party-state authority and came to form a new status group with its own privileges. While the administrative village became an important foundation of state organization under the collectivist regime, the corporate village that emerged during the reform era was similar to a "local state" whose leaders styled themselves as representatives of the collective interests of villagers.

Other political theorists have approached the notion of corporatism from the perspective of sectoral interest-group representation (e.g., Schmitter 1974; Chirot 1980). The vertical administrative structures imposed by a highly centralized party-state government restricted autonomous horizontal exchange and interaction between collective work units, families, and individuals. Although many attempted to cope by constructing their own alternate, particularistic nexus of *guanxi*, or "personal connections" (Mayfair Yang 1994; Yan 1995, 1996; Kipnis 1997), local cadres dominated most resource channels. Since the advent of the post-Mao reforms and the loosening of centralized controls, state authorities, local collective leaders, and independent entrepreneurs have competed to expand their respective interests. Voluntary associations and government institutions have tried to organize interest-group communities, both from above, by state agencies, and at the grass-roots level, by local representatives (Mayfair Yang 1989; Chan 1993; Pearson 1994).

During the reform era, Qiaolou cadres attempted to restyle themselves as both the technocratic managers of collective enterprise and the democratically elected representatives of village families. They tried to foster a developing popular consciousness of collective village enterprise as a community of mutual interests. They positioned themselves, vis-à-vis both state superiors and local families, as effective representatives of the interests of village "peasants." The creation of the new administrative category of villager (*cunmin*) to replace that of commune member (*sheyuan*) coincided with the consolidation of the village corporate community. Village cadres promoted a civil morality and downplayed (old and new) class tensions through the "village compact" (*cungui minyue*) they drafted. Yet their own particular interests were embedded in the managerial regime they controlled, and it was they who defined the interests of the village collective.

Finally, the social organization of village economy and polity—particularly the management of collective property rights, the use of shareholding practices, and the employment of symbolic imagery in Qiaolou—bore hallmarks of corporate groups and corporate power as studied by political anthropologists (e.g., Fortes and Evans-Pritchard 1940; M. G. Smith 1975;

Peters 1990). In the intellectual traditions of Maine, Durkheim, and Weber, corporate groups have often been characterized by ideological and organizational aspects, including identifiable boundaries, charters of origin, internal organization and regulatory procedures, institutional permanency beyond the lifetime of individual members, exclusively defined common affairs, coordinated autonomous action, and a sense of collective identity. Historically, corporate organization has been adapted in a wide variety of forms in China (e.g., J. Watson 1975b; Sangren 1984; Cohen 1993b). Evoking the idiom of family to characterize their corporate community, Qiaolou cadres attempted to legitimize their managerial power over village "kin."

Cadres and Kin

Over the past half century, the effects of power under collectivism have become etched onto the local landscape, transforming the physical and social topography of Qiaolou. Mao's vision of a New China promoted among the population new identities and organized new communities of exchange. The government policies, organizational initiatives, and administrative practices of the Maoist era rechanneled the flow of goods and people, transforming the landscape in the process. Villages were created, roads widened, paddies consolidated, railways constructed, and towns expanded. Irrigation channels were excavated, flood levees raised, and reservoirs built. Hillsides were terraced, deforested, and sometimes leveled completely. Shrines were demolished, temples torn down, ancestral graves disinterred, and new built forms erected. Like symbols of state power and monuments of collective authority, many administrative buildings rose above the landscape: the Supply and Marketing Cooperative, the township offices, the junior middle school, the brigade building. Fifty years ago, the tallest structure in Baimapu township was the two-story Bridge Building along the Meishan road. Today, the tallest structures are the chimneys of Qiaolou's factories, the new symbols of territorial village identity, representing the land that village families have traded for jobs (*tudigong*).

Reimagined communities of various sorts are being formed by local elites throughout China, and by state elites at the national level. As Jing Jun (1996) has shown in his study of the Kongs of Gansu province, memories of trauma experienced under mobilizational collectivism have provided an important organizational focus for emerging communities of interest and emotion. The cooperativization movement of the early 1950s was generally received with enthusiasm, but collectivization caused growing disillusionment among peasantized farmers. During the Great Leap Forward, party-state authorities initiated a highly idealistic political campaign that attempted to transform popular cosmologies of the relationship between humans and nature. Attacking notions of symbiosis, they promoted a militant confrontationalism that depicted nature as an obstacle to overcome. This extreme expression of collectivist effort resulted in a national tragedy that took the lives of an estimated twenty million people, or more. In Qiaolou, almost every family lost a member to starvation or famine-related illness. The trauma of this experience had a profound influence on the shaping of popular consciousness. For many, it came to symbolize the illusory promises of the new Communist society; for others, it was evidence that their interests were ultimately subordinate to—or expendable for the sake of—those of "the state."

Throughout the collective era, "peasants" and urban "residents" inhabited largely separate administrative spheres and markedly different social worlds, rarely intermarrying. Urban-registered Baimapu townspeople enjoyed government-issued rations for food and other key commodities, disposable cash incomes, retirement pensions, access to a range of consumer goods, and employment opportunities in other towns or at different jobs in the commune settlement. The recurtailment of marketing and the suppression of individual family entrepreneurial activities heightened the segregation imposed on farmers, restricted as they were to their cash-poor agricultural collectives. Unlike their town neighbors, who enjoyed monthly salaries and staple rations, "peasants" received remuneration for their labor only once a year—and then largely in grain—and hence were obliged to budget their consumption and expenditures for the next twelve months. In Wenwu, they even had to obtain authorization from brigade cadres before visiting the Baimapu commune town.

The state procurement system contributed to the marginalization of China's "peasants" in the cash economy. Beginning in the early 1950s, all rice, maize, sweet potatoes, cotton, peanuts, sorghum, soya, and other beans (and later wheat) had to be delivered to the Baimapu Supply and Marketing Cooperative. Farmers were obliged to accept relatively low prices that enabled state authorities to subsidize the allocation or resale of foodstuffs to urban-registered consumers. Yet the costs of fertilizer, pesticide, and other agricultural inputs distributed by government agencies remained relatively high. Through such "price scissors," the state government attempted to subsidize the costs of urban industrial development and to maintain stability in densely populated cities.

A quarter century of Maoist collectivism created deep schisms between China's rural and urban populations. Despite perceived inequalities in corporate Qiaolou and discontent over the privileges enjoyed by an elite few, most villagers directed their frustrations at the economic discrimination and social prejudice they endured as "peasants" at the hands of their urban counterparts. Recommercialization of the economy has presented opportunities for mobility beyond the village collective. But as families have diversified into entrepreneurial activities in the marketplace, a growing consciousness has developed of the apparently contradictory interests of rural farmers and urban business proprietors, as well as an awareness of state officials' bias toward the latter.

When two young, enterprising state cadres assigned to the Baimapu township government contracted use of an empty storage house along Baimapu Street in 1991, they opened a Youth Activity Center with pool tables, a VCR, and karaoke tapes. At first, they permitted local residents free use the equipment, and the center quickly became a favorite gathering place for young and old alike. Most were from farming families, young and old men with time on their hands. Sometimes groups of young unmarried women would come and socialize. After a week, however, the managers began to charge fees. One afternoon there was a loud altercation between the two young *jumin* cadres and an old farmer who scoffed at the idea of paying admission to watch a videotape with a roomful of young people. The tape was stopped, the lights turned on, and they forcibly led the old man out the door by his arm. He was indignant over their disrespect. "I have eaten a lifetime of bitterness," he shouted at them. "How dare you try to pull money out of me? This is our land!"

His sentiments reflected the view, expressed by more than a few village residents, that much had been taken from them but little returned. In the teashops of Baimapu on market days, many often voiced their discontent with a system of institutionalized inequality that regulated "peasants" to second-class status. Reflecting on the student demonstrations of 1989, another farmer found little sympathy for the protestors. "What did they have to complain about? They are *jumin*. They live in cities. They have jobs. They eat the state's grain. We can do without them, but they cannot do without us. We peasants are the pillars of the state."

Reference Matter

Qiaolou Village Compact

(Cungui Minyue)

In order to carry out the spirit of the Fourth and Fifth Plenary Sessions of the Thirteenth Party Congress; in order to take further steps to support reform, to develop the collective economy, to administer economic areas, to rectify the economic order, and to maintain proper public order, stability, and unity; in order to promote the development of Qiaolou's commodity production and the laudatory growth of agricultural production; and in order to enable Qiaolou to construct a material and spiritual civilization that will make the unification of this village a reality, we hereby promulgate Qiaolou's village compact.

I.   In accordance with Marxism-Leninism, Mao Zedong Thought, and the spirit of the Fourth and Fifth Plenary Sessions of the Thirteenth Party Congress, all villagers must adhere resolutely to the Four Basic Principles and use the party's line, principles, and policies as a guide for administering this village. In order to foster a sense of the nation within the village and to give consideration to the interests of the state, the collective, and the individual, public duties must be carried out with responsibility. Villagers must conscientiously study, understand, and implement the law, meet their tax obligations and grain quotas, and strive to love their country, their collective, and their native place.

II. Developing the campaign of the Five Emphases, Four Beauties, and Three Loves, promoting the study of Lei Feng, and establishing a "new wind" are all good things for the masses. Villagers must be practical, must create a spirit of serving the people, must prevent occurrence of bad things, and must refrain from arguing and fighting or hitting or cursing people. They must be civilized in production tasks, must be mutually courteous and polite, and must unite together for mutual aid. They must undertake to make more than 80 percent of the village Households that Follow Discipline and Adhere to the Law, to make 25 percent Households of the Five Goods, and to make 5 percent Households of Material and Spiritual Civilization.

III. In order to implement birth planning, to respond to the state's call, and to control population growth, each couple must have only one child.

    A. Nine months after the birth of a first child, all newlywed women of reproductive age must be fitted with an IUD and adopt other [birth control] measures. If these measures prove ineffective, an abortion will be required. The village will cover expenses for the first operation, but women will be responsible for covering medical costs of any subsequent abortions.

    B. Women of reproductive age must undergo a physical examination every four months, according to schedule. Those who miss an examination will have Y15 deducted from their single child subsidy.

    C. If any team has more than two unplanned pregnancies, in addition to the fines that will be imposed according to birth planning regulations, no member of that team will receive bonuses or dividends in the village's annual redistribution.

IV. Lovingly protect the collective property of village enterprises and public property of the state. All villagers must lovingly protect the machinery and electrical production equipment of the two brick factories, as well as the trees and fruit of the orchard. It is forbidden to damage trees or to pilfer fruit, or to graze water buffalo [in the orchard], or to cut grass [for animal fodder]. Villagers in every group must carefully maintain their winter water fields and ponds, and work with the team to coordinate pumping water for irrigation or for animal use. It is forbidden to drain winter water fields into dry fields or to plant crops in them. The irrigation of fields each spring will be carried out according to the arrangements of each team. After fields are flooded, water must be turned off immediately. Violators will be fined.

V. Respect discipline, adhere to the law, and promote self-respect. Prosperity lies in industriousness. Resolutely oppose wasteful extravagance. It is forbidden to marry before reaching legal age. It is forbidden to gamble or to promote gambling. Eradicate all ill winds and do not neglect agricultural production.

VI. All villagers must alter their customs and change their habits. Be hardworking and save on expenditures. Struggle hard to be clean, tidy, and sanitary, to renounce superstitions, to promote thrift, and to use science and scientific technology as a guide to agricultural production.

VII. All villagers must conscientiously implement the Land Law and Forest Law. It is forbidden to construct houses, build graves, dig fish ponds, or otherwise damage or occupy arable land without permission. All must help develop the forests. Trees are to be cut only after obtaining permission. Do not recklessly cut down trees.

VIII. Create a secure social order that links public safety with governance. Resolutely eliminate the Six Evils, protect unity and stability, and change the thinking of government to educate the people. Stress prevention first, and intervene only when necessary. Resolutely drive out all bad people and criminal elements, and protect the state as well as the property and lives of the people.

IX. All villagers must respect elders and love children. Show filial respect to old people. Brothers and sisters must get on harmoniously. Neighbors must unite in friendship. Earnestly provide care and support for the elderly, and education for children.

X. All villagers must evaluate the quality of their political thought and culture, and must carry out production in a planned and secure manner, in accordance with a material and spiritual civilization. Create a sanitary environment, and rectify the appearance and looks of the village. Make Qiaolou into a new socialist village.

All residents of every village group must actively uphold the implementation of the above regulations, [not only] those pertaining to birth planning. Any violators will be criticized and educated. In serious circumstances, subject to investigation, those found responsible [for violations] will also be subject to fines [ranging from] Y10–Y300.

Promulgated by the Qiaolou Villager Committee
February 7, 1990

Notes

1. Since the early 1600s, there had been growing unrest and destructive fighting in Sichuan. A large uprising associated with the millenarian White Lotus religious sect embroiled seven counties and prefectures in Sichuan from 1565 to 1621. In 1637, armies loyal to rebel Li Zicheng moved through the province before he eventually captured Beijing and toppled the Ming dynasty in 1644.

2. Although Zhang himself was killed in battle in 1646, much of the destruction wrought in Sichuan during the next few decades is often attributed to him and his infamous "Kill! Kill! Kill!" order. In Baimapu, as elsewhere in Sichuan, popular narratives of ancestral origins often invoke the name and imagery of Zhang Xiangzhong (see Endicott 1988; Sun, Jiang, and Chen 1989).

3. With the devastation of the early seventeenth century, the population of Sichuan fell precipitously, by one count from over 3 million in 1578 to less than 100,000 in 1663 (Li Shiping 1987: 152). In the 1660s, the total area of tax-paying land in Sichuan, China's largest province, amounted to only 1.1 million *mu*, roughly equivalent to that in an average county in the lower Yangzi region (Ho 1959; Entenmann 1980). Yet a decade after the suppression of Zhang Xianzhong's forces, the "San Fan" rebellion brought renewed

fighting to Sichuan, where general pacification under the Qing was achieved only in the 1680s. By 1685, the twenty-fourth year of Kangxi's reign, the registered population of the entire province was less than 90,000 (Sun, Jiang, and Chen 1989: 237).

4. A variety of material incentives were officially offered to migrants, including free oxen (or water buffalo) and seed grain, as well as a five-year tax exemption on all land newly brought under cultivation. Acting on a memorial presented to him by the governor of Sichuan, the Yongzheng emperor later instituted land grants for settlers. Each (male) head of family was to be given title to 15 *mu* of paddy (*tian*) or 25 *mu* of unirrigated land (*di*) for each able-bodied member of his family. Supplemental allotments were issued for children and elderly family members. Tax exemptions were rolled back to three years on new paddy and five years on dry land. Each settler was also to be granted 12 taels (ounces) of silver for the purchase of draft animals, seed, or feed grain (Entenmann 1980: 42). By 1724, the second year of Yongzheng's reign, the population of Sichuan had grown to almost 2.5 million and more than 200,000 *mu* of land were once again on government tax registers.

5. Such an account should not be taken as a literal history of ancestral origins. Not only is it doubtful that Zhang Xianzhong brought the Haos to Sichuan, but many Sichuanese claim their ancestors came from Macheng county (M. Zelin, personal communication), which is in Hubei—not Hunan—province. Even the anecdote about "freeing a hand" was common throughout Sichuan (Sun, Jiang, and Chen 1989).

6. Like many earlier civilian militia, these group and drill (*tuanlian*) units were funded, managed, and in some cases commanded by prominent local leaders. But they were intended to be more centrally organized than their predecessors, and more firmly accountable to official state authorities.

7. For eight months in 1861, a combined force of 190,000 soldiers under Li Yonghe and Lan Chaoding fought with some 240,000 regular and militia troops commanded by the Qing imperial army. Casualties in this "Li-Lan Uprising" were put at over 100,000 (Wan 1988: 141–46; see also MSG 1992: 388–89). Whether new settlers in Baimapu were drawn to the area for reasons related to the uprising remains unclear, although the events were apparently closely linked in time.

8. In the summer of 1911, with agitation against Manchu rule growing in many parts of China, civilian militia in Sichuan, led by local elites and supporters of the provincial "Railway Protection Movement," attacked imperial offices in many parts of the province. In Meishan, militia forces a thousand strong, some coming from market towns in the western hills near Baimapu, stormed the prefectural magistrate's office (*yamen*) and temporarily seized power, forcing Qing garrison troops to withdraw from the area (MSG 1992: 389).

9. Sheridan (1975: 88) noted that one source counted 400 wars, large and small, fought in Sichuan during the Republican era (1911–49). Much of the

civilian population lived in fear of violence from the military, with those most vulnerable living in areas where no single commander emerged as dominant (Lary 1984).

10. In 1926, Chiang Kai-shek led an expeditionary force under the banner of the KMT northward from Guangzhou (Canton) in a campaign to subjugate or neutralize regional warlords in eastern China. The first stage of this "Northern Expedition" concluded with the capture of Nanjing, the former Ming capital, where a new national government was established. The Northern Expedition largely bypassed Sichuan, however, where KMT influence remained weak until the relocation of the national capital to Chongqing ten years later.

11. Kapp (1973: 70–71) argued that the nominal character of national government control in Sichuan was evidenced in the relatively little information on the province published in KMT annual statistical reports, yearbooks, and almanacs. He maintained that although revenue collected through land taxes and other miscellaneous levies in Sichuan was equivalent to roughly one-third of the total annual revenues of the KMT in Nanjing, few of these funds reached national government coffers.

12. In 1928, a year after KMT authorities opened their first offices in Meishan, Communist organizers led an agrarian uprising in the northwestern hills of the county (MSG 1992: 9). After its suppression, activists moved their base to Simeng, in southern Meishan (ibid., pp. 389–90), leading another unsuccessful uprising there in 1934 (p. 10). The following year, Meishan was designated the seat of a newly established Special Administrative Inspectorate Region covering ten counties (p. 37), partly in response to growing Communist activity.

13. Huang Qichang (1993: 17) claimed that a branch of the eighty-first generation of the Hao clan (*shi*) came to Meishan, although he did not date the migration.

14. By the time of the Song dynasty (960–1279), farmers on the Chengdu plain were producing double and even triple crops of rice, making the region one of China's key grain areas. The fertility of the plain has been attributed to the ingenious water control system built in the third century at Dujiangyan, on the northern edge of the plain where the Min River emerges from the Min Mountain range. As early as the fourth century, the Sichuan basin had become known as Heaven's Storehouse (Tian Fu Zhi Guo; P. Smith 1991). During the Song, new irrigation channels extended the water control system as far south as Meishan (P. Smith 1988: 24–29).

15. Leshan, to the south, had long served as a major transit point for traffic on the Minjiang, as well as the principal staging site for pilgrimages to Mt. Emei (3,099 m), one of China's sacred peaks, which stood to its west. Downriver from Leshan, the Minjiang was navigable by deeper draft boats, including steamships, coming up from Yibin (Suifu) and Chongqing on the Yangzi. Northbound cargo and passengers were transferred to shallow-draft

sailing barges at Leshan for transport farther upriver, such as to Chengdu, via Meishan.

16. At Danling, the footpath joined other routes leading to the county towns of Pujiang and Hongya, in adjacent river valleys to the north and south, respectively. In Hongya, it joined a larger road that ran up to Ya'an, a commercial center in the mountains near the Tibetan frontier.

17. Highbaugh (1948) described a popular children's game in rural Sichuan, called "hunting the house." While out in the fields with parents or babysitters, children learned to read the local landscape by identifying from a distance which family homes were hidden within particular bamboo stands.

18. Hao Daixiu's son, Hao Tianyan, married and fathered three sons of his own. According to the inscription on his widow's tombstone, she died in 1920 at the age of sixty. If husband and wife were roughly the same age, then Hao Tianyan was born in Meishan sometime around 1860. This would suggest that he and his father arrived in the Baimapu area after the uprising of 1861.

19. Although such ideals were commonly shared by many Chinese, few families actually grew to such size. In fact, achieving "five generations under a single roof" was so rare that such families were officially recognized for their accomplishment in the 1923 Meishan county gazetteer (MSG 1967). Locally, families that attained even four generations under a single roof (*si-dai tongtang*) held popularly recognized status in Baimapu.

20. Friedman, Pickowicz, and Selden (1991: xviii) also noted the way local inhabitants read status into structures such as family doorways.

21. On or near each stove was a placard representing the stove god (*zao-shen*), who mediated each family's relationship to the spiritual Underworld. In popular religion, once a year, at the Lunar New Year spring festival, the stove god reported on the family to the Jade Emperor, ruler of the cosmos. As the holidays approached, families often placed special offerings, especially sweets, before the stove god in hopes of influencing the report.

22. In some cases, the construction of separate stoves (or separate use of a single stove) preceded formal family division. An adult son and daughter-in-law, for example, might begin to shop, cook, and eat separately from the rest of the family even before the division of family property was finalized. Division often entailed protracted negotiations, usually mediated by relatives (often a matrilateral uncle [MB]) and finalized in written contracts detailing the equitable redistribution of assets as well as liabilities, from furniture, tools, and land to animals, credit, and debts.

23. Individual ancestral tablets were reportedly not used in the Baimapu area. The ancestral scrolls used in Baimapu also differed from those described in North China (cf. Cohen 1990), on which the names of individual ancestors were written, and which were often rolled up and stored for safekeeping until needed for formal rituals. Those in Baimapu bore only the family

surname, with no other individualizing markers, and remained mounted on the wall all year long.

24. Some evidence suggests that ancestral halls in the Baimapu area may originally have been the homes of early settlers that were subsequently set aside by descendants as corporate property of their local ancestral associations. Ancestral associations without corporately owned ancestral halls convened their banquets and meetings at the family homes of elders.

25. Different assertions were made about the origin of these wooden columns. Some claimed they had come from the mountains to the west, in Wansheng, Danling, or even Ya'an. Others insisted they had been brought from Leshan. A third view was that they had originated in neighboring Renshou county, where the main ancestral hall (*da citang*) of the Wens was located. A man named Wen Zhonglu was said to have come from there and resettled in Baimapu around the middle of the nineteenth century.

26. None of the ancestral halls in the area had individual tablets for specific ancestors, but only single tablets, about a meter high. The ancestral tablets in the Hao and Xi halls were fashioned of wood; that of the Wens was made of stone. Inscribed on each were the generational names (*paihang*) of their respective patrilines, but not the names of individual ancestors.

27. Wealthier families erected tombstones in the front of grave mounds. Tombstones were an important source of genealogical information, particularly in the absence of other written records. Their inscriptions usually included the surname of the deceased, her or his family status (e.g., "venerable grandmother"), date of death, age at death, and the names of surviving relatives who had contributed to the costs of the monument. In most cases, these were family members whose kinship ties to the deceased were within the five grades of mourning (*wufu*), and who were therefore most vulnerable to the symbolic polluting influences of death (see Baker 1979: 107–13; A. Wolf 1970). In addition to such details, one of the oldest tombstones in the area, that of woman Deng, the daughter-in-law of founding Hao ancestor Hao Daixiu, was engraved with the generational names of the Hao lineage branch to which her husband Hao Tianyan and his descendants belonged.

28. For studies of *fengshui* beliefs and practices, see Feutchtwang (1974), Freedman (1979a), R. Watson (1988), and Bruun (1996).

29. Graves sometimes also marked the genealogical ties of particular families within large patrilineal descent groups. The cemeteries of the Hao, Wen, Xi, and Yan lineages, for example, had been organized in gridlike fashion, graphically representing collateral branches. That is to say, graves belonging to men in the same generation (i.e., brothers or cousins) were placed in a rough horizontal line, while those of their ancestors and descendants were located to the rear and front, respectively (see also Cohen 1990).

30. As in other parts of South China where banyan trees grew, many earth god shrines were placed in front of such trees, which sometimes grew

to encompass the shrines within their trunks. In Meishan such trees were often regarded with a sacred deference due to their embodying (as it were) a local earth god and its spiritual powers. This may explain the claims of Graham (1928), who wrote of animistic religious beliefs in tree spirits among the Chinese in Sichuan. Yet even without earth gods inside their trunks, banyan trees of great age and wide, sprawling branches were popularly viewed as symbols of community longevity. Many residents believed that cutting down such trees would lead to calamity.

31. Occasionally, organized and sometimes competitive community cults developed around earth god shrines (Ahern 1973).

32. The centrality of rural periodic markets as a primary organizational focus of social and economic activity in Sichuan was accentuated by the predominantly dispersed residential pattern in the countryside (cf. Skinner 1964–65; P. Huang 1985).

33. An itinerant seed peddler, for example, might have attended the Meishan markets on the 16th day of the lunar month, then traveled to Baimapu for the local market there the following day, and then on to Dongguan (Fudong) on the 18th before arriving in Wansheng on the eve of the 20th (see Map 2). Afterward, steps might be retraced, enabling a trader to conclude transactions started on the trip out as he or she traveled back through Fudong on the 21st, Baimapu on the 23rd, and perhaps Hanjiachang (Shangyi) on the 24th before returning to Meishan for a day's rest and then venturing into the countryside again on a new cycle.

34. Marketing activities were influenced by a variety of concerns, including the type and quality of goods or service one was looking to buy or sell, weight of load, travel distance and terrain, time availability, safety and security, *as well as* the location of friends, kin, or affines one might visit during the excursion. Inhabitants of the Baimapu area regularly frequented the markets in Hanjiachang [Shangyi] (1–4–7), Dongguan [Fudong] (1–5–8), and Wansheng (3–7–10), where many had marital affines. Despite its proximity, few regularly marketed at Xianger (2–4–6–8), finding it more sensible to walk a few additional *li* down to the markets in Meishan, where the variety and quality of goods and services was much greater. The relatively infrequent marketing exchange between residents of Baimapu and Liang Jinyuan's native Dongguachang [Xiuwen] (2–4–6–8), where trade flowed to Meishan town via Simeng rather than to Xianger, was marked by subtle differences in vernacular dialect (see Hao 1985).

35. In eastern China during the Song dynasty (960–1276), the God of the Eastern Peak was a particularly popular deity among merchants, perhaps because he was not associated with specific localities or descent groups (Hansen 1990: 115). The Dongyue temple in Beijing was once one of the city's most important and popular temples (Goodrich 1964).

36. Both Hansen (1990: 181) and Goodrich (1991: 358) traced the development of the Dongyue cult, which placed the judgment halls of Hell under

Taishan, to the period following the Han dynasty (206 B.C.E.–220 C.E.). Like many popular religious deities that enjoyed large numbers of followers, the God of the Eastern Peak was promoted to the status of emperor (*Dadi*) during the Song dynasty (Hansen 1990: 82n4). He came to be regarded as the supreme deity presiding over the Underworld, to whom all city gods and their subordinate, local earth gods answered (ibid., pp. 128–29n2). Goodrich (1991) noted that, despite the common association with Taishan, the God of the Eastern Peak should not be confused with the God of Taishan (Taishan Wang), who ruled the seventh court of Hell.

37. Chinese kinship terminology distinguishes between *tang* ("within the hall," or patrilineal) cousins and *biao* cousins (the children of one's father's sister [FZ] or one's matrilateral kin [MBC, MZC]).

38. There were several temples in the countryside surrounding Baimapu, including a Jingju temple reportedly dating to the Ming dynasty (MSG 1992: 52). The largest of these temples, dedicated to Guanyin, the Buddhist goddess of mercy, was located a kilometer or two south of the market settlement. There was also a Qingfutang, or vegetarian hall (*zhaitang*), just northeast of Baimapu, although the Dongyue procession did not call there (see Chapter 2).

39. The archway in Baimapu was torn down after the Communists came to power in 1949, and no one with whom I spoke could remember to whom it had been dedicated or when it had been constructed. One man, son of a former "landlord," claimed that one of his ancestors had earned an imperial examination degree, but I found no such record among the lists of degree-holders published in county gazetteers.

40. The Martial Temple (Wu Miao), a central architectural icon in cities and large towns throughout China, was associated with the patron deity Guan Di.

41. This transcendence of local territorial communities was a characteristic shared by many patron deities, from the God of the Eastern Peak (Hansen 1990: 113) to Mazu (Sangren 1987).

42. Kuhn (1980: 212) noted that, by the Republican era, *tuanlian* ("group and drill") militia groups in some parts of Sichuan had come to operate as "omnibus" units responsible for tax collection, local policing, and militia conscription. In Meishan, subcounty districts opened new administrative offices for civil affairs, finance, education, construction, and security in an attempt to assert greater bureaucratic control over militia forces. Militia commands in rural market towns were renamed *zibao* ("named ward") units and were staffed by a director, security chief, secretary, household-registration clerk, and errand runners (MSG 1992: 39, 208).

43. Paramount among these Sichuan "warlords" were such men as Deng Xihou, Liu Chunhou, Liu Wenhui, Liu Xiang, Tian Songyao, and Yang Sen.

44. Liu Wenhui was one of Sichuan's wealthiest landowners and controlled his own personal army. After the Communist revolution, his family mansion near Chengdu was converted into a museum, complete with plas-

ter sculptures of oppressed farmers and implements of torture allegedly used on debtors and prisoners.

45. In 1924, Sichuan had twenty-six supplementary taxes on salt alone (Sheridan 1975: 90).

46. There existed, in fact, not only "opium prohibition fees" but also the so-called lazy tax (*lankuan*) levied on farmers who refused to cultivate the profitable poppy when ordered to do so by local authorities. In some areas of the province, new surcharges attached to the land tax exceeded revenues generated by grain cultivation, offering a strong incentive for local farmers to engage in cash-crop production of poppy during the winter months (Bramall 1989: 16). For an account of the widespread use of opium across social classes in Sichuan, see Franck (1925).

47. Kapp (1973: 45) asserted that leaders of local militia units in Republican-era Sichuan "commonly extorted funds for themselves" as they collected taxes and other levies. He also noted that they frequently "collected their own revenues, erected their own customs barriers on trade routes, and inflicted their penalties on delinquent taxpayers or their leaders' enemies. 'Militia lords' (*tuanfa*) engaged heavily in rural usury and in opium trading" (ibid., p. 52).

48. Under the Qing, land had been registered and taxed according to its type and quality (MSG 1923: 55). During the Republican era, however, land-owning families were assessed a flat tax of 30 catties (1 *dou*) per *mu*, a rate roughly equivalent to one-tenth of the rent most landowners charged tenants (see Chapter 2). After relocating to Sichuan, the KMT government launched an ambitious land-registration campaign (Bramall 1989: 13). By some estimates, as much as 50 percent of cultivated land in the province was unregistered in the late 1930s (Grunde 1976). As Bramall noted, this new land-registration campaign was largely voluntary; in Meishan, it was actively resisted by local elites (Jin 1977: 4, 127).

49. Among the levies collected by the Meishan county government (not including separate surcharges imposed by subcounty authorities) were taxes on alcohol, banqueting and entertainment, commercial goods, deeds and contracts, enterprises, firewood, houses, inheritance, ivory, licensing, livestock, oil, pawning of goods, ritual ceremonies, sugar, and tea, as well as a stamp tax, a postal tax, a tax on dry land (as opposed to those on paddy), a wartime consumer tax, and various sorts of income and profit (both personal and business) taxes (MSG 1992: 734–37). There were also surcharges imposed on market transactions, property leasing and sale, the sale of meat, public announcements and advertising, and even a "fee for paying taxes" (MSG 1923: 55–59).

50. In Meishan county, officially registered recruits and conscripts into military service totaled 25,438 men from 1937 through 1949 (MSG 1992: 377), or roughly 13 percent of the adult male population. Many conscripts, however, were unregistered. According to a Canadian missionary working as

a secret Office of Strategic Services (OSS) operative in the countryside near Leshan during the 1940s, heavy KMT conscription practices contributed to growing popular support for the Communists (Endicott 1980: 185).

51. I owe this observation to Myron Cohen.

52. To store revenue from tax levies and other extractive measures, authorities in Baimapu maintained what many referred to as a "warlord granary" (*junfa liangku*) next to the township offices at the Guan Ye temple. By all accounts, however, the granary was rarely full. Most revenues were alleged to have gone into the pockets of township officials or to have been distributed by them to allies, clients, and underlings. For most of the 1930s, cash from the granary was loaned out selectively to borrowers at what were said to have been exorbitant rates of interest. By the 1940s, however, soaring inflation had destabilized the currency, and the cash holdings of the granary were converted into unhusked rice.

53. Elderly residents of Baimapu recalled that four men, whom they referred to as "great local tyrants" (*da tuhao*), had dominated affairs in Meishan county during the 1940s, dividing the rural hinterland into four spheres of influence. All four had owned large landed estates, some consisting of more than 1,000 *mu* of prime paddy, and they had controlled militia forces personally loyal to them.

54. Devised in the eleventh century and employed intermittently over the next 900 years during periods of civil unrest, the *baojia* system in its extreme applications could compel mutual surveillance among neighbors through collective responsibility for crimes and offenses. The system had been officially revived by the Qing during the mid-nineteenth century, largely in response to growing unrest and rebellion (Kuhn 1980: 143; MSG 1992: 39), and remained in place in many areas throughout the Republican era. In Meishan, it was officially designated as the basis for subtownship administration in 1935 (MSG 1992: 10).

55. Note that the administrative households (*hu*) that constituted each *jia* unit within the *bao* did not necessarily conform with residential households or with family units. Over time, a family would eventually partition into independent economic units, and sons or brothers might build new houses of their own. Yet until *baojia* records were updated with family partition information, several de facto family households might be subjected collectively to conscription, taxation, and policing as a single administrative household.

56. Kapp (1973: 112) claimed that *jia* leaders were popularly elected from among the household heads in the unit. Elderly residents in Baimapu, however, insisted that *jia* headmen were never elected but rather appointed directly by *bao* leaders (see also MSG 1992: 208).

57. One elderly and now retired local cadre likened the power of the *bao* representative to that of the village Communist Party secretary.

58. Not all *jia* leaders, however, were necessarily men of wealth. Some,

it was said, were small landowners selected because of their reputations as capable farmers who enjoyed influence with neighbors. Many of the elderly in Qiaolou impressed upon me that *jia* leaders were generally "good people" and "ordinary people" who tried to mitigate the sometimes harsh policies they were directed to enforce.

59. With the Communist revolution, the appellation *"dizhu"* acquired new and markedly negative connotations, when it was used by Land Reform activists in reference to an exploitative landlord class (see Chapter 3). In its earlier usage, however, *dizhu* was a respected mark of distinction ascribed to families that took a leading role in local social affairs. Wealthy families that made major contributions to the building or repair of temples, for example, had the honorific "local notable" (*dizhu*) inscribed beside their names on memorial stelae. Not all local notables in Baimapu possessed large landholdings, although most owned some land and many did operate as rentiers.

60. Military strongmen in Meishan county commonly seized possession of and sold off the grain stores of land owned by officials (*guan*), the public (*gong*), enterprises (*ying*), temples (*miao*), and guilds (*huiguan*). Because grain from educational lands (*xuetian*) was exempt from requisition, many influential landowners attempted to protect their holdings by transferring registration to that category (Jin 1977: 4, 184n2). As school head, Hao Yuntai would have been manager of educational land registered to the Baimapu school.

CHAPTER 2

1. Some residents of Baimapu maintained that Hao Caiqin further enlarged these rental holdings by leasing additional plots from a wealthy landowner and militia lieutenant from Second Bao who reportedly went off to join the forces of Yang Sen, a prominent Sichuan "warlord" of the 1920s.

2. Recall that local conscription policies required that families with three or four sons send at least one for military duty, while those with five or more were obliged to send at least two. Hao Caiqin's family had five sons and eleven grandsons.

3. I am uncertain whether Hao Caiqin actually rented land from Hao Yuntai (who other elderly farmers claimed did lease his land to a Hao family), or whether "we" was used here in a generic sense.

4. Following Cohen (1970), "families" (*jia*) are defined here as members of a group related by notions of descent, marriage, or adoption, sharing a common budget, and with rights and obligations both to one another and to corporately owned assets or property. Members of a family may live together in a single (family) residential household, be dispersed in different households (e.g., Hao Caiqin's family), or board elsewhere as laborers, soldiers, or students. Households, in contrast, may contain boarders, hired laborers, or servants who have no latent rights to the property of the family that maintains the residential group. Households exclude family members

residing elsewhere but include members of more than one economically in-dependent family who share a single residence. Note that the administrative households (*hu*) used in official Chinese records were defined by authorities in different ways—sometimes in ways that approximated families as defined here, and other times in ways that attempted to undermine such family units (see Judd 1994).

5. As corporate groups, patrilineal families held assets as family prop-erty (*jiachan*). The authority of the family head, as public representative of the group in official matters, was symbolized by his seal (*yinzhang*). Because seals were required on all legal documents, such as loans, leases, deeds, and tax receipts, they were instruments of authority possession of which was sometimes an object of contention. Seals or "chops" are an important sym-bol of authority in China, crafted of various materials and sizes. In Baimapu, families sometimes tried to convey a sense of status through their seals. Those wealthy enough to afford it had family seals cut from various types and grades of stone, while the poor possessed simple wooden seals.

6. As socially recognized heirs, sons and brothers had rights to an equal share (*fen*) of the patrilineal family estate headed by their fathers, although they generally could not claim control over that share until they married and established their own conjugal branch (*fang*) of the family. Most women could expect some form of dowry at marriage, but this was neither an en-titlement nor a form of pre-mortem inheritance (McCreery 1976; Shiga 1978; R. Watson 1984; Ocko 1991). The very poor were sometimes married with no dowry at all. Despite customary guidelines, patrilineal families had discretion over the content, size, and value of a daughter's dowry, which was almost always of lesser value than any brothers' shares of family property. Moreover, dowry became conjugal branch property (*fangchan*) of the couple rather than a bride's own.

7. Whereas brothers and male cousins within a descent group shared a common generational name (*hang*), sisters and female cousins usually did not. Girls were generally given generic names, such as Suzhen ("Plain Trea-sure") or Shufang ("Gentle Fragrance") that were commonly used through-out the Baimapu area.

8. Margery Wolf (1972) described these informal yet pervasive mother-child groups within each patrilineal family (*jia*) as "uterine families" and suggested that patrilineal family development, management, and division were fundamentally influenced by women competing to create their own maternally based communities of interest, exclusive of their husbands and daughters-in-law or sisters-in-law. Critics have asserted, among other things, that there is no Chinese term for the concept, pointing to Wolf's own caveat that the uterine group had "no ideology, no formal structure, and no public existence" (ibid., p. 37). Yet in the Baimapu area, and elsewhere in Sichuan, the term "*niangniangmu*" was widely used to refer to a mother-child unit, a conceptual group that excluded a husband/father and daughters-

in-law. Note, however, that no one with whom I spoke, including some urban intellectuals, knew how to write this colloquial term.

9. Historically, Chinese women have had few formal property rights, especially since the Song dynasty. Women in 1940s Baimapu did not customarily inherit family property, despite new national laws introduced in the early 1930s that both gave daughters inheritance rights equal to those of sons and guaranteed a widow's right to maintenance (R. Watson 1984: 2; Lang 1946: 115–19). Several empirical studies have shown that these laws were rarely observed in rural areas (Fei and Chang 1949; C. K. Yang 1959; Cohen 1976).

10. Husbands had no formal claim to their wives' "private room money" (M. Wolf 1975; Cohen 1976; Gallin and Gallin 1982; Gallin 1984; R. Watson 1984; Stockard 1989), although this did not deter them from trying to assess its value or gain control over it. Despite the claims of some men that such *sifangqian* was conjugal branch property (*fangchan*) owned jointly by husband and wife, all women—and most men—insisted that it was a bride's personal property, and that it remained so even after a couple formally divided out from the husband's patrilineal family and established themselves as economically independent (cf. Cohen 1976: 176). Thus private room money was distinguished from valuables publicly displayed among the bride's dowry, and also from monetary gifts (*baikeqian*) presented to both the bride *and* groom as they knelt and bowed to elderly relatives at wedding feasts. Private room money might best be regarded as the property of "uterine" groups headed by mothers (M. Wolf 1975: 135; cf. Cohen 1976: 186n3). It was frequently asserted that a woman's autonomy, influence, and long-term security as a wife was predicated on her ability to retain control of her private room money.

11. Both "labor exchange" (*tiaogong*) and "help" (*bangmang*) were based on notions of delayed reciprocity and were commonly used during peak periods of the agricultural cycle and when constructing a new house (see Cohen 1976). The more formalistic labor exchange often involved a detailed accounting of parity over time, and was most frequently employed between close patrilineal relatives. The more informal arrangements of help rarely entailed such meticulous tracking, being based more loosely on affective sentiments (*ganqing*) between families—usually marital affines, matrilateral relatives, close friends, and dry kin (*ganqin*).

12. "Dry kinship" was a popular means by which families or individuals who shared close affective relations could formally institutionalize those ties. In a simple ritual involving the presentation of a bowl of uncooked rice (*shengmi*), a pair of chopsticks, and a small monetary gift (*hongbao*), a male or female sponsor "gave a name" to the child of a close friend, often (but not necessarily) a name modeled on the generational names (*paihang*) of the sponsor's patrilineal descent group. The symbolic bond ritually established

between the two families was renewed each year through reciprocal presentations of small gifts during banquets at festive occasions, such as the Lunar New Year. Repeated failure to offer or accept such gifts effectively terminated "dry kin" relationships. One poor farmer included a wealthy neighbor among his dry kin as the "dry father" (*gandie*) of his son, but acknowledged that his former friend no longer recognized the tie since he had made his fortune.

13. There has been considerable debate among scholars about the extent of tenancy in early-twentieth-century China and general economic conditions in the countryside, with analytical categories, sampling techniques, econometric modeling, and conclusions all falling under dispute. This study is too limited in scope to address those debates, although conditions in Sichuan were apparently worse than in other parts of China. For an overview, see Esherick (1981); see also Stross (1984), Faure (1985), P. Huang (1985, 1990), Shepherd (1988), and Brandt and Sands (1992). Reworking data collected by Buck (1964), Arrigo (1986: 280) estimated that in Sichuan the largest farms were six times the size of average holdings in the province, and that 10 percent of families held almost 40 percent of the land.

14. In the 1940s, little more than 50 *mu* (10 percent) of cultivated land in Second Bao belonged to the corporate trust estates of ancestral associations, temples, or other institutional owners. Note that these calculations are provisional; more precise estimates await the availability of government archives.

15. By the 1930s, nearly one-third of farm families nationwide reportedly owned no land, and more than 40 percent of all land was rented out (Eastman 1988: 75).

16. Elderly farmers claimed that in the 1940s a single *mu* of paddy might yield anywhere from 270 to 340 catties (*jin*) of unhusked rice a year, depending on the quality of land and the availability of labor, fertilizer, water, and other resources. Barnett (1963: 112–13) noted that rent contracts in the 1940s Chongqing countryside generally split the harvest 50:50, 60:40, or 70:30, although "in areas not far away, some [tenants got] as little as 20 percent." Near Chongqing, land was measured and rented on the basis of potential yield rather than area, with what was viewed as 1 *dan* (300 catties) of rented paddy being roughly equivalent to 1 *mu* in area (Barnett 1963; Crook n.d.). In the Baimapu area, some leases also stipulated rents of 1 *dan* of unhusked rice per *mu* of paddy.

17. Many petty-merchant families in Baimapu also owned land (often 10 *mu* or less) in the countryside, which they maintained as a source of economic security and collateral. For such part-time farmers, agriculture was secondary to commerce. The annual returns on commercial investments were often two or three times those in agriculture, and moneylending was twice as profitable still (Eastman 1988: 76). But during periods of peak labor

demand, many small shopowners closed up their stores, left their homes under the watchful eye of an elder, and joined other family members at work in the fields. Those short of labor, or who could not afford to leave their businesses unattended, hired short-term farm laborers for a few days.

18. Often glossed as "sideline occupations," subsidiary enterprises (*fuye*) were rarely marginal to a family economy. On the contrary, they were directly subordinate to and supportive of a family's principal source of livelihood and often meant the difference between prosperity and a more marginal existence. In more commercialized regions, nonagricultural activities were often a major part of farm family income. Hog rearing, chicken raising, spinning and weaving, and foraging for animal dung and firewood were among the most important nonagricultural economic activities for both area farmers and merchants in the 1940s.

19. Based on county-level government statistics published in 1917, one source calculated the average size of farm holdings in Sichuan at 9.2 *mu* (see Tawney 1966; cf. Brown and Li 1927, 1928). Crook (n.d.) put the size of a "medium" or "viable" farm in 1930s Sichuan at 11 to 20 *mu*, but did not specify family size. In one of the most comprehensive agricultural surveys conducted in 1940s Sichuan, Buck (1980) maintained that family-owned and -operated farms averaged 17 *mu* in area. Buck's studies have been criticized, however, for biased sampling toward larger farms in more commercialized core areas (see Esherick 1981; Arrigo 1986).

20. A study of land transfers in early 1940s (lowland) Meishan found that three-quarters of all purchases were made by merchants and the rest by "large landlords" (*da dizhu*) owning 200 *mu* or more. Three-quarters of land sales were made by "landlords" (*dizhu*), most of whom reportedly had difficulties extracting rents from tenants, often their own patrilineal kin. The remaining 25 percent of land was sold by "middle self-cultivators" (*zhongping zigeng*). An overwhelming majority of land transfers involved middle- and lower-grade paddy, whereas sale of upper-grade paddy was extremely rare (Li Yuzhang 1945: 421).

21. The status distinction between the landless and those families that owned even a single *mu* or less was evident in the fact that the latter could, under certain circumstances, serve as guarantors for others or even mortgage their property, whereas the landless were dependent on the patronage of others. For details on contractual practices in late imperial China, see Myers and Chang Chen (1976, 1978).

22. In the 1940s, rent deposits—like taxes, rents, loan payments, and even some market purchases—were made in unhusked rice. Deposits were usually the equivalent of one year's rent.

23. For more detailed studies of how so-called affect (*ganqing*), human feelings (*renqing*), and personal connections (*guanxi*) work in China, see Fried (1953), Mayfair Yang (1994), Yan (1996), and Kipnis (1997).

24. Buck (1980) calculated that although rent in Sichuan claimed, on av-

erage, about 70 percent of a tenant family's rice crop, this amounted to less than one-third of most tenant family income. He concluded that tenant farms were generally more profitable than those run by owner-cultivators, principally because they were usually larger in size, averaging 25 *mu* compared to a 17-*mu* average for owner-operated farms. Note, however, that the tenant farms in his sample were much larger than most of those in the Baimapu area, which were rarely more than 10 *mu*. Moreover, the importance of rice as a chief medium of exchange in the mid- and late 1940s suggests that the burdens of tenants were greater than Buck's study indicated.

25. One elderly woman claimed to have been a slave (*nuli*) in the household of a wealthy rentier family. Although her chores were similar to those of domestic servant girls (*yatou*), she had been frequently reminded that her servitude would last a lifetime.

26. For detailed studies on the relative importance of affinal and matrilateral relationships, see Gallin (1960), R. Watson (1981), Judd (1989), R. Watson and Ebrey (1991), and Gates (1996).

27. Quite often, matchmakers were common relatives of the families involved, usually matrilateral kin who were themselves related to both parties by marriage. Some, however, were (semi)professionals paid in cash or grain. Most matchmakers were women with a wide range of social contacts, not only within the local marketing community but also in other market settlements and rural townships.

28. The "new room" (*xinfang*) set aside for a groom and his bride symbolized the new conjugal branch unit (*fang*) their marriage created within his patrilineal family (*jia*).

29. Residents of Baimapu, like many Sichuanese, were sensitive to a person's height. It was commonly joked that a person 1.70 to 1.75 meters tall (5'7"–5'9") was considered a "half cripple," while anyone of less height was a "full cripple" who would face difficulty in finding an attractive spouse. Height measurements were meticulously recorded in the 1990 village household registry. Although I occasionally encountered (indeed, had been forewarned of) erroneous entries concerning names, dates and places of birth, or relationship to household head (one man, for example, was recorded as his mother's husband), each person's height statistic was generally regarded as accurate. Some people were said to have asked to examine their personal entry in the registry to ensure they were not short measured.

30. As mentioned in n. 6 above, this endowment of the couple was considered their conjugal property. In contrast to bridewealth payments, which became patrilineal family property (*jiachan*) controlled by the bride's natal family, a bride's dowry (*peijia*) was not merged with the property of her husband's father's family, nor was it included in negotiations over family division; rather, it went intact to the conjugal branch (*fang*) that divided out to become an independent family (*jia*). With this transition, a couple's conjugal property became the family property of their new *jia*.

31. Betrothal negotiations defined the value of the bridewealth and dowry exchanged. Poor families sometimes used incoming bridewealth payments to subsidize the costs of a daughter's dowry, but such practices could lead to a loss of "face." Gates (1996: 137) characterized "prerevolution" marriages in Chengdu as predominantly large dowry / small bridewealth, with betrothal gifts from the groom's family often given in the form of immediate consumables (e.g., pork, candy) that were not easily convertible to capital. In the Baimapu countryside, south of Chengdu, dowries also tended to be of greater value than bridewealth payments. Nevertheless, among farmers in particular, bridewealth payments could be substantial and were usually made in grain. This suggests that Gates's characterization of the Sichuan economy as a "tributary mode of production" may have less general validity than she presumed.

32. In some instances, local residents had difficulty recalling the amount of bridewealth or dowry that they (or others) had given or received. Yet almost all of them could remember how many tables had been hosted by their families and their spouses' families, and even at wedding banquets they had attended as guests.

33. Of the forty-seven first marriages (i.e., excluding widow remarriage) in the first half of the twentieth century for which I was able to obtain information, 36 percent (N = 17) of brides had been married by the age of fourteen *or earlier*, nearly half (N = 23) by age sixteen, and 64 percent (N = 30) by age seventeen. While *"simpua"* marriages in Taiwan (see M. Wolf 1972; A. Wolf and Huang 1980) involved girls of a much younger age, many elderly men and women in Baimapu considered any bride who moved in with her future husband's family before the onset of menarche to be a "little daughter-in-law."

34. Some families tried to mitigate the relatively low status associated with such early, dowry-less marriages by hosting a small feast or by sending an adopted-out daughter to her new home with a small trousseau, but this was rare. Most "little daughters-in-law" were escorted to their new homes by the matchmaker, without fanfare and usually on foot. One woman, however, recalled that her natal family had borrowed money to hire a sedan chair for her, in the hope of maintaining "face" (*mianzi*).

35. Such assertions of closeness between child brides and their mothers-in-law, however, belied the harsh treatment suffered by many "little daughters-in-law" (M. Wolf 1972). Elsewhere in Sichuan, Highbaugh (1948) noted that physical abuse of young daughters-in-law was so common in the countryside that it rarely provoked social commentary unless it caused grievous bodily harm or jeopardized the young woman's fertility. In Baimapu, the story was told of a woman who so mistreated her little daughter-in-law throughout the latter's adolescence that the girl ran away before bearing children. Other women ridiculed the mother-in-law for "wasting grain."

36. In some parts of China, uxorilocal grooms were viewed as having abandoned their own ancestors for another patriline (see A. Wolf and Huang 1980). In the Baimapu area, uxorilocally married men generally gave their own surnames to their children. The low status popularly accorded to such unions stemmed from the fact that such couples rarely divided out from the wife's natal family. A uxorilocal conjugal branch was expected to remain economically subordinate to the patrilineal *jia* of the wife's father. Yet, in at least one case, tensions between a uxorilocal son-in-law and his wife's parents became so acute that the latter acquiesced to family partition, despite normative conventions.

37. Substantial gifts of grain were sometimes offered to the family of a potential uxorilocal groom. In a few instances, landless laborers on particularly good terms with their employers accepted the patronage of the latter in arranging marriages for them. Such weddings were simple and austere, with only a small celebratory meal attended by members of the patron family. One young man from Second Bao who worked as a year-round hired laborer so impressed his employer with his diligence and enterprise that the landowner, who had no sons, eventually married him to one of his daughters in a uxorilocal arrangement.

38. These descendants of Hao Caiqin maintained that the 5.2 *mu* that he had received in his natal family's division was land located in an adjacent *bao*, and that he had moved there with his wife to farm it. Although his relocation left him physically distant from the neighbors of his youth, it also provided his family members with important new social ties that offered sanctuary when his adversaries in Second Bao began to pursue them.

39. Of the twelve polygynous marriages I have been able to reconstruct through family oral histories, three involved Hao men. Two Jin, two Wen, and two Yan men also married polygynously, as did one Lin, one Tian, and one Xi man.

40. Xi Yuhua's status rose further in 1938, when she bore her second husband a son of his own. Afterward, she apparently came to supplant his primary wife as a family manager. After the death of Xi's second husband, the widowed co-wives divided the family and set up separate stoves for their respective uterine groups, although they continued to live in the same household compound. When the daughter of the primary wife married out in 1959, during the Great Leap Forward (see Chapter 4), her mother went along with her. The two women starved to death within a year.

41. The two grandsons were first cousins and had once been members of the same large joint family. Although the remarriage took place after Hao Caiqin's joint family had divided, it nevertheless reflected the strong sense of agnatic solidarity that persisted among those particular patrilineal kin. Considering that, in local kinship parlance, patrilineal cousins referred to each other as "brothers" and "sisters," such a marriage might be regarded

as a classificatory levirate, a marriage practice found in societies with strong unilineal descent groups. Several Haos recalled that there had been much talk among themselves of preserving unity (*baochi tuanjie*) through the remarriage. Others described it as simply a convenient solution to a common problem.

42. An unmarried son, regardless of age, was generally considered a jural minor, and his share remained part of his father's patrilineal family property.

43. Family division explicitly redefined the obligations that partitioning sons would have to their parents in the future. In most cases, parents continued to reside with at least one son, who received an extra share to cover their expenses. Sometimes, a rotational scheme was devised among brothers for feeding and lodging parents. In other cases each parent became the dependent of a different son (see Hsieh 1985).

44. One share of rent each was given to the new families of the two eldest sons. The remaining three shares were held collectively by Hao Caiming's retrenched extended family in the name of his three younger sons.

45. Voluntary rotating credit societies were common throughout China (e.g., Fei 1939; Gamble 1963; Freedman 1979b). Women sometimes managed their own private room money (*sifangqian*) as investment funds to form their own grain associations (Martin Yang 1945; Cohen 1976; R. Watson 1984).

46. For example, the initial recipient in a one-*dan* association typically received 10 *dan* and repaid 10.9 *dan* over the next nine years (at 1.1 *dan* a year), whereas the last family to claim the draw received 10.9 *dan*, having invested only 10 *dan*. In this way a family could borrow as much as 10 *dan* (3,000 catties) of grain and repay it in annual installments at a maximum of 9 percent interest.

47. Ancestral associations in Baimapu convened collective gatherings at the Lunar New Year, at Qingming, and again in late summer or early fall, reportedly during the Ghost Festival (Gui Jie or Yulanpen Jie). Of the three occasions, the activities and ceremonies surrounding Qingming were the most elaborate and best attended. For more on the Grave Sweeping festival and *Qingminghui*, see Hu Hsien-chin (1985), Gamble (1963), P. Huang (1985), Ebrey (1986), Hazelton (1986), Duara (1988a), and Cohen (1990); see also Teiser (1988).

48. Following Ebrey and J. Watson (1986), I distinguish here between *descent groups* (self-conscious groups of patrilineal kin linked by descent from a common ancestor) and *lineages* (descent groups with an institutional economic base in corporately held assets). In Baimapu, small, more loosely organized ancestral associations were formed by local descent groups, but most lacked the ritual elaboration, organizational sophistication, property holdings, and strong collective identity often attributed to lineages. Yet the *Qingminghui* of both local descent groups and local lineages were often linked to

similar but higher-order ancestral associations spanning broader geographic areas and sometimes owning hundreds of *mu* (MSG 1992: 999).

49. Although commemorative ancestral rituals focused on and were performed by men, women were also present at such gatherings. Those who had married into a descent group and mothered heirs for the patriline were welcomed guests. Unmarried daughters of association families also attended, for they shared their father's patrilineal affiliations and would one day provide association members with new affinal connections. Yet neither married daughters nor adopted-out sons were permitted at these celebrations. Daughters-in-law who had not given birth to a son were not formally barred from the *Qingminghui* celebrations of their husbands, but they were neither expected nor encouraged to attend.

50. The Wens, for example, with the grandest hall and largest estate of the ancestral associations in the township, reportedly seated more than twenty tables (over 160 people), while the Haos hosted twelve to fifteen tables (96 to 120 people), and the Xis, six to eight tables.

51. Building on a model of lineage as family writ large, Cohen argued that rotational leadership in *Qingminghui* symbolized the equal status of each branch (*fang*) segment in a corporate descent group. He suggested that this recognition of branch equality over genealogical rank (of eldest son lines) was instrumental in fostering sentiments of collective identity and agnatic solidarity (Cohen 1990: 522, 524).

52. The only exception I found to universal membership in ancestral associations involved a Yan family that had converted to Christianity in the early twentieth century. The husband had been an itinerant chicken peddler who married a Catholic woman from Meishan. Before that, they had attended *Qingminghui* celebrations in a township to the west, suggesting that they were more recent settlers in Baimapu. After becoming Christians they no longer made the trip (some alleged that they were no longer welcomed). Their contact and cooperative exchange with patrilineal Yan kin declined, in both ritual and practical contexts. Their two eldest sons left home and were not heard from again; another volunteered for the KMT army. Remaining family members fell under the suspicion of new Communist authorities in the 1950s, and one was executed (see Chapter 3).

53. Such patterns among ancestral associations are suggestive of asymmetrical segmentation in theories of lineage development, as modeled by Freedman (1958, 1966) and many others. But in practice, these associations were formed "from the bottom up," so to speak. Individual families made their own choices about whether or not to participate in broader, more overarching patrilineal ancestral associations, and did so to whatever extent they deemed appropriate. Although patrilineal descent ideology depicted the development of descent groups in terms of branch segmentation from common roots, ancestral associations were created through "fusion" rather than "fis-

sion" (see also Siu 1993; Faure 1989). Yet unlike many areas of the south-eastern coastal region, settlement rights in the Baimapu area were not dependent on descent group affiliation.

54. Although elderly Hao men claimed affiliation with a grand ancestral hall (*dazong citang*) in Leshan, none could recall any of his local kin having attended rites or banquets there.

55. Control of the local Hao ancestral hall remained with the descendants of Hao Binghui, the first Hao ancestor to be born in the Baimapu area. With decollectivization in the early 1980s, the Hao ancestral hall was similarly allotted to a family in the senior branch of the descent group (see Chapter 5).

56. The origins of the Dongyue temple association in Baimapu remain obscure. I found no mention of the temple in available historical documents on Meishan. Local residents claimed that the Dongyue temple had once owned a substantial corporate estate of paddy, but they could not recall how large these holdings had been nor how or when they had been acquired or endowed.

57. Before pleading their arguments, parties to a dispute knelt in front of the temple's gate-guard, a statue with bulging eyes, crossed fingers, protruding tongue, and raised foot similar to the chief of devils (*lingguan*) that stood as protector before many Sichuan temple doors (Wood 1937). There they swore an oath calling for lightning to strike them down if they gave false testimony.

58. Selection of contestants was a matter of great interest in the days leading up to the procession. Inside the temple, at the base of each statue, was a wooden title plaque (see Hansen 1990: 82n3, 162). Young Wen and Xi men who aspired to compete would often try to steal the name plaque of their deity or attempt to bribe the temple watchman into hiding it until the day of the procession. Whoever held the plaques that morning had the right to compete as a carrier.

59. The new Meishan Gazetteer (MSG 1992) identified the temple in Baimapu's present Jingju village as a protected cultural relic dating to the Ming dynasty but did not mention the Guanyin temple in present-day Yangtang village. This may well be due to county party authorities' reluctance to grant status or recognition to the strong women's community at the Guanyin temple that reemerged in the 1980s. The Guanyin temple association was disbanded at Land Reform, and most of its original architectural structure was destroyed during the Cultural Revolution. In the 1980s, local efforts began to rebuild the temple, and its women's association, to its former glory and prestige.

60. Oral traditions of Guanyin temple devotees claimed that, in the early twentieth century, a number of male monks from Jianyang county were sent in succession to assume management of the temple, but each refused to stay. The first, a "Master Wang," allegedly felt that the temple was too decrepit (*tai polan*), while the second, "Master Li," left soon after his bedding was

stolen. The third, "Master Ren," arrived in the early 1940s and remained a few years. A fourth monk, "Master Mao," was sent to succeed him but reportedly left before even unpacking his bags when he saw that temple residents were so poor that they were eating sweet potatoes.

61. Although the 1923 Meishan county gazetteer (MSG 1967) identified the school as a government-run (or state-sponsored) facility, several former pupils, including Liang Jinyuan, insisted that it had been privately operated by the women attendants at the Guanyin temple itself.

62. As an unmarried virgin, Guanyin was a deity associated at times with the Eternal Mother, the supreme being in some "heterodox" sectarian ideologies such as the White Lotus (Sangren 1983, 1987; see also Topley 1963; Naquin 1985).

63. Qingfutang and vegetarian halls have been described in southeastern China and Singapore (Greenway 1987; Sankar 1978; Stockard 1989; Topley 1958, 1978), although these institutions generally have been associated largely with women and the commercial silk industry.

64. Thirty *mu* consisted of rice paddy; the other ten *mu* was dry land (*di*) on which vegetables were cultivated. Some members were said to have donated land to the association when they joined; others reportedly bequeathed property upon their deaths, although this would contradict customary practices (and provisions of the Qing legal code) concerning the rights of succession.

65. The Qingfutang hosted ritual banquets on Buddhist holidays as well. Participation in these vegetarian feasts was open to members and nonmembers alike, the only stipulation being that visitors were asked to donate one catty (*jin*) of rice, some cooking oil, and a small monetary gift.

66. The dead members of the Qingfutang thus made the transition to the status of ancestors, as the idiom of ritual kinship provided them with "descendants" (*houdai*). In this way, it was said, there was no impropriety, and the spirits of the dead would not haunt the countryside as hungry ghosts.

67. Dressing one's own hair was a practice followed by the *zishunu* sisterhoods of the Canton delta, for it usurped the elaborate hairdressing ceremony that was common in marriage rituals (Stockard 1989; Topley 1978). Notions of purity are often associated with vegetarian practices, and the second character in the term *chi su* ("to eat vegetarian") refers to things that are plain, simple, native, or elemental.

68. Several amateur local historians in Meishan claimed that militant White Lotus sects had once been active in the county, although I found no such references in available archival documents. During my stay in Baimapu, local authorities discouraged my inquiries on the Qingfutang, which was also one of few topics many local residents were themselves reluctant to discuss.

69. For more on the heterodoxy of female goddesses, see Weller (1987: 50), Topley (1963), and Sangren (1987).

70. See, for example, Chesneaux (1971, 1972) and Hu Hansheng (1988); see also Liu Cheng-yun (1985).

71. See Crook (n.d.), Kapp (1973: 55), Endicott (1988), Hu Hansheng (1988: 123–95), and MSG (1992: 1000–1001).

72. Skinner (1964–65: 37) claimed that although the Gowned Brothers "wielded supreme power at all levels of society," the name "Gelaohui" (Elder Brothers' Society) was actually applied collectively to a number of "secret societies" of similar organizational structure. Some were composed of more enlightened landowning and mercantile elites associated with a "clear water" (*qingshui*) faction that promoted community welfare services. Others, labeled a "muddied water" (*hunshui*) faction, engaged in self-aggrandizing and often illicit activities such as extortion, kidnapping, opium dealing, and running gambling dens and brothels.

73. By the late Qing, the Gowned Brothers' presence had been noted in more than twenty market towns across Meishan county. At the peak of their activities, the Gowned Brothers had at least 323 local lodges throughout Meishan, totaling some 70,000 members, or nearly 20 percent of the county population (MSG 1992: 1001). In 1911, they organized an armed force in support of the provincial "Railway Protection Movement" and its failed uprising against Qing rule. In late 1949, members of some lodges fought against the People's Liberation Army in the battle for Meishan.

74. The Gowned Brothers were organized into a number of ranked grades, from a single top leader, referred to by the honorific "grandfather" (*daye*), down to numerous "little younger cousins" (*xiao laoyao*). As one elderly man put it, "Everything [the *daye*] ate and wore had been given to him by his subordinates." Other members were said to have been ranked based largely on the size of the annual contributions they made to the association at Lunar New Year festivities.

75. Crook (n.d.) maintained that, in the Chongqing countryside, the Gowned Brothers (Pao Ge) formed an alternative power structure to the formal organs of local government. But in Baimapu, Pao Ge leaders wielded power from within the official township bureaucracy. Several prominent Republican-era county officials in Meishan, including the director of the Meishan KMT party bureau and the head of the county public-security apparatus, were alleged to have had close ties with the Gowned Brothers.

76. Such a combination of effigies would have been unusual because official Guan Di temples and urban Martial Temples (Wu Miao) rarely featured the mortals Liu Bei or Zhang Fei, who, unlike Guan Yu, had not been deified after death. Note, however, that local residents in Baimapu spoke of the "Guan Ye" rather than "Guan Di" temple, suggesting that the hall may have been built without official state recognition. No reference to it appeared in county gazetteers (MSG 1967, 1992). I have been unable to date its construction, but its location close to the end of Baimapu and east of the memo-

rial archway (many of which were built at the entrances of settlements), suggested relatively recent origins.

CHAPTER 3

1. In 1937, the Meishan section of the stone-slab footpath that connected the county seat with Danling and Hongya to the west was widened and converted to a dirt road large enough to support motor vehicle traffic. This was one of several projects in the region during the War of Resistance against Japan, when thousands of laborers were pressed into service for the construction of airfields and roads (MSG 1992: 11). These efforts brought American military engineers to the region, including two camera-toting GIs who, elderly Baimapu residents recalled, came on a sight-seeing visit to the local market carried in open sedan chairs.

2. Several "underground" groups of Communist organizers had been active in the county since the mid-1920s, some working out of the Meishan Teachers' School while others mobilized farmers in townships in northwest and southwest Meishan (MSG 1992: 8–13, 136–37; see also Ning 1988). Despite several armed uprisings in the countryside (including one in 1927 at Wansheng, not far from Baimapu; MSG 1992: 389–90), their efforts were poorly coordinated and harshly suppressed by military authorities. In 1949, as the PLA approached Meishan, party strength and mobilization activities were reportedly weak in the county.

3. One chronicler of official Communist history in Meishan (Liu Chuanmei 1990) asserted that the organizers of the Meishan People's Self-Defense Committee were a group of concerned conservative elites who sought to avoid a disaster like the one that had befallen the town of Xichang, in southern Sichuan, which had been razed in the course of fighting between Communist and KMT armies.

4. For official accounts of the Battle of Baimapu, see Liu Chuanmei (1990) and MSG (1992: 390–91). Some KMT troops and other defenders at Baimapu retreated to the north, while others fled westward toward the Sichuan-Xikang frontier and Tibet, although a PLA division had been dispatched to Danling the previous day in an attempt to cut off their anticipated retreat (MSG 1992: 390). By the time the PLA arrived at the walls of Meishan town, county authorities and their security forces had fled, and a crowd of townspeople waving red flags greeted the arriving victors from atop the town's South Gate. In the days that followed, PLA forces pursued retreating forces northward, capturing Chengdu after a fierce seven-day battle at the Minjiang river crossings near Xinjin. Nevertheless, it took another two years before remnant resistance in the high mountains of northern and western Sichuan could be suppressed (Endicott 1988).

5. Many of these terms, such as "feudal" (*fengjian*) and "superstition" (*mixin*), were loan words that made their way into the Chinese lexicon by

way of Japanese translations of European Marxist literature around the turn of the twentieth century (Li Yu-ning 1971). Although Chinese Communist Party rhetoric ostensibly elevated the "peasantry" as a favored political group, this was part of a broader agenda of revolutionary change that viewed rural cultivators and their productive techniques as premodern and in need of radical transformation. The reality of the Maoist era was that farmers and other rural inhabitants continued to face prejudice and discriminatory economic policies that favored urban areas (S. Potter 1983; Selden 1993; Whyte 1996). For critiques of the concept of peasantry in general, see Hill (1986) and Kearney (1996).

6. For firsthand accounts of Land Reform, see Hinton (1966), Crook and Crook (1979), C. K. Yang (1959), and Chang Su (1979).

7. See *West Sichuan Finance and Economic Bulletin*, no. 13 (1951), pp. 12–13.

8. The land tax (which had already been collected through the early twenty-first century) was abolished and replaced by a progressive agricultural tax (*nongye shui*) ranging from 3 to 42 percent (MSG 1992: 731). Nevertheless, with the advent of the cooperativization movement (see Chapter 4), taxes began to grow again, rising fivefold from 1950 through 1956 (MSG 1992: 737).

9. CCP work teams also attempted to introduce a new paper currency, but experience had taught them that the population might be reluctant to accept printed bills of nominal value. In the meantime, to win the respect and support of local farmers and merchants, soldiers and party workers paid for their food and supplies with silver coin, which PLA soldiers had carried into Baimapu on strings strapped to their chests.

10. The precise amount of land awarded to recipients in this provisional redistribution varied between 1.3 and 1.4 *mu* per person, based on the number of mouths a family had to feed and the total amount of land confiscated for redistribution.

11. These neighboring townships were said to include Sanbao, Shangyi (formerly Hanjiachang), and Xinsi (formerly Sihe).

12. Note that the seat of subcounty district government for this area was subsequently moved briefly to Shangyi, and then again to Duoyue. After Land Reform in 1952, district boundaries were redrawn once again, and Baimapu became part of Wansheng district. The influence of the Gowned Brothers was also reputed to have remained strong in Wansheng, which lay amid deeper hills west of Baimapu.

13. During the Republican era, there had been twenty *bao* units in Baimapu township. Around the time of Land Reform, however, four former *bao* units in the western part of the township were administratively reassigned to neighboring Sihe township (which was then renamed Xinsi, or "New Four"). Elderly residents in Baimapu claimed that this had been part of an effort by the new Communist authorities to undermine the continuing in-

fluence of the Gowned Brothers. Note that the mother of Hao Yuntai, a top leader in the Baima Gowned Brothers, was from Sihe, and at least two of his sisters married there. After Hao's execution, his surviving family members also moved there.

14. "Peasant associations" were the main vehicle of CCP rural organizational work. They had provided the core force of a failed 1927 agrarian uprising in northwestern Meishan county, and at Land Reform these organizations led the denunciation of, and expropriation of the property of, the old ruling elite (MSG 1992: 181–83).

15. "Peasant associations" were organized first at the subcounty district level, then around market townships, and finally in villages and subvillage small groups (*xiaozu*), the former *baojia* units. As a whole, this segmented branch structure provided an organizational foundation for basic-level, or "grass-roots," administrative government and mass mobilization. Township "peasant associations" were led by an appointed chairman who eventually became the township head. A deputy township head was usually nominated by the township "peasant association," approved by the township "peasant assembly" (*nongmin daibiaohui*), and officially appointed by the county government. Under these leaders worked a staff of five to seven people, most of whom were identified by the work teams as leading "activists." They managed public finances, marketplace exchange, agricultural production, irrigation, grain taxes, public order, and the development of youth and women's organizations (MSG 1992: 234). The process was apparently much the same when eventually extended to villages (former *bao*).

16. Initially, the first administrative villages established in Baimapu were an amalgamation of two or more *bao* units. In 1950, for example, First Bao and Second Bao were combined to form a single administrative village. Within a year, however, they had been separated into the independent villages of Yunpan and Qiaolou, respectively.

17. I was unable to determine precisely when Wei was removed as liberation chairman, but note that the CCP launched a rectification (*zhengfeng*) campaign in the summer of 1951 to deal with alleged cadres abuses (MSG 1992: 15).

18. The couple had met at the French Catholic Mission in Simeng, where the young woman was being raised in an orphanage. Both the man and, later, his sons were educated at the mission school. The mission, according to one former student, had owned more than 200 *mu*.

19. This landowner resided in Qingshen county, across the border from Simeng in southern Meishan, where the French Catholic Mission was located.

20. Xiu's appointed successor, as best I could reconstruct, was "poor peasant" Hao Yuanan, the first new village official affiliated with a major patrilineage in Qiaolou. Hao served as liberation chairman until Land Reform in 1952, when elections were instituted for village heads and deputies.

21. Despite the fact that "peasant associations" were to be open to so-called middle peasants, leaders were expected to be drawn from the ranks of the poor and landless. Nevertheless, owing in part to the privileged status these organizations enjoyed under new Communist authorities, membership remained selective. By the time of Land Reform, although more than 80 percent of county farmers were eligible for membership, less than half that number had been admitted. New militia recruitment among association members was even more selective, including only about 5 percent of villagers countywide (MSG 1992: 244).

22. Other elderly villagers, however, claimed that Yan Guifang had been forced from her position during the rectification campaigns in the early 1960s (see Chapter 4). Some claimed that her grandfather [FF] had been a feared *bao* head who was executed at Land Reform. Yan herself declined to discuss her family history or even to tell me her father's name.

23. In 1951, the newly established Meishan branch of the "Committee of the Chinese People to Protect World Peace and to Oppose American Imperialist Aggression" put out a recruitment call for a "Chinese People's Volunteer Army" being mobilized for Korea. In June 1952, the first group of nearly 1,200 Meishan recruits, Liang Jinyuan among them, left the county for training and, eventually, the front lines. During the course of the war, more than 30,000 men in the county registered for service, of whom more than 5,000 were enlisted (MSG 1992: 15, 375–76).

24. Friedman, Pickowicz, and Selden (1991) also noted the role children played in keeping tabs on "suspicious strangers" (p. 47), and that of rural youth in militia work (pp. 272, 276).

25. One of the county cadres was nicknamed "Blind Eye" (Xia Yan) by local villagers, who recalled that they had joked that his poor eyesight would botch up the redistribution. Another was a farmer from neighboring Yunpan village who had distinguished himself as an early activist and who was promoted to the status of temporary state cadre (*lingshi guojia ganbu*) for the Land Reform campaign. One retired village official, who had been a young adult at the time, maintained that a committee composed solely of local villagers would have been vulnerable to favoritism and factionalism, rendering a fair redistribution impossible. For accounts of Land Reform elsewhere in Sichuan, see Chang Su (1979) and Endicott (1988).

26. For studies on the class status system and its implications for social stratification in rural China, see, for example, Kraus (1977), J. Watson (1984), Whyte (1975, 1981), and Unger (1984).

27. See "Decisions Concerning the Differentiation of Class Status in the Countryside" in Selden (1979: 218–25).

28. Local Land Reform activists recalled that, in Baimapu, each of these major class designations was divided into a number of grades or subtypes. "Landlords," for example, were classified as tyrant (*eba*), exploitative (*boxue*), commercial (*gongshangye*), or bankrupt (*pochan*). "Rich peasants"

were divided into commercial and self-cultivator (*zigeng*). "Middle peasants" included profiteers (*laosan*), self-cultivators, owner-renters (*zigeng dian*), and tenants (*dian*). "Poor peasants" were also subclassified as self-cultivators, owner-renters, or tenants.

29. Land Reform in Sichuan came five years after the violent "excesses" carried out under revolutionary governments in older Communist-controlled areas during 1947, and party policy had already swung toward protecting key elements of the rural economy that would lead investments in future productivity. See "Some Important Problems of the Party's Present Policy" and the 1950 "Agrarian Reform Law" in Selden (1979: 225–29, 240–43). Violent expressions of class struggle in Baimapu were directed mainly against "tyrant landlords."

30. This distribution of class designations is based on reconstructions made through interviews with Qiaolou residents. I was unable to consult any written records pertaining to family class designations. Classifications were officially rescinded by national decree in 1979 as part of the post-Mao reforms, and the new 1990 household registry of village residents contained no notation of family class designations. Some villagers discussed their class assessments (and those of others) quite openly, but others were more reticent or reluctant, and a few even declined altogether. The Qiaolou party secretary disapproved of my inquiries on this subject, although (or perhaps because) he himself had been a long-standing proponent of class struggle.

31. In 1957, under the advanced cooperative (or collective village), one Xi man and two Yan men served as cooperative financial officers, but for less than a year (see Chapter 4).

32. Relatively low levels of literacy among the rural population made education a valuable resource in the early years of Communist rule. Prior to the Cultural Revolution (1966–76), political appointments in the countryside sometimes favored those with more education over those with "good" class designations (Kraus 1982: 128). The so-called bloodline (or "natural redness") interpretation of class identity and revolutionary purity was revived as a litmus test of political loyalty during the Cultural Revolution.

33. The distinction made by the CCP between "exploited" hired labor and "nonexploited" family labor implicitly recognized the privileged property rights of patrilineal families as units of production and consumption (see Chayanov 1986). As corporate economic groups, families controlled the use, transfer, and income of their labor.

34. Note that when Hao Caiqin died, his descendants buried him not in the Hao ancestral cemetery (where almost all their kin, including Hao Yuntai, were buried) but in a separately sited grave closer to their homes. Since the mid-1950s, that small hillside has become an ancestral burial ground for all of Hao Caiqin's descendants. On a symbolic level, these graves marked their segmentation from the local Hao lineage and expressed the separate identity and status claimed by his branch (*fang*) of descendants.

35. All four "seasons" of Land Reform work in Meishan followed five basic steps: (1) propagandize Land Reform policies, denounce local bullies, hold memorial services for those who died under "feudal exploitation," and publicly exhibit wealth seized from landlords; (2) assign class designations; (3) confiscate properties of "landlords" and excess holdings of "rich peasants"; (4) redistribute land to the poor, burn old deeds and issue new certificates at mass rallies; and (5) establish government and youth league organizations, teach class struggle, socialism, and patriotism, and identify, cultivate, and test local activists to become basic-level cadres (MSG 1992: 244).

36. Self-declared agricultural families living along the eastern half of Baimapu Street were placed under the administrative jurisdiction of Qiaolou; those residing along the western half of the market street were registered as members of Yunpan village, which bordered Qiaolou to the west. Families opting for commercial livelihoods as merchants, artisans, restauranteurs, or service specialists were organized under a newly created Street Village (Jiecun), which was administered by an "Industrial and Commercial Alliance" (see also Siu 1989: 143, 148). With the establishment of the "household registration" (*hukou*) system in the mid-1950s, these families were registered as "urban residents" (*jumin*) and became eligible for salaried positions, staple food rations, and privileged access to schools. Their experiences under collectivization differed markedly from those of their neighbors who were registered as "peasants" (*nongmin*).

37. Some of these recipients were given outright ownership of draft animals or agricultural tools, while others received a share (*fen*) in such property, which was thus held jointly by several families.

38. The countywide average per capita allotment was 1.09 *mu* (MSG 1992: 244).

39. The temple structure was eventually torn down during the collective era, although a new commune (township) junior middle school was built on its former grounds.

40. Some elderly Baimapu residents refused to say the names of executed landlords aloud, or did so only in barely audible whispers, for fear of ghosts. The "tyrants" of the Old Society may have been eliminated, but they suffered violent, unnatural deaths that, for some, left apprehension about lingering malevolent spirits.

41. A few local notables, judged less "despotic" than others, received death sentences that were subsequently commuted to provisional parole. For example, Wen Shisan, the local *fengshui* master and township head, was executed. However, his eldest son, who had divided out in the mid-1930s and who later served as a tax collector and *jia* headman, was classified as a "poor peasant," and his second son, who had served as *bao* headman and *bao* representative, was labeled a "political criminal" (*zhengzhi fan*) but given a suspended death sentence. His other sons were also classified as "poor peasants" (members of a family of nine with less than 10 *mu* of land).

CHAPTER 4

1. Although the optimal pace of "socialist transformation" was debated among top CCP officials, few party leaders questioned the ultimate goal of collectivization. Advocates of rapidly increasing the state's procurement of agricultural goods to subsidize the ambitious, heavy-industry-oriented first Five Year Plan eventually prevailed, although others had proposed a more gradualist approach (see MacFarquhar 1974; Selden 1993: 62–108).

2. While the household registration system provided the framework for state-managed redistribution of food and other staple commodities, it was also intended to impede a large-scale rural exodus to urban areas. China's urban population had swelled from 57 million to 89 million from 1949 to 1957, precipitating "massive urban unemployment" that approached "crisis proportions" (Selden 1979: 55). For detailed discussions of the household registration system and the urban-rural status hierarchy it created, see also S. Potter (1983), Potter and Potter (1990), Cheng (1991), Selden (1993), and Cheng and Selden (1994).

3. Petitions to change one's registration—or to be transferred to a new job in a more highly ranked urban center—were rarely granted. "Peasants" might evade government monitoring and live surreptitiously with relatives in a town or city, but without access to urban "resident" ration booklets they could not survive there indefinitely. Although the *hukou* system created two largely endogamous social categories in China's population, it did not entail the complex religious cosmology, pollution concepts, or ritual symbolism generally attributed to caste systems in South Asia. Notwithstanding the ideological glorification of "peasants" in CCP propaganda, many urbanites came to regard them as a backward, dirty, or culturally inferior Other, as evidenced in autobiographical memoirs (e.g., Chang Jung 1991).

4. At least three different types of cooperative credit institutions were established by the CCP in rural China: small credit mutual aid groups, independent credit cooperatives, and credit departments attached to branches of the state-run Supply and Marketing Cooperative. The latter two forms were reportedly preferred in areas of dispersed population and where branch offices of the People's Bank had not yet been established (Shue 1980: 259–60).

5. Recall that, at Land Reform, the former *jia* units had been renamed subvillage "groups" (*zu*). This subsequent reorganization, in which new groups were created at a higher level of administrative coordination, represented an effort to enhance the integration of village and subvillage management.

6. Families participating in a mutual aid group decided among themselves whose fields would be worked in what order. Water buffalo, winnowing machines, and irrigation wheels were shared with other families in the group, or sometimes even rented out by the group for use by other families. Each MAG was assigned a government tax quota of grain, based on its combined

area of farm land and the size of its member families. After harvest, the group delivered this grain to the village government, which arranged for its transfer to the township branch Supply and Marketing Cooperative. Village cadres also handled distributions of cash payments to MAGs (and to independent families) that sold the state additional grain above and beyond their obligatory tax quotas. A family that found itself with a deficit in its labor exchange obligations to others in its MAG was expected to clear those debts before the Lunar New Year.

7. In some cases, Land Reform had disrupted previous labor exchange relations by redistributing land—and thus labor demands—among village families. Moreover, there were both formerly landless laborers who had returned to Qiaolou to receive land in the redistribution and newcomers settled there by the government, none of whom had labor exchange ties with local families.

8. The year before they were organized into the county's first experimental MAG, these families spent an aggregate total of twenty-two labor days bringing in their respective rice harvests. As a mutual aid group, they cut their labor almost in half while raising production nearly 25 percent (MSG 1992: 15, 246–47).

9. As a MAG leader, Jin Yuting soon acquired a solid reputation as a capable manager, skillful farmer, and effective broker. He enhanced his influence among other villagers after he arranged for the impoverished members of his mutual-aid group to obtain low-interest cash loans from the newly established township credit cooperative. Village and township administrators, for their part, were equally impressed that he persuaded his group members to purchase seed and production supplies from the new Supply and Marketing Cooperative with their loans, rather than spending the money on the growing diversity of consumer goods at the local Baimapu market. Jin also enjoyed affinal ties with the Hao brothers. Both an uncle and a close nephew [yBS] of his had married Qiaolou Hao women, and he subsequently married his own son to a niece [ZD] of the Hao brothers.

10. See "Decision on Mutual Aid and Cooperation in Agriculture" and "Decision on Development of Agricultural Producers' Cooperatives" in Selden (1979: 331–40).

11. The workpoint system went through various permutations during the course of the collective era and continued to be employed in some enterprises even in the 1990s. Remuneration was based on the number of workpoints accumulated by each laborer. Surplus food or money was distributed to families based on the number of workpoints earned by all family members. During "radical" campaigns of the collective era, workpoints were often issued on an egalitarian basis, varying sometimes because of a person's attitude toward work, bad class designation, or political label. Under periodic "reform" measures, workpoints were graded for skill, experience, and quality of work.

12. Potter and Potter (1990: 64) glossed *lianzu* as a noun, "United Groups." Qiaolou villagers, however, used the phrase as a verb-object construction meaning "to join [or to unite] the groups."

13. The boundaries between the two cooperatives, and their two respective administrative subdivisions, were adjusted by production supervisors in an attempt to balance land and labor ratios. These new boundaries eventually came to serve as the basis for the subvillage production teams established in Qiaolou under the post-Leap reforms.

14. In 1955, Mao had criticized cadres who were "tottering like women with bound feet and constantly complaining" about the fast pace of the socialist transformation of agriculture (see Mao 1975b; abridged in Selden 1979: 341–50).

15. Following Land Reform, "poor peasants" and "hired laborers" made up roughly 55 percent of county farmers. The reclassification of "poor and lower-middle peasants" raised the percentage of those rhetorically identified with the revolutionary social order to two-thirds (MSG 1992: 244, 247).

16. By the end of 1956, when "elementary cooperatives" were being established in Qiaolou, almost 90 percent of "peasant households" elsewhere in China had already been organized into "advanced cooperatives" (Riskin 1987: 89; Selden 1993: 79; Teiwes 1993: 58).

17. In another Baimapu village, almost the entire population reportedly had refused to participate in cooperatives until more coercive measures were adopted to compel their compliance.

18. The most comprehensive and well-documented study of the cooperative movement to date comes from the North China research of Friedman, Pickowicz, and Selden (1991).

19. As noted above, the push to establish an advanced cooperative in Qiaolou came a year later than in most parts of China. The first such collective villages were established in Meishan in early 1956 (one, again, in Baimapu township), but it was not until December 1957 that the county attained near full compliance from farmers (MSG 1992: 246–48). Despite the fact that the pace of collectivization in Meishan appeared to lag behind the rest of the country, it nevertheless was accomplished eight years ahead of the original schedule.

20. These private plots subsequently became the subject of intense debate within the CCP leadership, and would occasionally be rescinded or restored according to the changing "winds" of political campaigns.

21. For details on these critical debates among top party leaders, and the concerns and interests that shaped various positions, see MacFarquhar (1974, 1983), Riskin (1987: 87–88), Selden (1993: 62–108), and Lieberthal (1993).

22. The people's commune system was one of the most ambitious schemes ever devised to organize production and distribution, involving some 26,000 communes with an average of 20,000 to 30,000 laborers each during its early phase (Potter and Potter 1990: 68). The Greater Shangyi

Commune, of which Baimapu had been part, encompassed roughly 24,000 people. Skinner (1964–65: 394) argued that the artificial and "grotesquely large mold" of the communes failed to align these new comprehensive collective organizations "with the natural socioeconomic systems [i.e., standard marketing communities] shaped by rural trade." He maintained that this contributed to the grave economic problems and massive famine that developed over the next few years. As early as December 1958, county party authorities ordered these unwieldy units to be reduced in size, and the number of communes in the county more than doubled, from eleven to twenty-five. The following summer they were scaled back even further, to the level of former rural market townships (MSG 1992: 253–54).

23. The terminology of administrative organization under the people's commune system went through a confusing series of changes between 1958 and 1961. MacFarquhar (1983: 181–84) provided the most concise overview of this "rectification of names." Originally, the communes were based on former collective villages (i.e., advanced cooperatives), which were renamed "production teams" (*shengchan dui*) and which were run by an unnamed intermediate level of administration (the former townships), later termed "managerial districts" (*guanli qu*), or, in some places, "production brigades" (*shengchan dadui*). Critics of grand collectivism advocated devolving managerial authority to small units, which Mao (and Qiaolou farmers) referred to as "production small teams" (*shengchan xiaozu*). With the post-Leap reforms of 1961, the three-tiered terminology of communes, brigades, and teams was standardized, and generally corresponded to former townships, villages, and subvillage groups. (Although these reforms designated subvillage production teams as the "basic accounting units" of the collective era, tensions persisted among commune, brigade, and team cadres, whose interests were often at odds with one another (see Oi 1989).

24. The rescinding of private plots removed what little autonomy or security had remained to individual families under the collective village. During the Great Leap Forward, Qiaolou farmers were no longer permitted to grow their own green vegetables, supplemental grain, or cash crops. Even hogs, which had remained family property under the "advanced cooperatives," were now appropriated by the collective.

25. Although many collective canteens in Meishan county were closed in 1960 (MSG 1992: 254), farmers in Qiaolou insisted that they had maintained compulsory collective dining arrangements until at least 1961, and some claimed even longer. "Regiment commanders" supervised a staff that included a chief of foodstuffs (*shiwuzhang*), an account, one or more cooks, and a storage supervisor (*baoguan*) who guarded access to the regiment's collective grain supply. Each person was required to fulfill daily work assignments before being fed at mess. Although men and women often performed identical tasks, men generally received daily servings of grain that were one-third larger than those given to women. Youths, children, and other "half

able-bodied laborers" (*ban laoli*) were given half the standard fare for their gender.

26. The Wen ancestral hall was dismantled during the Great Leap Forward, and its materials were used to construct a collective storage house on a new site. Many of the families who had been living there since Land Reform were moved into the former Qingfutang compound.

27. In some districts, grain supplies intended to last half a year were consumed in less than a month (Potter and Potter 1990: 73).

28. The water control works at Dujiangyan, which date to the third century, helped make the Chengdu plain one of the most productive grain areas of China (see Needham 1995: 202–10). As early as 1955, work began on an expansion of this system southward, from a previous terminus at the Minjiang river town of Xinjin. During the Great Leap Forward, new canals and viaducts were constructed through the shallow hills west of the plain.

29. In 1958, more than half the rural population of Meishan was involved in the "iron and steel" campaign, which concluded in January 1959. Agriculture was left largely in the hands of women (MSG 1992: 18–19, 446).

30. Even working at the same tasks, women thus had to labor fifteen months or more to accumulate the workpoints men earned in twelve. While their participation in the work force grew during the collective era, their actual labor burden rose (Diamond 1975; see also Robinson 1985).

31. Most studies of the "rustification" movement have focused on the role and fate of urban students sent down to the countryside to live with, labor among, and learn from "the peasantry" in an effort to halt violent factionalism among youthful Red Guards during the Cultural Revolution (see, for example, Bernstein 1977). Indeed, several cohorts of students from Meishan and even some from Chengdu did come briefly to Qiaolou at that time. But the main thrust of the local rustification campaign occurred earlier and focused on the transfer of Baimapu town poor, who lacked capital or material resources to contribute to the Cooperative Store (*hezuo shangdian*) run by the commune.

32. To meet these grain production goals, farmers were instructed to adopt new "high output" (*gaochan*) cropping techniques, such as plowing deeper and planting more densely, with upward of 800,000 rice saplings per *mu*. So-called Sputnik fields (*weixing tian*) were established to produce rice yields of 1,000 or even 5,000 kilograms (rather than the average 160 kg) per *mu* (MSG 1992: 253, 505).

33. This renewed push followed a dramatic confrontation between top party leaders at the Lushan conference. There, threatening to break with critics and form a new revolutionary army, Mao orchestrated a purge of Defense Minister Peng Dehuai (replaced by Lin Biao), who had challenged the efficacy of the Leap and its abandonment of central planning and consultative decision-making processes (see MacFarquhar 1983; Domes 1985).

34. Originally, official estimates of the 1958 national grain harvest put

the figure at 375 million metric tons. By August 1960, this had been revised downward to 250 million metric tons. New statistics, issued after Mao's death, further reduced this estimate to only 200 million metric tons (Riskin 1987: 127). Huang Shu-min (1989) provided examples of how local cadres tried to deceive superiors about grain output in order to win recognition and acclaim.

35. See "Regulations on the Work of the Rural People's Communes" ("Sixty Articles") of 1962, abridged in Selden (1979: 521–26).

36. The new Meishan gazetteer offered contradictory claims on the timing of these reforms. The chapter on political matters reported that they were implemented as early as March 1959, whereas the chapter on agriculture dated them to 1961 (cf. MSG 1992: 254, 442). Residents in Baimapu claimed that they had been part of the Shangyi Greater Commune until 1961.

37. Team 1, for example, lay to the northwest, around the area of Big Wen Pond, while Team 2 covered most of northeastern Qiaolou. Team 3 consisted of the families in southernmost Qiaolou, near Big Hao Hill, while Team 4 stretched from the southern side of Baimapu Street across to Upper Xi Slope.

38. Beginning in the fall of 1962, production teams were authorized "to contract tasks to households" (*baogan daohu*) on a limited basis (MSG 1992: 254). Ten to twenty percent of unirrigated "dry land" in each team was assigned for use by individual family households. In return for pledges to meet certain output targets, they were permitted some discretion in using such land for additional productive activities. Many were encouraged to grow sweet potatoes, for example, to aid in famine recovery. The remainder of team land, however, including all paddy, continued to be cultivated collectively by team labor.

39. The Four Cleanups were actually a series of campaigns through which competing party factions attempted to rectify problems in pragmatic economic management and ideological political commitment. Many observers have attributed the Socialist Education Movement and the Four Cleanups campaign to a power struggle within the upper echelons of CCP leadership in the wake of the Great Leap fiasco. See, for example, Baum and Teiwes (1968), Baum (1975), MacFarquhar (1983), and Lieberthal (1993); see also "The First Ten Points," abridged in Selden (1979: 536–41). In Meishan, these began with the Small Four Cleanups in October 1963, which focused on management of accounts, warehouses, finances, and workpoints. A year later, a new Big Four Cleanups campaign was launched with a decidedly ideological orientation, redirecting critical attention on issues of politics, economy, organization, and thinking (MSG 1992: 258–59). Apparently, the Big Four Cleanups had the greatest effect on Qiaolou. For details on how these and other mass campaigns affected interpersonal relations in rural communities, see Chan, Madsen, and Unger (1992).

40. Khrushchev, villified by Mao as a "revisionist" for his critique of Stalin, had cut Soviet aid to China in 1960. As the split in the CCP leadership

heightened in the mid-1960s, supporters of Mao and mobilizational collectivism depicted Liu Shaoqi and his aide Deng Xiaoping, principal architects of the post-Leap reforms, as "revisionists" and "hidden capitalist roaders" in the party.

41. Jun Yueqing seemed to have the credentials to make a suitable revolutionary successor. His father had been a landless laborer hired by the Qingfutang. He was also a patrilineal relative of Qiaolou's first accountant-clerk, by then a retired "old revolutionary" (*lao geming*). Years later, the political alliance between Jun Yueqing and Hao Yuanliang was augmented by an indirect but mutually recognized affinal tie. Jun, it was said, took an active role in finding a suitable spouse for his younger brother, who eventually married a daughter of Jin Yuting, the organizer of Qiaolou's second MAG and a close affinal ally of the Haos.

42. The figure cited repeatedly by local respondents was 10,000 *yuan*, although this seems extraordinarily high and I suspect it may be an exaggeration. In "Chen Village," the brigade accountant had been accused of embezzling 2,000 *yuan*, but later the amount was pruned back to only 100 *yuan* (Chan, Madsen, and Unger 1992: 65).

43. It was said that the man escaped prosecution only through the intervention of an influential patron. Nevertheless, he and his family endured considerable hardship over the next decade because they were ordered to repay the money. The incident effectively ended his political career.

44. After the establishment of advanced cooperatives, or collective villages, grain was subtracted from harvests to cover procurement quotas, seed and feed supplies, and administrative costs before the net surplus was made available to farmers for workpoint-based redistribution at year's end.

45. The Destroy the Four Olds (*po si jiu*) campaign was vigorously carried out in Baimapu. Many families burned or demolished heirlooms, chests, carved-post beds, and tables. Local lineage genealogical history books were also said to have been lost at this time, and much of the Guanyin temple in Yangtang village was demolished. In 1966, as part of this campaign, some 4,700 original woodblock printing plates from the 1832 edition of *The Collected Works of the Three Sus (San Su Quanji)*, which had been sent to Chengdu for safekeeping the previous year, were burned (MSG 1992: 22–23).

46. The term "*wen*" refers to things literary and refined, such as being well-versed in letters, and was often associated with civil administration, whereas "*wu*" is associated with martial arts, weaponry, and the military, and may convey notions of valor or even fierceness. The Confucian temple, an important landmark in many Chinese cities and towns, was sometimes referred to as the Temple of Letters (Wen Miao), and many Guan Di temples were known as Martial Temples (Wu Miao). Images of Mao himself were often presented in a *wenwu* style, with a portrait of him in the military garb of younger days, accompanied by another depiction of him as a balding and

more corpulent elder statesman. Protective talismans bearing such dual images of Mao became popular during the 1980s and 1990s.

47. Throughout the collective era, "peasant" workpoints were remunerated mainly in foodstuffs. Meishan farmers earned, on average, less than Y100 a year per "mouth," or family member (MSG 1992: 448). Although many families continued to barter produce from their private plots, if only through so-called underground (or "black") markets, few were able to accumulate significant savings. In such circumstances, punitive cash fines imposed harsh economic burdens.

48. In most of the other eight production teams, year-end remuneration for each credited full day's labor averaged Y0.70. In a few teams, particularly those with extensive duck-breeding enterprises, daily remuneration was upward of Y1.00. Even so, such earnings remained below the reported Y1.50 rate of the Dazhai "model" (Zweig 1989: 29). Note, however, that the average per capita income for farmers throughout Meishan county in 1967 was only Y74, roughly the same as the average reported for Team 7 (MSG 1992: 448).

49. Most grain borrowing took place within the Baimapu commune, where personal friendships and interfamily relationships were denser and stronger. Moreover, this enabled borrowers to transport grain over shorter distances and thus evade detection. Patrilineal kin, it was said, were rarely a source of such loans. As they had done previously in relationships of "help" before the Communist revolution, most families turned to marital affines, close friends, and "dry kin" to borrow grain or to serve as intermediaries in arranging such loans. Local authorities officially disapproved of this practice but tacitly permitted it. Although such transactions were referred to as "borrowing" (*jie*) grain, most loans were repaid in cash rather than in kind. The government monopoly of the grain trade prohibited the unauthorized purchase and sale of grain, but families participating in these unofficial exchange relationships protected themselves by couching such exchange in an idiom of cooperation and mutual assistance.

50. The former head of Team 7 remained in Xinjiang for several years, securing a salaried position through an uncle who had received an influential PLA party post there during the Great Leap famine. In the later stages of the Cultural Revolution, this uncle himself became a target of criticism and struggle, and was dismissed from his position. Having lost his patron's protection, the former production team leader eventually returned to Wenwu, but no charges were ever brought against him.

51. Most former members of (Old) Team 7 were administratively reassigned to Teams 8 and 9. (Team 9, it might be noted, was renamed, "New Team 7.") Three families in particular, however, were viewed as so divisive or problematic that they were assigned to other teams. Two of them went to Team 6, while the family of the former leader of "Old Team 7" was assigned

to Team 1 after he returned from Xinjiang in the late 1970s. Street farmers were also split up: those living on the north side of Baimapu Street were assigned to "New Team 7," while those on the south side of the street became part of Team 8.

52. Party Secretary Lin Chengying was only in his early fifties at the time, and there was some suggestion that he had been maneuvered out of power by a more militant faction within the brigade leadership, a group of younger and more impassioned supporters of Chairman Mao led by Hao Yuanliang. No one in Qiaolou cast any direct aspersions on the character of "old revolutionary" Lin, now deceased, although allusions were made to certain improper conduct. Hao Yuanliang himself once remarked in passing that Lin had been "a little like" the entrepreneurs of the 1990s, "wanting to make money" all the time. More serious allegations were raised by other villagers, who complained about the brigade's sale of a former "landlord" home to Lin's eldest daughter shortly after her marriage. Half of the large *si-heyuan* was reportedly sold to Lin's daughter and her new husband for a modest price. The space had hitherto served as an office for the new village administration, which had to be relocated after the sale. Many villagers regarded the sale as improper, and one woman scornfully commented that it was the finest dowry ever seen in Qiaolou.

53. There was a double entendre implicit in such a name. In local vernacular dialect, "Jieshi" was pronounced "Gai-si," a homonym that could be glossed as "ought to die."

54. Another Liang man, a distant patrilineal relative of Liang Jinyuan who lived in another production brigade near Wenwu, was co-leader of all the Red Guard groups in Baimapu commune. The other youth leader was an "outsider" sent to Baimapu from the state granary in Duoyue, a large commune town north of Shangyi. Three Wenwu Red Guards—Liang's nephew, his nephew's "rich peasant" Hao cousin [MyBS], and the son of former women's cadre Yan Guifang—enhanced their status and influence after joining a 700-strong Meishan delegation in political pilgrimage to Beijing in October 1966, where they saw Chairman Mao in his fourth appearance before a mass youth rally in Tiananmen Square (MSG 1992: 260).

55. The son of young Lin and his Hao wife also married a Hao woman from Team 3, the daughter of "old revolutionary" Hao Yuanan, former Land Reform presidium cadre. His cousin [FeBS], son of former party secretary Lin Chengying, had been married to Liang Jinyuan's sister, but had been a victim of the Great Leap famine.

56. After the death of his beloved wife, Liang Jinyuan resigned his security post to care for their four children. Nevertheless, during the 1970s he served many years as leader of his production team. His proudest accomplishment, aside from raising his four children, was an irrigation channel he designed. It allowed for the conversion of much "dry land" to paddy

fields and brought a dramatic rise in the standard of living among families in his team.

57. During the mid-1960s, it was widely reported that Dazhai brigade had made phenomenal gains in grain harvests and living standards, despite its marginal and semiarid ecological setting. These successes were attributed to ideological commitment, brigade-level accounting and management, and spirited efforts to overcome hardship. Dazhai was championed by Mao himself in 1964, and its brigade chief was named to the CCP politburo in 1973. Only later was it disclosed that this model of "self-reliance" had fabricated many of its claims. For details on Dazhai, the politics surrounding its promotion as a national model, and the Study Dazhai campaign, see Tsou, Blecher, and Meisner (1979); Hinton (1983); and Zweig (1989).

58. In February 1968, a delegation of party leaders from Meishan toured Dazhai and returned to launch a Study Dazhai campaign in the county, but if faltered amid the chaos of the Cultural Revolution. In 1971, however, with the restoration of party organizations and government offices, county authorities renewed efforts to create a "New Meishan" within five years, based on the Dazhai model. At the first national Study Dazhai conference in 1975, Meishan county was one of 300 units awarded official recognition for their achievements (MSG 1992: 268–70).

59. During the collective era, new housing starts and home repairs required not only considerable cash, which many farm families lacked, but also official authorization. After approval by production team leaders, such petitions were submitted to brigade cadres who determined whether or not they could be forwarded to commune offices. Because state authorities sought to restrict the amount of land taken out of cultivation, permission was difficult to obtain and often required the political patronage of local cadres.

60. Qiaolou farmers continued to complain about their wheat "duty" well into the 1990s. Many made careful calculations and planted only as much land as was necessary to meet their wheat procurement quota. Most still did not eat wheat or flour products—few even ate noodles—preferring instead to feed surplus wheat to their hogs.

61. By 1978, a single *mu* of paddy in Meishan produced about 300 kilograms of rice, roughly twice the yield of fields before Liberation. Average annual per capita grain allotments had risen from 122 kilograms in the early 1960s to more than 488 kilograms, although production expenditures had more than doubled between 1958 and 1979, from 16 to nearly 40 percent of collective income (MSG 1992: 448–49, 505). Farmers in Qiaolou claimed that their rice yields tripled during the 1970s, largely through the introduction of new hybrid seeds. Whereas they typically had produced 150 to 175 kilograms of rice per *mu* of paddy, the new seed brought yields of 500 to 600 kilograms. But the hybrid seed was costly and had to be purchased anew each year, in contrast to natural rice grain, which, if left unhusked and

unpolished, could be replanted the following season. Moreover, some people found the new rice tasteless. One man complained that "I no longer enjoy eating it. It used to be delicious, very sweet and fragrant. Now it is no good."

62. This was one of the four houses originally purchased by their grandfather, Hao Caiqin, some thirty years earlier. Hao Yuanliang and his cousin Hao Yuanqian had a close personal relationship, and their families shared the household until the early 1980s. Following the decollectivization of agriculture and the success of the village's first brick factory, Party Secretary Hao Yuanliang moved into a new house he built a few dozen meters away.

63. The bride's family lived a few hundred meters from the Haos, across the border in neighboring Minzhu (Yangtang) brigade. This was the former *bao* in which Hao Caiqin's wife Zhen had been born, and where the couple lived for several years after their marriage. Also in Yangtang was the Guanyin temple, which had been largely demolished during the Cultural Revolution. The new couple apparently helped form a strong alliance between the two families, for their eldest son (b. 1969) was subsequently married to his matrilateral first cousin [MBD]. It might be noted that this son, like his father, also became "dry kin" of the Zhens in Yangtang.

CHAPTER 5

1. Since the establishment of the advanced cooperatives in the 1950s, rural collectives have been required to guarantee five basic necessities for elderly, infirm, disabled, widowed, or orphaned members who have no relatives to care for them: food, clothing, cooking and heating fuel, education, and a burial.

2. This system of "contracting production to [work] groups" (*baochan dao zu*) was a precursor to the more liberal "contracting production to households" (*baochan dao hu*) which followed. Such practices were already well underway in some parts of China before the Third Plenum in 1978 (A. Watson 1983; Kelliher 1992). Sichuan, under Zhao Ziyang, had been the site of many early experiments at economic reform. In May 1979, 80 percent of production teams in Meishan county, including those in Qiaolou, were using group contracting (MSG 1992: 28). It was another two years before nearly all teams nationwide employed *some* form of contract responsibility system (Riskin 1987: 289).

3. Although class designations were officially abandoned in 1979 (MSG 1992: 28), they continued to be listed in the Qiaolou household registry until the late 1980s.

4. Dry land distribution averaged roughly 0.25 *mu* per person across teams in Qiaolou. In addition, 0.1 *mu* of dry land was reallocated for each registered household member as a permanent private plot.

5. These procurement quotas, or "duties" (*renwu*), consisted of a stipulated amount of specific crops (rice, wheat, and rapeseed) that each Qiaolou

family household was obliged to sell to the state in return for its usufruct contract to the land. Farmers were paid for such deliveries, but at state-mandated prices that were below the market value of such crops. State officials also offered to buy surpluses from farmers at higher prices that were sometimes competitive with going market rates. Deliveries to the Baimapu granary were weighted and assessed for quality. Remuneration was then calculated, and farmers were given a receipt for the amount due to them. For security reasons, no payments were made at the granary itself. Instead, funds were subsequently disbursed through village administrators, to whom villagers brought their receipts. Note that quality assessments were vulnerable to subjective manipulation, and since procurement prices were ranked by product quality, disputes often erupted between granary workers and farmers anxious to obtain the highest rating (and best price) for their compulsory crop quotas. Many farmers maintained that the surest way to secure top ratings was to develop personal friendships with granary workers or their relatives. Qiaolou cadres were able to arrange temporary employment for several villagers at the granary during harvest season.

6. Under both methods of land redistribution, families in a given team were permitted to exchange their plots with other families in that team. Some traded in an effort to consolidate landholdings nearer their homes; others, to obtain concentrated parcels in the fields. A few families subcontracted (*zhuanbao*) with others in more formal arrangements. Subcontractors agreed to meet state procurement quotas and to provide the original contracting family with a specified amount of consumption grain (*kouliang*) each year, in return for control over land use and any remaining surplus. Although subcontracting was quite common in some parts of China, it was relatively rare in Qiaolou. Most subcontracting arrangements in Baimapu involved street farmers who decided to devote themselves full time to new commercial endeavors in their marketplace homes, and who therefore transferred their agricultural rights and responsibilities to others.

7. Certain restrictions on land use continued to be imposed, such as prohibitions against building, clearing forests, and planting crops on designated woodlands.

8. Earlier responsibility contracts issued in other parts of China in 1980 stipulated one-year usufruct tenure. This was then lengthened to three years, largely to encourage investment in land improvement measures. Fifteen-year tenure was instituted on the national level only in 1984 (Kelliher 1992: 182). The previous year, the CCP leadership had formally reversed collectivist policies by permitting farmers to hire labor, buy and own motor vehicles and machinery, market any surplus (i.e., after-quota) goods they produced, and cross administrative boundaries while on marketing errands (Riskin 1987: 289). In 1984, subcontracting practices also received official endorsement.

9. Note, however, that cadres and entrepreneurs alike often referred to

the acquisition of extra-long-term usufruct rights as "buying land" (*mai tudi*). In certain specially zoned areas of Meishan county, investors can purchase ninety-year tenure rights to land (including rights of succession for kin). In 1995, a single *mu* of land in the county's western hills, where many county officials were building summer cottages, could be leased for about Y15,000 (US $5,000). Prices in more prime real estate areas were much higher.

10. Although the "Sixty Articles" of 1962 stipulated that land was owned collectively by production teams, state authorities continued to determine crop choice and production targets, as well as agricultural inputs, prices, and the distribution and marketing of surpluses (Selden 1993). Brigade cadres, as agents of that state authority, could also redraw team borders and thus transfer assets (including land and labor) from one team to another, as they did in the case of "Old Team Seven" (see also Chan, Madsen, and Unger 1992). Even under household responsibility contracting, mandatory procurement quotas continued to influence cropping patterns and agricultural outputs.

11. Administratively imposed adjustments to landholdings were institutionalized every five years to restore equity after household demographic changes. Families that suffered a net loss of members (usually through death, division, or marriage) had their per capita land allotments and procurement quotas reduced accordingly. A portion of the land they had worked was appropriated for reallocation to families that had grown in size. As long as a family's demographic size remained stable, its landholdings were fairly stable. Some families took advantage of prospective fifteen-year use rights to invest in long-term improvements, such as converting some paddies to cement-walled fish ponds.

12. Sometimes, once plans for a marriage were finalized, a bride's father might explicitly announce which parcels of land among the family's holdings represented her share. Often these would be more distant from the house or of poorer quality. Although such strategies were discriminatory, they were not intended to hurt a daughter, but rather to induce team cadres to accept those plots as reclaimed shares after she married out. Most newlywed women signed subcontracts with their natal families which stipulated that a certain amount of grain would be delivered to them at each harvest as subsistence food. Nevertheless, it was not unusual for such women to receive less than the agreed-upon quantity. It was a common "squeeze tactic" for fathers or brothers to retain extra grain, claiming they needed to recoup the cost of agricultural inputs such as fertilizers and pesticides. A few married women have therefore insisted on retaining active use rights to their allocated land in Qiaolou, returning to work it as necessary and delivering their own procurement quotas to the state granary themselves.

13. Several families would share ownership in a buffalo, working out among themselves a schedule and budget for the care, feeding, and use of the animal. Most water buffalo were shared among families that voluntar-

ily formed such cooperative relations, usually with agnates or ritual "dry kin." In later years, as some families prospered and sought to purchase new buffalo, they often formed partnerships based on similar shareholding arrangements.

14. During the Maoist era, production team cadres in Qiaolou included a team leader, deputy team leader, accountant, treasurer, storage supervisor, workpoint recorder, and women's leader. In the 1990s, the new "villager small groups" were staffed only by a group leader, whose responsibilities were confined mainly to collecting taxes and electricity fees, coordinating irrigation pumping, and arranging fertilizer purchases for families in the group.

15. The construction team remitted all of its earnings to the brigade accountant, who credited team members with special workpoints to be remunerated with extra cash disbursements at the year-end redistribution (cf. Jervis 1987). Although such extra cash earnings contributed to family income differentials in the late 1970s, team members realized far greater value for their labor after the team disbanded in the 1980s and they were free to market their acquired skills independently.

16. A demobilized soldier and cousin of the Hao brothers was appointed manager of the brigade machine repair station. "Sent-down youths" were credited with making an artistic sign for the station, with decorative characters fashioned out of metal bars, that still adorned the gate of the administrative compound long after the station closed. Village residents continued to express pride in the sign, which they regarded as a symbol of "culture" and status.

17. In 1972, there had been only 42 tractors, large or small, in the entire county. By 1976, the Study Dazhai campaign had help to boost those numbers to more than a thousand, a figure that doubled in the next seven years (MSG 1992: 650–51). The transport sector of the county economy grew from 1.3 percent in 1966 to 2.3 percent in 1978 and almost 6 percent in 1987 (ibid., p. 402).

18. The orchard initiative came at the end of another grain crisis in Sichuan during 1974–76. Throughout the province, efforts were made to expand the amount of land devoted to grain cultivation. In Qiaolou, the land selected for the orchard had been considered too marginal for effective grain cultivation but appropriate for potentially lucrative cash crops, such as oranges and tangerines.

19. Sales were boosted after Meishan navel oranges, a variety cultivated in Qiaolou, won awards of excellence in a 1985 national competition (MSG 1992: 33).

20. Xianger, a rural town situated midway between Baimapu and Meishan and close to the county railway depot on the Chengdu-Kunming line (see Map 2), was the site of considerable state investment. It was host to sev-

eral state-run factories that produced bricks, cement, and petrochemical fertilizers, as well as a telecommunications station and a PLA garrison that saw action in Vietnam in 1979. During the late 1970s and early 1980s, the Xianger brick factory reportedly had such a large backlog of orders that it could not keep up with demand. Many collectively owned township and village enterprises established in the early years of reform served as outsourced subcontractors for state work units.

21. Additional shares were also offered to selected families in other Baimapu brigades, most of whom were either close patrilineal kin or marital affines of influential Qiaolou residents. These shares promised fixed dividends of 10 percent a year, several points higher than the interest offered to depositors at the Baimapu credit cooperative or state-run banks. Those willing to waive divided payments were also eligible for jobs at the brick factory. Since guaranteed dividends amounted to only Y10 a year, most opted instead for wage employment.

22. In Baimapu township, the housing boom of the 1980s was most intense in Qiaolou village itself. Land redistribution in 1983 gave many farmers a new sense of family affinity with the land, and restrictions against building on private plots were relaxed. As a result, new cash savings from brick factory jobs were widely invested in home renovation and reconstruction. In 1982, the year the brick factory opened, Qiaolou homes had mud-brick walls, and more than 80 percent had straw thatched roofs. Within the next ten years, over 90 percent of these were converted to fired brick and tile-roofed dwellings. Perhaps symbolic of his leading role in the factory's establishment, the first fired-brick house was built for Secretary Hao Yuanliang. This is not to imply that he garnished unfair personal economic gain from his position, although such trends were not uncommon in many parts of China under the reforms (e.g., Chan, Madsen, and Unger 1992). Although "rapid economic growth does not preclude the improved well-being of . . . local officials" (Oi 1992: 113n44), perceived disparities in the accruement of benefits and privileges did lead to alienation, frustration, and resentment.

23. This formerly wooded hilltop, completely deforested during the "iron and steel" campaign of the Great Leap Forward, had been the site of a collective orange orchard owned by Team 8. The village paid a modest annual cash rent (zu) to the erstwhile team, now a "villager small group," for use of the land. The orange trees were uprooted and redistributed to individual families in the former team.

24. The distillery was built by members of the former brigade construction team, who had reorganized under private management after the team officially disbanded in the early 1980s. Several private construction teams from outside Qiaolou also bid on the construction contract, but preference was reportedly given to Qiaolou residents.

25. In addition to land, which remained under the formal ownership of

(former) teams, several teams also retained other collective property, such as irrigation equipment. Two teams contracted out their own collective orange orchards to individual managers.

26. Villagers did not vote individual candidates into specific posts; instead, the winning candidates themselves decided, after the election, which administrative portfolios each would hold. Although the term "villager committee" might be a more accurate translation of *cunmin weiyuanhui*, I have opted for "village council" to avoid confusion with the "enterprise management committees" (*qiye guanli weiyuanhui*) discussed below.

27. Local elections in townships and villages were institutionalized as part of a broader agenda promoted by advocates of democratic reform working within the CCP, who regarded this as a key step toward eventual national elections. For details on local elections in rural China, see O'Brien (1994). Other activists, including some prominent national intellectuals, have been less enthusiastic about the mass participation of "peasants" in national elections and democratic government.

28. Proxy voting occurred most often between spouses. Although many Qiaolou villagers denied that they would ever abuse their authority as proxies by voting for candidates other than those specified by their spouses, a few admitted that there was no way to prevent a proxy from casting whatever ballot he or she chose. As one man put it, "A husband and wife can argue all they want about who to vote for, but in the end it is the hand of the proxy that casts the ballot." The authority of such proxies lies in possession of the seal, or "chop," of another family member. All formal transactions, from voting to picking up monthly wages at a village enterprise, required (only) the imprint of such a personal seal, which sometimes carried more legal authority than a signature. Most personal seals in the area were fashioned of wood. Those engraved in stone were rare and were considered a symbol of higher economic status, a distinction reminiscent of that between wooden and stone ancestral tablets in the early twentieth century.

29. Write-in candidates have appeared in every election, but none has ever been elected. Villagers who had voted for write-in candidates explained that the latter tend to split protest votes. Nevertheless, many asserted that a strong showing by a popular write-in candidate might lead to formal nomination to the election slate in the future.

30. The new village head, unrelated to Secretary Hao Yuanliang, was a successful farmer who had recently built the first two-story (*loufang*) home in Qiaolou, at a cost of over Y10,000. He had also acquired a popular reputation as a skilled mediator in family disputes. However, as a neophyte to village administration, he was openly deferential to the authority of both Secretary Hao and the long-incumbent village accountant, who generally oversaw daily management of village affairs. It was to Accountant Jun, rather than the village head or the deputy party secretary, that most matters were

referred in Secretary Hao's absence. During a 1991 dispute that I witnessed between distillery managers and prospective buyers from a neighboring county, staff members deferred a decision over price to Jun, whom they deliberately introduced as the village head, as if in de facto recognition of his power.

31. Many villagers claimed that when two women were nominated to the candidate slate in 1989, they understood that they were expected to vote for either one or the other, rather than both. The incumbent women's cadre, a Qiaolou native and the mother of four grown men, had been appointed during the Four Cleanups. She had been an outspoken radical during the Cultural Revolution, and the way she aggressively enforced new birth-planning regulations in the 1980s alienated many villagers. She was replaced by a young woman recently married into Qiaolou.

32. The new Meishan county gazetteer (MSG 1992: 572) noted that Qiaolou was designated a model (*dianfan*) of village-operated enterprises in 1987. It described its enterprises as having been "contracted to brigade management" and credited the village with fixed assets of Y1.1 million (a figure that rose several-fold by the mid-1990s). However, it also counted twenty-three enterprises in the village, a number that could only include private ventures run by individual families. These included two grain-processing machines, two contracted (former) team orchards, at least two private construction teams, and more than a dozen independent transport contractors with small tractors.

33. Such awards, particularly those conferred by provincial authorities, sometimes require strong lobbying efforts. Nevertheless, the high regard in which the village, and its leadership, were held by state officials no doubt influenced the decision to select Qiaolou as my research site. Particularly in the wake of events of 1989, it was an impressive showcase of collective management.

34. According to the Qiaolou party secretary, average per capita income in the village rose from Y148 in 1980 to Y380 in 1990, but remained well below the county average of Y468. The new Meishan Gazetteer (1992: 406, 408–10) noted that average per capita income in county villages rose from Y73 in 1977–78 to Y446 in 1987. This might suggest that Qiaolou lagged significantly behind other villages in economic development, except that county averages were skewed by the inclusion of highly commercialized periurban villages on the lowland county core, which had more productive land and better access to urban markets and long-distance transport. Note, however, that provincial statistics put average personal income for Meishan county farmers at nearly Y560 in 1989 (Y494 for farmers provincewide, up from Y188 in 1980; *Sichuan Yearbook* 1990: 501–02, 575). In 1990, currency exchange rates were roughly 5 *yuan* to the U.S. dollar.

35. The average value of betrothal gifts and payments in Qiaolou rose

more than tenfold in the 1980s, from roughly Y84 in 1982 to Y876 in 1991. Dowries also increased in average value over the same period, from Y250 to over Y2,000. At one particularly grand wedding, involving the daughter of a leading village cadre, the bride reportedly received some Y10,000 in "private room money."

36. Competitive admission criteria were applied to children from other villages in the township, who were required to score well on entrance exams, to demonstrate good social conduct, and to be from "single child families." However, all children from Qiaolou (and from Baimapu town [*jumin*] families) were guaranteed enrollment. This new central primary school in Qiaolou not only had better instructional talent than locally operated (*minban*) schools in neighboring villages, but also a large walled compound, exercise area, several classroom buildings, desks for all students, staff dormitories, running water, and electricity.

37. The introduction of fiscal reforms in the 1980s led to growing economic empowerment by local governments and a proliferation of new taxes and administrative levies (Oi 1992). Local administrative surcharges (*tiliu*) have been generally levied by township and village authorities in rural China to raise revenues for standard operations and special projects. During the 1980s, such levies became quite burdensome to many families and were widely resented throughout China. Unpopular *tiliu* surcharges were a factor in several incidents of civil unrest during the Deng Xiaoping era, including riots in neighboring Renshou county that attracted international attention in the early 1990s.

38. Couples who pledged to have only one child (or mothers who underwent voluntary sterilization) were issued a certificate and a small cash stipend by county authorities, which was supplemented with an additional cash award by village managers. As a deterrent to potential violators of birth-planning regulations, village officials threatened permanent dismissal of all family members from employment in collective village enterprises.

39. It is also noteworthy that village leaders in Qiaolou had little official interaction with immediate superiors in the Baimapu township government, but rather tended to consult directly with county authorities.

40. Anagnost (1992) noted that although such community compacts began to receive national media attention in 1982, they had well-established historical antecedents. Similar texts had been used by neo-Confucian local elites during the Song dynasty to promote ideological education through ritual practice. Under the Qing, "exhoratory lectures" (*xiangyue*) were delivered by local elites to help "reconstitute communities" following periods of turmoil and unrest (see also Hsiao 1967; Mair 1985).

41. Shareholding principles continued to find expression, and tacit official recognition, in family organization even during the more radical political campaigns of the Maoist era, as evidenced in local cadre mediation of

family partition negotiations (see Cohen 1992). In post-Mao Qiaolou, share-holding rights in the corporate village and its enterprises were held by families, not individual residents.

42. Shareholding rights did not confer any decision-making authority over enterprise management or control of other assets in the corporate collective. Rather, the interests of shareholders were represented by village council members and the party secretaries, who not only appointed the enterprise management committees but also headed those committees themselves.

43. These three employment categories are analytical abstractions intended to highlight aspects of social stratification in Qiaolou and generally do not reflect specific occupational job titles employed in the village, with the exception of "clay-diggers" (wa ni). The labor force at the brick factories alone, for example, was divided into at least fourteen specific job categories, ranging from clay diggers and furnace stokers to brick press operators and various management or supervisory positions.

44. However, on days with prolonged power outages, when mixing and pressing machines ceased operating, clay-diggers might be allowed to deliver only a couple of carts of soil, if that. Their income was thus vulnerable to wide fluctuation. Ten carts per man was considered a good day.

45. Enterprise management staff included directors, managers, and their deputies, as well as accountants, treasurers, supply and marketing agents, and production and storage supervisors.

46. Although village officials and enterprise managers denied that office staff received salaries (not to mention bonuses) during periods of suspended operations, many staff workers themselves confided privately that they did. They justified this practice by arguing that they still needed to work full time to sell overstocked products. The wage differential between managers and laborers was generally less than 2 : 1, yet managers enjoyed not only steadier salaries but also wider business contacts that aided their independent family income activities.

47. One driver accidentally struck and killed an elderly deaf man who reportedly stepped out onto a road in front of him. He continued to draw full pay while his license was suspended pending official investigation (which cleared him of criminal responsibility, although the village paid compensation to the victim's family). Another driver rolled his truck down a small hillside but walked away from the wreck. A third had the rear of his truck demolished by a locomotive when he attempted to run a railway crossing. Authorities warned him that he would have faced a prison sentence for destruction of state property had he caused a derailment.

48. The party secretary's son, one of the few villagers to graduate from senior high school in Meishan, was assigned a job at the county-run telecommunications station in Xianger. He quit a few years later, preferring, as

he put it, "to be free," and contracted operation of the Baimapu cinema from the township government. During this time, he reportedly had a leading position in the local Communist Youth League and was under intense pressure to join the party and prepare to succeed his father. He demurred, however, resigned his Youth League post, and contracted operation of a small phosphorous fertilizer factory in a nearby township, investing over Y30,000. He claimed to have accumulated this capital through sideline business deals conducted during driving assignments for the village.

49. By 1987, average wages in Meishan for workers employed in the transport sector were second only to those in major industries (MSG 1992: 407).

50. This villager-turned-state-cadre had been personally groomed for a leadership position by Secretary Hao, who arranged a village scholarship to send him to a cadre training school. After graduation, he served several years as a township head elsewhere in Meishan before being appointed to a post in the county government, where he became one of Qiaolou's most important personal contacts.

51. Distillery work was regarded as not overly demanding, and there was an atmosphere of comradarie among the small labor force of four. During lulls in the production process, workers often sat, talked, smoked, played cards, or even sipped a little alcohol—to sample its consistency, of course. They also ate there together, cooking their own meals on the old stove that had been part of the brigade's failed canteen and hostel.

52. When the distillery first opened and produced the more labor-intensive *qujiu* alcohol, it employed ten workers, nine of whom were from Secretary Hao's production team.

53. Some decisions over collective property use created emotional hardship for those affected (see Jing 1996). When the brigade orchard was expanded onto Yan Grave Hill in northern Qiaolou, ancestral remains were disinterred and graves destroyed. Many Yans were obliged to rebury their ancestors hurriedly elsewhere or send the remains for cremation. The incident, seen by some as an offense against the living and the dead, provoked outrage. Not even during the Great Leap Forward or the Cultural Revolution had ancestral graves in Qiaolou been disturbed. One elderly Yan man, visibly upset, recalled the "education" he had been given a decade earlier when he opposed the move: "If [a grave] occupies state land," he was told, "it is a crime."

54. A few others also raised allegations of corruption, although I have no evidence to substantiate such accusations. However, it might be noted that some enterprise staff engaged in ex officio business transactions, such as moneylending, in which collective assets were used for personal gain. Village leaders (and some other staff members) publicly opposed such practices, but generally tolerated them nonetheless.

55. Most farm families in the area have been reluctant to "specialize" in particular commodity products, preferring diversification strategies. Some

plant only enough grain to meet state procurement quotas and devote the rest of their land to various cash crops. Prevalent subsidiary activities included husbandry (mainly hogs, poultry, and fish), transport (mostly unlicensed hand tractors), and citrus cultivation. One family (that of Hao Yuanqian, a close cousin [FeBS] of Secretary Hao) received technical assistance from the county government in establishing an experimental chicken-breeding enterprise.

Works Cited

Ahern [Martin], Emily. 1973. *The Cult of the Dead in a Chinese Village*. Stanford, Calif.: Stanford Univ. Press.

Anagnost, Ann. 1992. "Socialist Ethics and the Legal System." In Jeffrey Wasserstrom and Elizabeth Perry, eds., *Popular Protest and Political Culture in Modern China: Learning from 1989*. 1st ed. pp. 177–205. Boulder, Colo.: Westview Press.

Andors, Phyllis. 1975. "Social Revolution and Women's Emancipation: China During the Great Leap Forward." *Bulletin of Concerned Asian Scholars* 7 (1): 33–42.

Arrigo, Linda Gail. 1986. "Landownership Concentration in China: The Buck Survey Revisited." *Modern China* 12 (3): 259–360.

Baker, Hugh D. R. 1979. *Chinese Family and Kinship*. New York: Columbia Univ. Press.

Barnett, A. Doak. 1963. "The Status Quo in the Countryside: Hsiehma-hsiang (Szechwan), June 1948." In idem, *China on the Eve of Communist Takeover*, pp. 103–54. New York: Praeger.

Baum, Richard. 1975. *Prelude to Revolution*. New York: Columbia Univ. Press.

Baum, Richard, and Frederick Teiwes. 1968. *Ssu-Ch'ing: The Socialist Education Movement of 1962–1966*. Berkeley: Center for Chinese Studies, Univ. of California at Berkeley.

Bernstein, Thomas. 1977. *Up to the Mountains, Down to the Villages.*
New Haven: Yale Univ. Press.

————. 1984. "Stalinism, Famine, and Chinese Peasants: Grain Procurements During the Great Leap Forward." *Theory and Society* 13 (3): 339–77.

Bird, Isabella. 1899. *The Yangtze Valley and Beyond.* London: John Murray.

Blok, Anton. 1974. *The Mafia of a Sicilian Village, 1860–1960: A Study of Violent Peasant Entrepreneurs.* Prospect Heights, Ill.: Waveland Press.

Bourdieu, Pierre. 1977. *Outline of a Theory of Practice.* Richard Nee, trans. Cambridge: Cambridge Univ. Press.

Bramall, Chris. 1989. *Living Standards in Sichuan, 1931–1978.* London: Contemporary China Institute, School of Oriental and African Studies.

Brandt, Loren, and Barbara Sands. 1992. "Land Concentration and Income Distribution in Republican China." In Thomas Rawski and Lillian Li, eds., *Chinese History in Economic Perspective,* pp. 179–206. Berkeley: Univ. of California Press.

Brown, Harold D., and Li Min-Liang. 1927. "A Survey of Twenty-five Farms on Mt. Omei, Szechwan, China." *Chinese Economic Journal and Bulletin* 1 (12): 1059–76.

————. 1928. "A Survey of Fifty Farms on the Chengtu Plain, Szechwan." *Chinese Economic Journal and Bulletin* 2 (7): 44–73.

Bruun, Ole. 1996. "The *Fengshui* Resurgence in China: Conflicting Cosmologies Between State and Peasantry." *The China Journal* 36 (July): 47–65.

Buck, John L. 1964 [1937]. *Land Utilization in China.* New York: Paragon.

————. 1980 [1947]. "An Agricultural Survey of Szechwan Province." In idem, *Three Essays on Chinese Farm Economy.* New York: Garland Publishing.

Byrd, William, and Lin Qingsong, eds. 1990. *China's Rural Industry: Structure, Development, and Reform.* Oxford: Oxford Univ. Press.

Chan, Anita. 1993. "Revolution or Corporatism: Workers and Trade Unions in Post-Mao China." *The Australian Journal of Chinese Affairs* 29: 31–61.

Chan, Anita, Richard Madsen, and Jonathan Unger. 1992. *Chen Village under Mao and Deng.* Berkeley: Univ. of California Press.

Chang, Jung. 1991. *Wild Swans: Three Daughters of China.* New York: Doubleday/Anchor.

Chang Su. 1979 [1952]. "A Cadre's Land Reform Diary." In Mark Selden, ed., *The People's Republic of China: A Documentary History of Revolutionary Change,* pp. 243–53. New York: Monthly Review Press.

Chayanov, A. V. 1986 [1966]. *Theory of Peasant Economy.* Madison: Univ. of Wisconsin Press.

Ch'en, Jerome. 1969. "Historical Background." In Jack Gray, ed., *Modern China's Search for a Political Form.* New York: Oxford Univ. Press.

———. 1985. "Local Government Finances in Republican China." *Republican China* 10 (2): 42–54.

Cheng, Tiejun. 1991. "Population Registration and State Control in the People's Republic of China." Ph.D. dissertation, SUNY-Binghamton.

Cheng, Tiejun, and Mark Selden. 1994. "The Origins and Social Consequences of China's Hukou System." *China Quarterly* 139: 644–68.

Chesneaux, Jean. 1971. *Secret Societies in China in the Nineteenth and Twentieth Centuries,* Gillian Nettle, trans. Ann Arbor: Univ. of Michigan Press.

———, ed. 1972. *Popular Movements and Secret Societies in China, 1840– 1950.* Stanford, Calif.: Stanford Univ. Press.

Chirot, Daniel. 1980. "The Corporatist Model and Socialism." *Theory and Society* 9: 363–81.

Cohen, Myron L. 1970. "Developmental Process in the Chinese Domestic Group." In Maurice Freedman, ed., *Family and Kinship in Chinese Society,* pp. 21–36. Stanford, Calif.: Stanford Univ. Press.

———. 1976. *House United, House Divided: The Chinese Family on Taiwan.* New York: Columbia Univ. Press.

———. 1988. "Souls and Salvation: Conflicting Themes in Chinese Popular Religion." In James Watson and Evelyn Rawski, eds., *Death Ritual in Late Imperial and Early Modern China,* pp. 180–202. Berkeley: Univ. of California Press.

———. 1990. "Lineage Organization in North China." *Journal of Asian Studies* 49 (3): 509–34.

———. 1992. "Family Management and Family Division in Contemporary Rural China." *China Quarterly* 130: 357–77.

———. 1993a. "Cultural and Political Inventions in Modern China: The Case of the Chinese 'Peasant.'" *Daedalus* 112 (2): 151–70.

———. 1993b. "Shared Beliefs: Corporations, Community, and Religion among the South Taiwan Hakka During the Ch'ing." *Late Imperial China* 14 (1): 1–33.

Croll, Elisabeth J. 1981. *The Politics of Marriage in Contemporary China.* Cambridge: Cambridge Univ. Press.

———. 1984. "Marriage Choice and Status Groups in Contemporary China." In James Watson, ed., *Class and Social Stratification in Post-Revolutionary China,* pp. 175–97. Berkeley: Univ. of California Press.

Crook, David, and Isabel Crook. 1979. *Ten Mile Inn: Mass Movement in a Chinese Village.* New York: Pantheon.

Crook, Isabel. n.d. "Prosperity Township: A Sichuan Community in Wartime." Unpublished manuscript based on observations in the 1940s.

Diamond, Norma. 1975. "Collectivization, Kinship, and the Status of Women in Rural China." In Rayna R. Reiter, ed., *Toward an Anthropology of Women,* pp. 372–95. New York: Monthly Review Press.

Domes, Jurgen. 1985. *Peng Te-huai: The Man and the Image*. London: C. Hurst.

Duara, Prasenjit. 1988a. *Culture, Power, and the State: Rural North China, 1900–1942*. Stanford, Calif.: Stanford Univ. Press.

———. 1988b. "Superscribing Symbols: The Myth of Guandi, Chinese God of War." *Journal of Asian Studies* 47 (4): 778–95.

Eastman, Lloyd. 1988. *Families, Fields, and Ancestors: Constancy and Change in China's Economic and Social History, 1550–1949*. New York: Oxford Univ. Press.

Ebrey, Patricia B. 1986. "Early Stages in the Development of Descent Groups." In Patricia Ebrey and James Watson, eds., *Kinship Organization in Late Imperial China, 1000–1940*, pp. 16–61. Berkeley: Univ. of California Press.

Ebrey, Patricia B., and James Watson, eds. 1986. *Kinship Organization in Late Imperial China, 1000–1940*. Berkeley: Univ. of California Press.

Endicott, Stephen. 1980. *James G. Endicott: Rebel Out of China*. Toronto: Univ. of Toronto Press.

———. 1988. *Red Earth: Revolution in a Sichuan Village*. London: I. B. Tavris.

Entenmann, Robert. 1980. "Sichuan and Ch'ing Migration Policy." *Ch'ing-shih Wen-t'i* 4 (4): 35–54.

Esherick, Joseph W. 1981. "Numbers Games: A Note on Land Distribution in Prerevolutionary China." *Modern China* 7: 387–412.

Esherick, Joseph W., and Mary Backus Rankin, eds. 1990. *Chinese Local Elites and Patterns of Dominance*. Berkeley: Univ. of California Press.

Faure, David. 1985. "The Plight of the Farmers: A Study of the Rural Economy of Jiangnan and the Pearl River Delta, 1870–1937." *Modern China* 11 (1): 3–37.

———. 1989. "Lineage as Cultural Invention: The Case of the Pearl River Delta." *Modern China* 15: 4–37.

Fei, Hsiao-t'ung. 1939. *Peasant Life in China: A Field Study of Country Life in the Yangtze Valley*. London: Routledge and Kegan Paul.

Fei, Hsiao-t'ung, and Chang Chih-i. 1949. *Earthbound China: A Study of Rural Economy in Yunnan*. London: Routledge and Kegan Paul.

Feutchtwang, Stephan. 1974. *An Anthropological Study of Chinese Geomancy*. Vientiane: Editions Vithagna.

Franck, Harry A. 1925. *Roving Through South China*. New York: The Century Company.

Fortes, Meyers, and E. E. Evans-Pritchard, eds. 1940. *African Political Systems*. London: Oxford Univ. Press.

Foucault, Michel. 1995 [1975]. *Discipline and Punishment: The Birth of the Prison*. 2nd ed. Alan Sheridan, trans. New York: Vintage.

Freedman, Maurice. 1958. *Lineage Organization in Southeastern China*.

LSE Monographs on Social Anthropology, vol. 18. London: London School of Economics.

———. 1966. *Chinese Lineage and Society: Fukien and Kwangtung.* LSE Monographs on Social Anthropology, vol. 33. London: London School of Economics.

———. 1979a [1968]. "Geomancy." In G. William Skinner, ed., *The Study of Chinese Society: Essays by Maurice Freedman*, pp. 313–33. Stanford, Calif.: Stanford Univ. Press.

———. 1979b. "The Handling of Money: A Note on the Background to the Economic Sophistication of Overseas Chinese." In G. William Skinner, ed., *The Study of Chinese Society: Essays by Maurice Freedman*, pp. 22–26. Stanford, Calif.: Stanford Univ. Press.

———. 1979c [1970]. "Ritual Aspects of Chinese Kinship and Marriage." In G. William Skinner, ed., *The Study of Chinese Society: Essays by Maurice Freedman*, pp. 273–95. Stanford: Stanford Univ. Press.

Fried, Morton. 1953. *The Fabric of Chinese Society: A Study of the Social Life of a Chinese County Seat.* New York: Octagon.

Friedman, Edward, Paul Pickowicz, and Mark Selden. 1991. *Chinese Village, Socialist State.* New Haven, Conn.: Yale Univ. Press.

Gallin, Bernard. 1960. "Matrilateral and Affinal Relations in a Taiwanese Village." *American Anthropologist* 62 (4): 632–42.

Gallin, Bernard, and Rita Gallin. 1982. "The Chinese Joint Family in Changing Rural Taiwan." In R. W. Wilson, S. L. Greenblatt, and A. A. Wilson, eds., *Social Interaction in Chinese Society.* New York: Pergamon.

Gallin, Rita S. 1984. "Rural Industrialization and Chinese Women: A Case Study from Taiwan." *Journal of Peasant Studies* 12 (1): 76–92.

Gamble, Sidney. 1963. *North China Villages: Social, Political, and Economic Activities before 1933.* Berkeley: Univ. of California Press.

———. 1968. *Ting Hsien: A North China Rural Community.* Stanford, Calif.: Stanford Univ. Press.

Gates, Hill. 1996. *China's Motor: A Thousand Years of Petty Capitalism.* Ithaca, N.Y.: Cornell Univ. Press.

von Glahn, Richard. 1991. "The Enchantment of Wealth: The God Wutong in the Social History of Jiangnan." *Harvard Journal of Asiatic Studies* 51 (2): 651–714.

Goodrich, Anne S. 1964. *The Peking Temple of the Eastern Peak: The Tung-yueh Miao in Peking and Its Lore.* Nagoya, Japan: Monumenta Serica.

———. 1991. *Peking Paper Gods: A Look at Home Worship.* Nettetal, Germany: Steyler Verlag.

Graham, David Crockett. 1928. *Religion in Szechuan Province, China.* Washington, D.C.: Smithsonian Institution.

Gray, Whitmore, and Henry Ruiheng Zheng, trans. 1986. "General Principles of Civil Law in the People's Republic of China." *The American Journal of Comparative Law* 34 (4): 715–43.

Greenway, Alice. 1987. "Ah Bing and Her 'Sisters.'" *Wilson Quarterly,* Summer, pp. 152–61.

Grunde, Richard. 1976. "Land Tax and Social Change in Sichuan, 1925–1935." *Modern China* 2 (1): 23–48.

Guo Hong. 1990. "Nongcun Hunyin de Jianli: Hunqian Jiaowang" [The Establishment of Village Marriages: Contacts Before Marriage]. In Zhao Xishun, ed., *Nongmin Hunyin: Sichuan Nongcun Hunyin Yanjiu,* pp. 57–110. Dujiangyan: Sichuan Renmin Chubanshe.

Hansen, Valerie. 1990. *Changing Gods of Medieval China, 1127–1276.* Princeton, N.J.: Princeton University Press.

Hao Yitong. 1985. "Guanyu Sichuan Fangyan de Yuyin Fenqu Wenti" [Concerning the Question of Pronunciation Differences in Sichuan Dialects]. *Sichuan Daxue Xuebao* 2: 71–85.

Harding, Harry. 1993. "The Chinese State in Crisis, 1966–69." In Roderick MacFarquhar, ed., *The Politics of China, 1949–1989,* pp. 148–247. Cambridge: Cambridge Univ. Press.

Hayford, Charles. 1990. *To the People: James Yen and Village China.* New York: Columbia Univ. Press.

Hazelton, Keith. 1986. "Patrilines and the Development of Localized Lineages: The Wu of Hsiu-ning City, Hui-chou, to 1525." In Patricia Ebrey and James Watson, eds., *Kinship Organization in Late Imperial China, 1000–1940,* pp. 137–69. Berkeley: Univ. of California Press.

Herzfeld, Michael. 1991. *A Place in History: Social and Monumental Time in a Cretan Town.* Princeton, N.J.: Princeton University Press.

Highbaugh, Irma. 1948. *Family Life in West China.* New York: Agricultural Missions.

Hill, Polly. 1986. *Development Economics on Trial: The Anthropological Case for a Prosecution.* Cambridge: Cambridge Univ. Press.

Hinton, William. 1966. *Fanshen: A Documentary of Revolution in a Chinese Village.* New York: Vintage.

———. 1983. *Shenfan: The Continuing Revolution in a Chinese Village.* New York: Vintage.

Ho, Ping-ti. 1959. *Studies on the Population of China, 1368–1953.* Cambridge, Mass.: Harvard Univ. Press.

Hsiao, Kung-chuan. 1967. *Rural China: Imperial Control in the Nineteenth Century.* Seattle: Univ. of Washington Press.

Hsieh, Jih-chang. 1985. "Meal Rotation." In Hsieh Jih-chang and Chuang Ying-chang, eds., *The Chinese Family and Its Ritual Behavior,* pp. 70–83. Taipei: Institute of Ethnology, Academia Sinica.

Hu Hansheng. 1988. *Sichuan Jindaishi Shi San Kao* [Three Studies in Recent Sichuan History]. Chongqing: Chongqing Chubanshe.

Hu, Hsien-chin. 1985 [1948]. *The Common Descent Group in China and*

Its Functions. Viking Fund Publications in Anthropology, vol. 5. New York: Viking Fund.

Huang, Philip C. C. 1985. *The Peasant Economy and Social Change in North China.* Stanford, Calif.: Stanford Univ. Press.

———. 1990. *The Peasant Family and Rural Development in the Yangzi Delta, 1350–1988.* Stanford, Calif.: Stanford Univ. Press.

Huang Qichang. 1993. *The [Hao] Surname.* In the series "Zhonghua Xing-shi Tongshu" [Collection of Chinese Clan Surnames]. Yiyang Region Xiangzhong Printing House.

Huang, Shu-min. 1989. *The Spiral Road: Change in a Chinese Village Through the Eyes of a Communist Party Leader.* Boulder, Colo.: Westview Press.

Jervis, Nancy. 1987. "Retracing a Chinese Landscape: The Interaction of Policy and Culture in a North China Village." Ph.D. diss., Columbia Univ.

Jin Haitong. 1977. *Meishan Jianwei Tianfu Yanjiu [Research on Land Tax in Meishan and Jianwei (Counties)].* In the series "Minguo Ershi Niandai Zhongguo Dalu Tudi Wenti Ziliao" [Materials on the Land Question in Mainland China During the 1930s], vol. 9. Taiwan: Cheng-wen Publishing House.

Jing, Jun. 1996. *The Temple of Memories: History, Power, and Morality in a Chinese Village.* Stanford, Calif.: Stanford Univ. Press.

Judd, Ellen. 1989. "Niangjia: Chinese Women and Their Natal Families." *Journal of Asian Studies* 48 (3): 525–44.

———. 1994. *Gender and Power in Rural North China.* Stanford, Calif.: Stanford Univ. Press.

Kapp, Robert A. 1973. *Szechwan and the Chinese Republic: Provincial Militarism and Central Power, 1911–1938.* New Haven, Conn.: Yale Univ. Press.

Katz, Paul R. 1995. *Demon Hordes and Burning Boats: The Cult of Marshal Wen in Late Imperial Chekiang.* Albany: State Univ. of New York Press.

Kearney, Michael. 1996. *Reconceptualizing the Peasantry: Anthropology in Global Perspective.* Boulder, Colo.: Westview Press.

Kelliher, Daniel. 1992. *Peasant Power in China: The Era of Rural Reform, 1979–1989.* New Haven, Conn.: Yale Univ. Press.

Kipnis, Andrew. 1997. *Producing Guanxi: Sentiment, Self, and Subculture in a North China Village.* Durham: Duke Univ. Press.

Kraus, Richard. 1977. "Class Conflict and the Vocabulary of Social Analysis in China." *China Quarterly* 69: 54–74.

———. 1982. *Class Conflict in Chinese Socialism.* New York: Columbia Univ. Press.

Kuhn, Philip. 1980. *Rebellion and Its Enemies in Late Imperial China: Militarization and Social Structure, 1796–1864.* Cambridge, Mass.: Harvard Univ. Press.

Lang, Olga. 1946. *Chinese Family and Society*. New Haven, Conn.: Yale Univ. Press.

Lary, Diana. 1984. "Violence, Fear, and Insecurity: The Mood of Republican China." *Republican China* 10 (2): 55–63.

Lavely, William. 1991. "Marriage and Mobility Under Rural Collectivism." In Rubie Watson and Patricia B. Ebrey, eds., *Marriage and Inequality in Chinese Society*, pp. 286–312. Berkeley: Univ. of California Press.

Lévi-Strauss, Claude. 1969. *The Elementary Structures of Kinship*. James Bell and John von Sturmer, trans., Rodney Needham, ed. Boston: Beason Press.

Li Shiping. 1987. *Sichuan Renkou Shi* [*Sichuan Population History*]. Chengdu: Sichuan Daxue Chubanshe.

Li, Yu-ning. 1971. *The Introduction of Socialism into China*. New York: Columbia Univ. Press.

Li Yuzhang. 1945. "Meishan Xian Zhenjiang Xiang Di Er Bao Nongcun Jingji Gaikuang" [General Economic Situation in Second Bao Village of Meishan County's Zhenjiang Township]. *Sichuan Jingji Jikan* 2 (3): 419–22.

Lieberthal, Kenneth. 1993. "The Great Leap Forward and the Split in the Yan'an Leadership, 1958–1965." In Roderick MacFarquhar, ed., *The Politics of China, 1949–1989*, pp. 87–147. Cambridge: Cambridge Univ. Press.

———. 1995. *Governing China: From Revolution Through Reform*. New York: W. W. Norton.

Lin, Nan. 1995. "Local Market Socialism: Local Corporatism in Action in Rural China." *Theory and Society* 24: 301–54.

Liu, Cheng-yun. 1985. "Kuo-Lu: A Sworn Brotherhood Organization in Szechwan." *Late Imperial China* 6 (1): 56–82.

Liu Chuanmei. 1990. *Lishi, Shanchuan, Meishanren* [*History, Scenery, and Meishan People*]. Chengdu: Sichuan Renmin Chubanshe.

Liu Jun. 1988. "Er Liu Dazhan Qianhou Sichuan Junfa Gejuxia de Tianfu Zhengshou" [Imposition of Land Tax Under Sichuan Warlord Separatist Regimes Before and After the Two Liu War]. *Sichuan Junfa Shiliao* 5: 79–102.

Lowenthal, David. 1985. *The Past Is a Foreign Country*. Cambridge: Cambridge Univ. Press.

MacFarquhar, Roderick. 1974. *The Origins of the Cultural Revolution, I: Contradictions Among the People, 1956–1957*. New York: Columbia Univ. Press.

———. 1983. *The Origins of the Cultural Revolution, II: The Great Leap Forward, 1958–1960*. New York: Columbia Univ. Press.

Madsen, Richard. 1984. *Morality and Power in a Chinese Village*. Berkeley: Univ. of California Press.

Mair, Victor. 1985. "Language and Ideology in the Written Popularization of the Sacred Edict." In David Johnson, Andrew Nathan, and Evelyn Rawski, eds., *Popular Culture in Late Imperial China*, pp. 325–59. Berkeley: Univ. of California Press.

Mao Zedong. 1975a [1927]. "Report on an Investigation of the Peasant Movement in Hunan." In *Selected Works of Mao Tse-tung*, 2nd ed., vol. 1, pp. 23–59. Beijing: Foreign Language Press.

———. 1975b [1955]. "On the Co-operative Transformation of Agriculture." In *Selected Works of Mao Tse-tung*, 2nd ed., vol. 5, pp. 184–210. Beijing: Foreign Language Press.

McCreery, John L. 1976. "Women's Property Rights and Dowry in China and South Asia." *Ethnology* 15: 163–74.

Medick, Hans, and David Sabean, eds. 1984. *Interest and Emotion: Essays on the Study of Family and Kinship*. Cambridge: Cambridge Univ. Press.

MSG (Meishan Gazetteer). 1967 [1923]. Taipei: Taiwan Xuesheng Shuju.

———. 1992. Chengdu: Sichuan Renmin Chubanshe.

Meyers, Ramon H., and Fu-mei Chang Chen. 1976. "Customary Law and the Economic Growth of China During the Ch'ing Period" (Part I). *Ch'ing-shih Wen-t'i* 3 (5): 1–32.

———. 1978. "Customary Law and the Economic Growth of China during the Ch'ing Period" (Part II). *Ch'ing-shih Wen-t'i* 3 (10): 4–27.

Naquin, Susan. 1985. "The Transmission of White Lotus Sectarianism in Late Imperial China." In Andrew Nathan, David Johnson, and Evelyn Rawski, eds., *Popular Culture in Late Imperial China*, pp. 255–91. Berkeley: Univ. of California Press.

Naughton, Barry. 1991. "Industrial Policy During the Cultural Revolution: Military Preparation, Decentralization and Leaps Forward." In Christine Wong, William Joseph, and David Zweig, eds., *New Perspectives on the Cultural Revolution*, pp. 153–82. Cambridge, Mass.: Harvard Univ. Council on East Asian Studies.

Nee, Victor. 1989. "A Theory of Market Transition: From Redistribution to Markets in State Socialism." *American Sociological Review* 54: 663–81.

———. 1991. "Social Inequalities in Reforming State Socialism: Between Redistribution and Markets in China." *American Sociological Review* 56: 267–82.

———. 1992. "Organizational Dynamics of Market Transition: Hybrid Forms, Property Rights, and Mixed Economy in China." *Administrative Science Quarterly* 37: 1–27.

Needham, Joseph. 1995. *The Shorter Science and Civilization in China*. Abridged by Colin Ronan. Cambridge: Cambridge Univ. Press.

Ning Jideng. 1988. "Meishan Guomin Shifan Xuexiao Huiyi" [Reflections on the Meishan Public Teachers' School]. *Leshan Wenshi Ziliao* 6: 121–23.

O'Brien, Kevin. 1994. "Implementing Political Reform in China's Villages." *Australian Journal of Chinese Affairs* 32 (July): 33–60.

Ocko, Jonathan K. 1991. "Women, Property, and Law in the People's Republic of China." In Rubie Watson and Patricia Ebrey, eds., *Marriage and Inequality in Chinese Society*, pp. 313–46. Berkeley: Univ. of California Press.

Oi, Jean C. 1989. *State and Peasant in Contemporary China: The Political Economy of Village Government*. Berkeley: Univ. of California Press.

———. 1990. "The Fate of the Collective After the Commune." In Deborah Davis and Ezra Vogel, eds., *Chinese Society on the Eve of Tiananmen*, p. 15–36. Cambridge, Mass.: Harvard Univ. Council on East Asian Studies.

———. 1992. "Fiscal Reform and the Economic Foundations of Local State Corporatism in China." *World Politics* 45 (1): 99–126.

———. 1995. "The Role of the Local State in China's Transitional Economy." *China Quarterly* 144: 1132–1149.

Pearson, Margaret M. 1994. "The Janus Face of Business Associations in China: Socialist Corporatism in Foreign Enterprises." *The Australian Journal of Chinese Affairs* 31: 25–46.

Perry, Elizabeth J. 1976. "Worshippers and Warriors: White Lotus Influence in the Nien Rebellion." *Modern China* 6 (1): 83–112.

Peters, Emrys L. 1976. "Aspects of Affinity in a Lebanese Maronite Village." In J. G. Peristiany, ed., *Mediterranean Family Structures*, Cambridge: Cambridge Univ. Press.

———. 1990. *The Bedouin of Cyrenaica: Studies of Personal and Corporate Power*. Jack Goody and Emanuel Marx, eds. Cambridge: Cambridge Univ. Press.

Potter, Jack, and Sulamith H. Potter. 1990. *China's Peasants: An Anthropology of Revolution*. Cambridge: Cambridge Univ. Press.

Potter, Sulamith H. 1983. "The Position of Peasants in Modern China's Social Order." *Modern China* 9 (4): 465–99.

Riskin, Carl. 1987. *China's Political Economy: The Quest for Development Since 1949*. Oxford: Oxford Univ. Press.

Robinson, Jean. 1985. "Of Women and Washing Machines: Employment, Housework, and the Reproduction of Motherhood in Socialist China." *China Quarterly* 101: 32–57.

Sage, Steven. 1992. *Ancient Sichuan and the Unification of China*. Albany: State Univ. of New York Press.

Sangren, P. Steven. 1983. "Female Gender in Chinese Religious Symbols: Kuan Yin, Ma-tsu, and the Eternal Mother." *Signs* 9 (1): 4–25.

———. 1984. "Traditional Chinese Corporations: Beyond Kinship." *Journal of Asian Studies* 43: 391–415.

———. 1987. *History and Magical Power in a Chinese Community*. Stanford, Calif.: Stanford University Press.

Sankar, Andrea. 1978. "The Evolution of the Sisterhood in Traditional Chinese Society: From Village Girls' Houses to Chai T'ang in Hong Kong." Ph.D. diss., Univ. of Michigan.

Schmitter, Philippe C. 1974. "Still a Century of Corporatism?" In Frederick Pike and Thomas Stritch, eds., *The New Corporatism: Social-Political Structures in the Iberian World*, pp. 85–130. Notre Dame, Wisc.: Univ. of Notre Dame Press.

Selden, Mark. 1993. *The Political Economy of Chinese Development*. Armonk, N.Y.: M. E. Sharpe.

———, ed. 1979. *The People's Republic of China: A Documentary History of Revolutionary Change*. New York: Monthly Review.

Shepherd, John. 1988. "Rethinking Tenancy: Explaining Spatial and Temporal Variation in Late Imperial and Republican China." *Comparative Studies in Society and History* 30 (3): 403–31.

Sheridan, James E. 1975. *China in Disintegration: The Republican Era in Chinese History, 1912–1949*. New York: Free Press.

Shiga, Shuzo. 1978. "Family Property and the Law of Inheritance in Traditional China." In David C. Buxbaum, ed., *Chinese Family Law and Social Change*, pp. 109–50. Seattle: Univ. of Washington Press.

Shue, Vivienne. 1980. *Peasant China in Transition: The Dynamics of Development Towards Socialism, 1949–1956*. Berkeley: Univ. of California Press.

———. 1988. *The Reach of the State*. Stanford, Calif.: Stanford Univ. Press.

Sichuan Yearbook. 1990. Chengdu: Sichuan Yearbook Editorial Committee.

Siu, Helen F. H. 1989. *Agents and Victims in South China: Accomplices in Rural Revolution*. New Haven, Conn.: Yale Univ. Press.

———. 1993. "Cultural Identity and the Politics of Difference in South China." *Daedalus* 122 (2): 19–44.

Skinner, G. William. 1964–65. "Marketing and Social Structure in Rural China." *Journal of Asian Studies* 24 (1): 3–43, (2): 195–228, and (3): 363–99.

Smith, Arthur. 1970 [1899]. *Village Life in China*. New York.

Smith, M. G. 1975 [1974]. *Corporations and Society: The Social Anthropology of Collective Action*. Chicago: Aldine.

Smith, Paul J. 1988. "Commerce, Agriculture, and Core Formation in the Upper Yangzi, 2 A.D. to 1948." *Late Imperial China* 9 (1): 1–78.

———. 1991. *Taxing Heaven's Storehouse*. Cambridge, Mass.: Harvard Univ. Council on East Asian Studies.

Stafford, Charles. 1995. *The Roads of Chinese Childhood: Learning and Identification in Angang*. Cambridge: Cambridge Univ. Press.

Stockard, Janice. 1989. *Daughters of the Canton Delta: Marriage Patterns and Economic Strategies in South China, 1860–1930*. Stanford, Calif.: Stanford Univ. Press.

Strauch, Judith. 1983. "Community and Kinship in Southeastern China: A View from the Multilineage Villages of Hong Kong." *Journal of Asian Studies* 43 (1): 21–50.

Stross, Randy. 1984. "Numbers Games Rejected: The Misleading Allure of Tenancy Estimates." *Republican China* 10 (3): 1–17.

Sun Xujun, Jiang Song, and Chen Weidong, eds. 1989. *Sichuan Minsu Daguan* [*Spectacles of Sichuan Popular Customs*]. Chengdu: Sichuan Renmin Chubanshe.

Szonyi, Michael. 1997. "The Illusion of Standardizing the Gods." *Journal of Asian Studies* 56 (1): 113–35.

Tawney, R. H. 1966 [1932]. *Land and Labor in China*. White Plains, N.Y.: M. E. Sharpe.

Teiser, Stephen F. 1988. *The Ghost Festival in Medieval China*. Princeton, N.J.: Princeton Univ. Press.

Teiwes, Frederick C. 1993. "The Establishment and Consolidation of the New Regime, 1949–1957." In Roderick MacFarquhar, ed., *The Politics of China, 1949–1989*, pp. 5–86. Cambridge: Cambridge Univ. Press.

Topley, Marjorie. 1958. "The Organization and Social Function of Chinese Women's *Chai T'ang* in Singapore." Ph.D. dissertation, Univ. of London.

———. 1963. "The Great Way of Former Heaven: A Group of Chinese Secret Religious Sects." *Bulletin of the School of Oriental and African Studies* 26 (2): 386–87.

———. 1978 [1976]. "Marriage Resistance in Rural Kwangtung." In Arthur Wolf, ed., *Studies in Chinese Society*, pp. 247–68. Stanford, Calif.: Stanford Univ. Press.

Treudley, Mary Bosworth. 1971. *The Men and Women of Chung Ho Ch'ang*. Asian Folklore and Social Life Monographs, vol. 14. Taipei: The Orient Cultural Service.

Tsou, Tang, Mark Blecher, and Mitchell Meisner. 1979. "Organization, Growth, and Equality in Xiyang County." *Modern China* 5 (2): 139–86.

Unger, Jonathan. 1984. "The Class System in Rural China." In James Watson, ed., *Class and Social Stratification in Post-Revolution China*, pp. 121–41. Cambridge: Cambridge Univ. Press.

———. 1985. "Remuneration, Ideology and Peasant Interests in a Chinese Village, 1960–1980." In William Parish, ed., *Chinese Rural Development: The Great Transformation*, pp. 117–40. Armonk, N.Y.: M. E. Sharpe.

———. 1989. "State and Peasant in Post-Revolution China." *Journal of Peasant Studies* 17 (1): 114–36.

Walder, Andrew G. 1986. *Communist Neo-Traditionalism: Work and Authority in Chinese Industry*. Berkeley: Univ. of California Press.

———. 1995. "Local Governments as Industrial Firms: An Organizational

Analysis of China's Transitional Economy." *American Journal of Sociology* 101 (2): 263–301.

Wan Sun, ed. 1988. "Li-Lan Qiyi Yanjiu Zhuan" [Special Research Collection on the Li-Lan Uprising]. *Leshan Wenshi Ziliao,* vol. 5.

Wang Hansheng, Cheng Weimin, Yan Xiaofeng, and Yang Weiming. 1995. "Industrialization and Social Differentiation: Changes in Rural Social Structure in China Since Reform." Special Issue: "Social Stratification in Rural China," Peng Yusheng, ed., Ai Ping, trans. *Chinese Law and Government* 28 (1): 9–38.

Watson, Andrew. 1983. "Agriculture Looks for 'Shoes that Fit': The Production Responsibility System and Its Implications." *World Development* 11 (8): 705–30.

Watson, James L. 1975a. "Agnates and Outsiders: Adoption in a Chinese Lineage." *Man* 10: 293–306.

———. 1975b. *Emigration and the Chinese Lineage: The Mans of Hong Kong and London.* Berkeley: Univ. of California Press.

———. 1985. "Standardizing the Gods: The Promotion of T'ien Hou (Empress of Heaven) along the South China Coast, 960–1960." In Andrew Nathan, David Johnson, and Evelyn Rawski, eds., *Popular Culture in Late Imperial China,* pp. 292–324. Berkeley: Univ. of California Press.

———. 1988. "The Structure of Chinese Funerary Rites: Elementary Forms, Ritual Sequence, and the Primacy of Performance." In James Watson and Evelyn Rawski, eds., *Death Ritual in Late Imperial and Early Modern China,* pp. 13–19. Berkeley: Univ. of California Press.

———, ed. 1984. *Class and Social Stratification in Post-Revolution China.* Cambridge: Cambridge Univ. Press.

Watson, James, and Evelyn Rawski, eds. 1988. *Death Ritual in Late Imperial and Early Modern China.* Berkeley: Univ. of California Press.

Watson, Rubie S. 1981. "Class Differences and Affinal Relations in South China." *Man* 16: 593–619.

———. 1982. "The Creation of a Chinese Lineage: The Teng of Ha Tsuen, 1669–1751." *Modern Asian Studies* 16: 593–615.

———. 1984. "Women's Property in Republican China: Rights and Practice." *Republican China* 10 (1a): 1–12.

———. 1985. *Inequality Among Brothers: Class and Kinship in South China.* Cambridge: Cambridge Univ. Press.

———. 1986. "The Named and the Nameless: Gender and Person in Chinese Society." *American Ethnologist* 13 (4): 619–31.

———. 1988. "Remembering the Dead: Graves and Politics in Southeastern China. In James L. Watson and Evelyn S. Rawski, eds., *Death Ritual in Late Imperial and Early Modern China,* pp. 203–27. Berkeley: Univ. of California Press.

———. 1990. "Corporate Property and Local Leadership in the Pearl River Delta, 1898–1941." In Joseph Esherick and Mary Rankin, eds., *Chinese*

Local Elites and Patterns of Dominance, pp. 239–60. Berkeley: Univ. of California Press.

―――, ed. 1994. *Memory, History, and Opposition Under State Social-ism*. Santa Fe, N.M.: School of American Research.

Watson, Rubie S., and Patricia B. Ebrey, eds. 1991. *Marriage and Inequal-ity in Chinese Society*. Berkeley: Univ. of California Press.

Weller, Robert. 1987. *Unities and Diversities in Chinese Religion*. Seattle: Univ. of Washington Press.

White, Tyrene. 1990. "Political Reform and Rural Government." In Deborah David and Ezra Vogel, eds., *Chinese Society on the Eve of Tiananmen: The Impact of Reform*, pp. 37–60. Cambridge, Mass.: Harvard Univ. Council on East Asian Studies.

Whyte, Martin King. 1969. "The Tachai Brigade and Incentives for the Peasants." *Current Scene* 7 (August): 1–13.

―――. 1975. "Inequality and Stratification in China." *China Quarterly* 64: 684–711.

―――. 1981. "Destratification and Restratification in China." In Gerald Berreman and K. Zaretsky, eds., *Social Inequality: Comparative and Developmental Approaches*. New York: Academic Press.

―――. 1996. "City Versus Countryside in China's Development." *Prob-lems of Post-Communism*, January/February, pp. 9–22.

Williams, Raymond. 1983 [1976]. *Keywords: A Vocabulary of Culture and Society*. rev. ed. New York: Oxford Univ. Press.

Wolf, Arthur. 1970. "Chinese Kinship and Mourning Dress." In Maurice Freedman, ed., *Family and Kinship in Chinese Society*, pp. 189–208. Stanford, Calif.: Stanford Univ. Press.

―――. 1974. "Gods, Ghosts, and Ancestors." In Arthur Wolf, ed., *Reli-gion and Ritual in Chinese Society*, pp. 131–82. Stanford, Calif.: Stan-ford Univ. Press.

Wolf, Arthur, and Chieh-shan Huang. 1980. *Marriage and Adoption in China, 1845–1945*. Stanford, Calif.: Stanford Univ. Press.

Wolf, Margery. 1972. *Women and the Family in Rural Taiwan*. Stanford, Calif.: Stanford Univ. Press.

―――. 1975. "Women and Suicide in China." In Margery Wolf and Roxane Witke, eds., *Women in Chinese Society*, pp. 111–41. Stanford, Calif.: Stanford Univ. Press.

―――. 1985. *Revolution Postponed: Women in Contemporary China*. Stanford, Calif.: Stanford Univ. Press.

Wood, Chester F. 1937. "Some Studies of the Buddhisms of Szechuan." *Journal of the West China Border Research Society* 9: 160–79.

Xiong Du. 1988. "Junfa Hunzhang Shiqi de Sichuan Jingji" [Sichuan Economy during the Period of Warlord Chaos]. *Sichuan Junfa Shiliao* 5: 129–49.

Yan, Yunxiang. 1995. "Everyday Power Relations: Changes in a North

China Village." In Andrew Walder, ed., *The Waning of the Communist State: Economic Origins of Political Decline in China and Hungary*,
pp. 215–41. Berkeley: Univ. of California Press.

———. 1996. *The Flow of Gifts: Reciprocity and Social Networks in a Chinese Village*. Stanford, Calif.: Stanford Univ. Press.

Yang, C. K. 1959. *Chinese Communist Society*. Cambridge, Mass.: MIT
Press.

Yang, Dali. 1996. *Calamity and Reform in China: State, Rural Society,
and Institutional Change Since the Great Leap Forward*. Stanford,
Calif.: Stanford Univ. Press.

Yang, Martin. 1945. *A Chinese Village: Taitou, Shandong Province*. New
York: Columbia Univ. Press.

Yang, Mayfair M. H. 1989. "Between State and Society: The Construction
of Corporateness in a Chinese Socialist Factory." *The Australian Journal
of Chinese Affairs* 22: 31–62.

———. 1994. *Gifts, Favors, and Banquets: The Art of Social Relationships
in China*. Ithaca, N.Y.: Cornell Univ. Press.

Yang, Minchuan. 1994. "Reshaping Peasant Culture and Community:
Rural Industrialization in a Chinese Village." *Modern China* 20 (2):
157–79.

Zhou Kaili. 1993. "Sichuan Sheng Meishan Xian Qiaolou Cun de Shequ
Diaocha" [A Community Study of Qiaolou Village, Meishan County,
Sichuan Province]. In *Zhongguo Nongcun Jiating*, Xue Suzhen, ed.,
pp. 251–91. Shanghai: Shanghai Academy of Social Sciences.

Zweig, David. 1989. *Agrarian Radicalism in China, 1968–1981*. Cambridge, Mass.: Harvard Univ. Press.

———. 1991. "Agrarian Radicalism as a Rural Development Strategy,
1968–1978." In Christine Wong, William Joseph, and David Zweig,
eds., *New Perspectives on the Cultural Revolution*, pp. 63–82. Cambridge, Mass.: Harvard Univ. Council on East Asian Studies.

———. 1997. *Freeing China's Farmers: Rural Restructuring in the Reform
Era*. Armonk, N.Y.: M. E. Sharpe.

Character List

baxianzhuo 八仙桌
baikeqian 拜客錢
bangmang 幫忙
bao 保
baoban 包辦
baochan dao hu 包產到戶
baochan dao zu 包產到組
baogan daohu 包干到戶
baoguan 包管
baojia 保甲
baomin daibiao 保民代表
baozhang 保長
baozhengren 保證人
biao 表

caijin 財金
caili 彩禮
changgong 長工
changnian 常年
chengbao 承包
chenghuang 城隍
chi popo fan 吃婆婆飯
chi su 吃素

chi guojia liang 吃國家糧
chi ziji liang 吃自己糧
citang 祠堂
cungui minyue 村規民約
cunmin weiyuanhui 村民委員會
cunmin xiaozu 村民小組
cunzhang 村長
cun zhuren 村主任

dachun 大春
dajiating 大家庭
da tuhao 大土豪
daye 大爺
dazibao 大字報
dazong 大宗
daibiren 代筆人
daipiao 代票
dan 石, 擔
dangjia 當家
dangpu 當鋪
de le fen 得了分
di (dry land) 地
di (emperor) 帝

235

dizhu	地主	guzi	谷子
dian (rent)	佃	guan	關
dian (hall)	殿	guanli qu	管理區
dianfan	典範	guanxi	關係
dinghun fei	訂婚費	Gui Jie	鬼節
dongshuitian	多水田	guiding fanwei	規定範圍
Dongyue Gong	東岳公	guoban	國辦
Dongyue Niang	東岳娘	guojia ganbu	國家幹部
dou	斗	guojia mimi	國家秘密
duangong	短工		
		hantian	寒天
eba	惡霸	hang	行
Er Bao	二保	haotoucun	好頭村
		heshang	和尚
fadong	發動	hezuo shangdian	合作商店
fanshen	翻身	hongbao	紅包
fanwei	範圍	hongshu hunyin	紅薯婚姻
fang	房	houdai	後代
fangchan	房產	hu	戶
fang qu	防區	hukou	戶口
fen	分	huzhu	戶主
fenhui	分會	huzhu zu	互助組
fenjia	分家	huangshan	荒山
fenjia dan	分家單	huiguan	會館
fenzao	分灶	huishou	會首
fengjian mixin	封建迷信	hunshui	混水
fengmiche	風米車		
fubai ganbu	腐敗幹部	jia (family)	家
fudan	負擔	jia (administrative unit)	甲
funong	富農	jiachan	家產
funu ganbu	婦女幹部	jiafa	家法
funu zhuren	婦女主任	jiapu	家譜
fuye	副業	jiazhang (family head)	家長
fuyu	富裕	jiazhang (administrative unit leader)	甲長
gandie	乾爹	jiazhuang	嫁妝
ganqin	乾親	jianguo	建國
ganqing	感情	jianzheng	建政
gangtie	鋼鐵	jianzheng ren	見證人
Gelaohui	哥老會	jiceng ganbu	基層幹部
geming qianfeng qu	革命前鋒區	jicheng ren	繼承人
geming weiyuanhui	革命委員會	jiebai xiongdi	結拜兄弟
gong	公	jiefang zhuxi	解放主席
gongfen	工分	jiegeshou	解個手
gongshangye	工商業	jieji chengfen	階級成分
gufen	股份	jienong	街農
gugong	雇工	jifenyuan	計分員

jiji fenzi	積極分子	nongxian	農閑
jipai	極派	nongye shui	農業稅
jiti	集體		
jiti cun	集體村	paihang	排行
jiti daolu	集體道路	paikuan	排款
jiti nongzhuang	集體農莊	pailou	牌樓
jingshang	經商	Pao Ge	袍哥
jiu shehui	舊社會	peijia	陪嫁
jumin	居民	pingba	坪壩
junfa	軍閥	pinnong	貧農
junfa liangku	軍閥糧庫	pin xiazhong nong	貧下中農
		pochan	破產
kong ke	空殼	po si jiu	破四舊
kouliang	口糧		
kuzhan yidong	苦戰一多	qiguhui	起谷會
kuaiji	會計	qiye guanli weiyuan-hui	企業管理委員會
la niang yue	拉娘約		
lankuan	蘭款	Qiaolouzi	橋樓子
laobaixing	老百姓	Qingfutang	清褔 (情婦?) 堂 (characters uncertain)
laobiao	老表		
lao geming	老革命		
lao jiefang qu	老解放區	Qingming	清明
li	里	Qingminghui	清明會
lian (company)	連	qingshui	清水
lianshe	聯社	qu	區
lianzu	聯組		
liangzhang	糧長	renqing	人情
ling	靈	renwu	任務
longmen	龍門		
loufang	樓房		
luohou qunzhong	落後群眾	san da hezuo	三大合作
		sandai wuchan	三代無產
mai tudi	買土地	saozi	嫂子
meiren	媒人	sheyuan	社員
mi	米	shenkan	神龕
mixin	迷信	shenwei	神位
mianzi	面子	shenzupai	神祖牌
miao	廟	shengchan dadui	生產大隊
minban	民辦	shengchan dui	生產隊
minzhu jianzheng	民主建政	shengchan qingkuang	生產情況
mu	畝	shengchan xiaozu	生產小組
		shengmi	生米
niangjia	娘家	shi (clan)	氏
niangniangmu	娘娘母	shiwuzhang	食物長
nongmin	農民	shuoku	說苦
nongmin xiehui	農民協會	si da renwu	四大任務

sidai tongtang	四代同堂	xueming	學名
sifangqian	私房錢	xuetian	學田
siheyuan	四合院	yajin	押金
		yatou	丫頭
Taishan Wang	泰山王	yaobar	幺半兒
tanxin	談心	yibu dengtian	一步登天
tang	堂	yinyang xiansheng	陰陽先生
tian	田	ying (battalion)	營
tiaogong	調工	you yichuan xing	有遺傳性
tiaozheng	調整	Yulanpen Jie	玉蘭盆節
tiliu	提留	yuanshi senlin	原始森林
tongyangxi	童養媳		
tudi gong (land for jobs)	土地工	zao shen	灶神
		zhaitang	齋堂
tudi gong (earth god)	土地公	zhandou	戰斗
tudi xiafang	土地下放	zhangbei	長輩
tufei	土匪	zhangfang	長房
tugai zhuxituan	土改主席團	zhao nuxu	招女婿
tuanfa	團閥	zhen	鎮
tuanlian	團練	zhengfang	正房
tuanzhang	團長	zheng shezhang	正社長
		zhengfeng	整風
wa niba	挖泥巴	zhengmi	征米
weixing tian	衛星田	zhengzhi guashua	政治掛帥
wen	文	zhengzhi fan	政治犯
Wen Miao	文廟	zhidian	支點
wenshu	文書	zhiyuan nong	志願農
wenwu	文武	zhongnong	中農
Wu Miao	武廟	zhongpin zigeng	中貧自耕
wuda nongju	五大農具	zhou	州
wudai tongtang	五代同堂	Zhuamindang	抓民黨
wu fu	五服	zhuanbao	轉包
wunong	務農	zhuozi	桌子
		zhushi	豬食
xian	縣	zibao	字保
xianjin wenming cun	先進文明村	zigeng	自耕
Xiantian Dadao	先天大道	zigeng dian	自耕佃
xiang	鄉	ziliudi	自留地
xiangyue	鄉約	ziran cun	自然村
xiangzhang	鄉長	zishunu	自梳女
xiao chidian	小吃店	zong	宗
xiaochun	小春	zu (rent)	租
xiao laoyao	小老幺	zu (groups)	組
xiao xifu	小媳婦	zu daibiao	組代表
xiaozu	小組	zuxian	祖先
xinfang	新房	zuzhang (group leader)	組長
xin si bi pei	心死必配	zuzhang (lineage master)	族長
xingzheng cun	行政村		

Index

In this index an "f" after a number indicates a separate reference on the next page, and an "ff" indicates separate references on the next two pages. A continuous discussion over two or more pages is indicated by a span of page numbers, e.g., "57–59." *Passim* is used for a cluster of references in close but not consecutive sequence.

Library of Congress Cataloging-in-Publication Data

Ruf, Gregory A.
    Cadres and kin : making a socialist village in West China, 1921–1991 /
Gregory A. Ruf.
       p.   cm.
    Includes bibliographical references and index.
    ISBN 0-8047-3377-5 (cloth) : ISBN 0-8047-4129-8 (pbk.)
    1. Villages—China—Case studies. 2. Villages—China—History—
20th century. 3. Communism—China—History—20th century.
4. Socialism—China—History—20th century. I. Title.
HN733.R85   1998
307.76'2'0951—dc21   98–16522
                                                       CIP
                                                       Rev.

⊗ This book is printed on acid-free, recycled paper.

Original printing 1998
Last figure below indicates year of this printing:
07   06   05   04   03   02   01   00